Asia-P...

Security, Globalisation
and
Development

Editors

M.L. Sondhi
K.G. Tyagi

Indian Council of Social Science Research

Manas Publications
New Delhi-110 002 (INDIA)

MANAS PUBLICATIONS
(Publishers, Distributors, Importers & Exporters)

4819, Varun House, Mathur Lane,
24, Ansari Road, Daryaganj,
New Delhi - 110 002 (INDIA)
Ph.: 3260783, 3265523, 3984388
Fax: 011 - 3272766
E-mail: manaspublications@vsnl.com

© ICSSR

First Published 2001

ISBN   81-7049-129-0

Typeset at
Manas   Publications

Printed in India at
R.K. Offset, Delhi
and Published by Mrs. Suman Lata for
Manas Publications, 4819, Varun House,
Mathur Lane, 24, Ansari Road, Daryaganj
New Delhi 110002 (INDIA)

◄ Introduction ►

The political, strategic and economic situation in different parts of Asia-Pacific is volatile. It needs to be examined carefully because of its importance for the pattern of relationship and the structure of power within Asia-Pacific and the rest of the world. There is a significant process of realignment taking place among major and secondary powers in Asia. The end of the Cold War did not lead to US unipolarity or global economic interdependence as a dominant scenario. Instead, there are challenging approaches to economic, political and social change which are shaping the global agenda. Because of the major changes in Asian domestic and external policies, national decision making process is facing dilemmas and new debates.

What are the political, strategic and economic risks in the Asia-Pacific at present and in the foreseeable future? How does domestic politics affect regional security? What is the future of regional economic groupings in Asia-Pacific and how do they relate to the issue of economic and military security in the region and sub-regions? What are the parameters and limits of Super Power involvement and interests in the coming decade?

The Indian Council of Social Science Research (ICSSR) celebrated its 30th anniversary of establishment. As a part of its commemorative activity, ICSSR organised an International Conference on Asia-Pacific and the Global Order from October 2-4, 2000 at Ashok Hotel, New Delhi.

It was attended by over 300 delegates from India and abroad. In this conference leading scholars, policy makers and experts in the social sciences analysed the fundamental trends that are shaping the challenges of the 21st century.

The goal of the Conference was to strengthen the basis for continued and informed discussion of policy choices and develop research policy linkages for strengthening democracy, economic reforms and security.

The Conference focused on the following four major topics under the broad theme `Asia-Pacific and the Global Order'.

1. An emerging order for Regional Peace and International Security

2. The New Economic Order

3. The New Information Order

4. An emerging social and cultural trends

Selected papers and proceedings of this conference are published in two seperate books as per details below:

Book I   :   Asia-Pacific: Security, Globalisation and Development

Book II   :   India in the New Asia-Pacific

Book I covers topics like National Security and Peace, Globalisation, Regional Development and Asia-Pacific etc.

Book II covers topics like Information Technology and Higher Education, Economic Order and Globalisation, Social and Cultural aspects of Globalisation, etc.

A special word of appreciation for Shri VK Garg of Manas Publications for brining out the two volumes nicely.

Several professional colleagues working in the ICSSR helped in accomplishing the task in different capacity in getting these two volumes published. In particular, I would like to mention names of Mrs. Meena Walia, Mrs. Nutan Johri, Mr. Mahesh P. Madhukar, Mrs. Mythili Raman,

Mr. Aosenba Jamir, Ms. Pushpa Rani, Mr. Manish Oberoi, Mr. BC Sharma, and Mr. Sudeshwar Prasad.

We hope that these papers in published form will provide a significant contribution to the debate on some of the major issues related to Asia-Pacific and will sharpen our understanding of the western and national preferences on these issues.

Professor M.L. Sondhi
Chairman

Dr. K.G. Tyagi
Secretary-General

‹ Contents ›

‹ Contributors List ›

Yoginder K. Alagh	:	Ex-Vice Chairman, Sardar Patel Institute of Economic and Social Research, Ahmedabad; Ex-Vice-Chancellor, JNU, New Delhi and Chairman, Civil Services Examination Review Committee (UPSC), New Delhi, India.
Debasis Bagchi	:	Inspector General of Police (Enforcement), Delhi Vidyut Board, Delhi, India
András Balogh	:	Head, Deptt. of Modern and Contemporary History, ELTE University, Budapest, Hungary; Chairman, Committee of International Studies at the Hungarian Academy of Sciences, Hungary.
Arya Bhushan Bhardwaj	:	Founder Director, Gandhi-in-Action Constructive Worker's Home, New Delhi, India
K. Borichpolets	:	Prof., Moscow State Institute of International Relations (MGIMO University) Lobachewsky, Moscow, Russia.
Zbigniew Brzezinski	:	Former National Security Adviser to the President of the United States and Counselor, Centre for Strategic and International Studies, Washington DC, United States.
Son Ngoc Bui	:	Institute of World Economy, Hanoi, Vietnam.

A.K. Chirappanath	:	Prof. and Director, School of Gandhian Studies, Mahatma Gandhi University, Kottayam, Kerala, India
R.S. Dube	:	Prof., Department of General & Applied Geography, Dr. H.S. Gour University, Sagar, Madhya Pradesh, India
Hoshiar Singh	:	Pro-Vice Chancellor, Kurukshetra University, Kurukshetra, Haryana, India & President, Indian Political Science Association.
Ashok Kapur	:	Prof., Department of Political Science, University of Waterloo, Ontario, Canada.
Bharat Karnad	:	Research Prof., Centre for Policy Research, New Delhi, India
Changsu Kim	:	Korea Institute for Defence Analyses, Seoul, Korea
Taeho Kim	:	Korea Institute for Defence Analyses, Seoul, Korea.
Sergei Lounev	:	Research Fellow, Institute of Oriental Studies; Institute of World Economy and International Relations, Russian Academy of Sciences, Moscow, Russia.
Tran Thi Ly	:	Head, Centre for Indian Studies, Institute for South East Asian Studies, Hanoi, Vietnam.
Bhaskar Majumder	:	Govind Ballabh Pant Social Science Institute, Jhusi, Allahabad, Uttar Pradesh, India
Meyer Mikhail	:	Director, Institute of Asian and African Countries, Moscow State University, Moscow, Russia.

Pramod Mishra	:	Fellow, Developing Countries Research Centre, University of Delhi, Delhi, India
Sushanta Kumar Nayak	:	Senior Lecturer, Department of Economics, Arunachal University, Itanagar, Arunachal Pradesh, India
Yong-Ok Park	:	Senior Research Advisor, Korea Institute for Defense Analyses, Seoul, Korea.
Govinda Chandra Rath	:	G.B. Pant Social Science Institute, Allahabad, Uttar Pradesh, India
Martin Sherman	:	Department of Political Science, University of Tel Aviv, Israel.
Arun Kumar Singh	:	Reader, Department of Political Science, Arunachal University, Itanagar, Arunachal Pradesh, India
Ramesh Thakur	:	Vice Rector (Peace and Governance), United Nations University, Shibuya, Tokyo, Japan.
Vijay Kumar	:	Prof., Department of Political Science, T.M. Bhagalpur University, Bhagalpur, Bihar, India
J. George Waardenburg	:	Centre for Development Planning, Erasmus University, Rotterdam, Netherlands
R.S. Yadav	:	Reader, Department of Political Science, Kurukshetra University, Kurukshetra, Haryana, India

‹1›

United States and the Asia-Pacific Region

*Prof. Zbigniew Brezezinski**

I have participated in many international conferences, but I have never participated in a conference with such a remarkable commencement as this one. And I say that in all seriousness, it was in much respect a truly evocative beginning. And it is in a way as it should have been in a country that itself personifies spirituality and philosophical debt, a country which gave the world Mahatma Gandhi. I listened to that mysteriously captivating and mystically hypnotizing music. And I thought that this was something which in a sense expressed the spirit of the man who spinned the wheel symbolically. I have the honour to garland him. To me those introductory moments have a double significance. For I am first of all an American—by commitment and by affection. Secondly, I am a Polish by birth and sentiments. And Mahatma Gandhi has a message that has proven to be historically relevant to the experience of the two countries with which I have a very personal and special relationship. Mahatma Gandhi symbolizes the power of the spirit and his triumph in this country is the testimony to the universality of his message. In my experience as an Americans, the civil right, movement the struggle for racial equality the undoing of the decades long racial injustice was inspired directly by Mahatma Gandhi.

* Former National Security Adviser to the President of the United States and Counsellor, Centre for Strategic and International Studies, Washington DC, USA.

But Martin Luther came, preached and a direct legacy. Of the same that enchanting music he evoked and what Mahatma Gandhi stood for. That was an important element in my own growing up as an American.

In the last 20 years the principle catalyst for the collapse of communism and Soviet power was the solidarity movement in Poland. And the essence in the movement of solidarity in Poland was the power of commitment. Peaceful and non-violent power, but power committed to certain fundamental notions which have come historically on time. Namely that human rights must not be politically repressed and that people stand up together to assert their rights.

So in this highly personal statement generated by the introductory movements of this morning sesion of this International conference, I found a great deal of meaning. And I wanted to share it with you. In that context it is almost sacrilegious to be talking about other realities. Such as geopolitics. But that is a task which is assigned to me and which has brought me here. Let me begin by noting something which though fairly obvious is worthy of being noted nonetheless, namely that we live in a time of a truly extra ordinary acceleration of history. And this acceleration of history is posing in the not too distant future, nothing less than perhaps a fundamental discontinuity in human affairs. Do consider the implications of the following three examples.

First the quantum leap in our individual capability to a fact to control or to destroy the world around us and external to us. For example within the next ten or 50 years every individual in this room will have in his breast pocket a tiny instrument which will be equivalent of the total calculating computing capability of the largest corporations that exist today. And of course one can also mention in that context the increasing possibilities of access by individuals to means of affecting massive destruction, external to oneself.

Secondly we should note the growing acceleration in the quantum leap in our collective human capability to alternate the world around us but ourselves. And to do so while endowing that process with enhanced capabilities particularly in the area of intelligence. While we are talking about cloning artificial intelligence or general enhancement of the human organism we are talking about powers, the exercise of which will involve some very fundamental questions regarding the very essence of the human identity. Questions, which, in a sense that Mahatma Gandhi previewed. And thirdly because of the onset of new technologies in the area of information communications and weaponry, the all-European originated vestalian system based on nation–state sovereignty it is going to fade. And will be replaced by, perhaps, here a preview and to be found in the process of unification that the European Union embodies in Europe but perhaps in different ways. Perhaps also we see previews in orbit in the already existing large entities as the Indian Union. I used the word Union deliberately. Or for that matter China. All of that implies fundamental changes. But fortunately I have not been asked to discuss them. But to discuss rather the anticipated strategic scenario for Asia by the year 2020.

In reference to that time-frame, let me mention that throughout the 20th century—the century which has just ended, world politics was dominated by struggles over the future of Eurasia. But they largely originated and were concentrated in Europe—the western periphery of Eurasia. In the 21st Century I think we all now realize it is the eastern extremity of Eurasia. The Far East Asia most generally - that is probably going to be the source of conflict. And now efforts must be increasingly addressed to then avoidance to evade it that eventually. In the western extremity of Eurasia we only have variety of institutions which reduce or mitigate or render unlikely the eruption of major-inter state conflicts. I have in mind, particularly, the political security realities created by the existence of the viable and expanding NATO which links America and Europe together and of the process of consolidation and enlargement of the European Union.

In Asia, the structural framework is much less defined. We are likely to see the increased role of three major states. And their interaction is likely to determine the strategic scenario of the national decades. I speak, obviously, of China, Japan and of India. One could perhaps also add in some respects Indonesia whose future is very uncertain. One could also add Russia, but its major thrust is also still fully defined and in any case it is more and more likely gradually to oscillate towards Europe if it succeeds in dealing with its internal problem. China, Japan and India are already in some respects, regional powers. And each has the potential for further growth and influence indirect power. Well relations among them has still in the process of identification and clarification. Relations among them are also affected by legacies of hostility, of suspicion and of rivalry. That introduces of course significance elements of unpredictability.

Beyond that each of them is also potentially vulnerable to domestic volatility which could impinge on political stability and affect the over-all quality of Asia's geo-strategic condition. In that context obviously a complicating issue will be the possible interaction between international conflicts and internal instability, each affecting the other and each to some extent being a catalyst for the other. In that broadly defined context the nature of the Chinese–Japanese relationship will clearly influence the role that each plays merely in the Far East. But not in North–East Asia. And much the same can be said in case of India and China. And not only in South Asia. But with other Asian countries, direct bilateral relations and the role of each of the Asian big three will be influenced by their specific relationship with the USA.

Whether one likes it or not for the next two decades or so the reason for that is that the USA is and will continue to be the pre-eminent global power. That is not a boast but a statement of fact with one objective that has to be taken into account. How long will that pre-eminence last, no one can tell. But I would hazard the judgement that it will last at least as long as the life of anyone in this room. And probably in the lives of the children of those present here. And may be few beyond, If one closely monitors the relationship of power in terms of the various indicators of power in the modern age one reaches the conclusion. That the gap is not only the wide but it is widening in most of the key centres of power of modern age. That could be changed. But at the moment there is no one in the horizon that can be viewed as a serious potential rival in the next 20 years, that is a reality.

Multi-polarity may be a desirable goal for a world more equally balanced but the fact that it is a desirable goal still does not bridge the enormous gap between the aspirations and reality. Hence America will be critically engaged in this part of the world positively or negatively, depending on the wisdom or stupidity of its own conduct. Depending on the reactions of others towards USA. My own judgement is that the factor most likely to undermine the American pre-eminence in the next 20 years or so. It is not an external challenge to America but the challenged American power posed by the American people and the changing culture of the American society which might condition in America an attitude, which would be inimical to the US continuing to play an active international role. But that should happen quickly before new structures have developed and the consequence I hastily add will not be the emergence of stable multi-polarity. The consequence can be described in a very simple word—Anarchy—global anarchy which will has tea the conflicts in various parts of the world.

Hence the American role in the Asia-Pacific region is going to be quite more leading than either Indo-China relations or China-Japan relations. If American relations with China were to deteriorate, and sometimes the conduct of the political links of China and America respectively seem to suggest that both are determined to make this relationship deteriorate, then I think some negative consequences will. follow.

I would also like to mention here the inclination of worsening relationship and the attitude on the parties concerned at different times over sensitive issues of Taiwan or national missile defence. But if it does deteriorates Japan will become increasingly insecure And if that happens, then there is only one remedy, it is likely to be the one that Japanese adopted—promptly re-militarisation and Japan has the capability to achieve it promptly and to an extent it will make it immediately - the preeminent Asian military power.

Secondly the deteriorating American-Chinese relationship will make Next detegioraty American—Chinese relationship: China will move away from its posture of minimum strategic deterrence which it has maintained till now and will adopt instead efforts to enhance and modernize its nuclear force. That clearly will impact on India's own sense of security giving further stimulus to India's own efforts in the strategic military sector. And that in turn will further generate unpredictable impulses in Japan. And that's what leading us into a vicious circle. Indeed I think the contagious effect, as we all know of nuclear weapons should not be under-estimated when we see the future. Can we truly estimate how long it will be to forge Japan to undersides to acquirement? In my own view it would pull off either an American disengagement from the Far East because of general fatigue in the US with burdens of engagements.

And the removal of the American umbrella will have that effect on Japan and it could also as a consequence of conflict over Taiwan which great aids increases insecurity in the Far East and it could also be the dynamic stage effect of the reunification of Korea leading to Korean demands that America will withdraw from Korea thereby undermining the strategic and political justification for continued American military presence in Japan. These are certain possibilities that can not be entirely dismissed.

And if Japan would go nuclear probably it would do so in the Israeli fashion. That is to say go nuclear semi-covertly without announcing it's acquired nuclear capability, which clearly become a political and strategic fact of life in the Far East. The consequences of that in turn are even more difficult to predict. But we cannot ignore the reality of several flash points in Asia which do contain the potential for direct conflict. And it is susceptible to greatly emotionalizing the respective publics. Taiwan is an obvious example - Sanctaku islands are another. The island between Japan and Korea, the islands in South China sea and not even bohter to mention here Kashmir. How stable then will be a situation in which there are four nuclear powers, roughly equal as to how will they interact especially, given the fact of highly emotionalizing territorial conflicts between them. I stress that because in the long lasting American-Soviet nuclear competition there was no direct highly emotionalizing territorial conflicts between America and Russia. There were only strategic conflicts of Europe. And broadly over the world at large reaching even one pointed with Cuba-Africa but there was no direct territorial conflict with its highly emotionalizing politically triggering effect. I do not know the answer to this question. But I would submit to those of you who are scientifically minded that the statistical probability of conflict in that context is inevitably higher. Then in the bilateral more controlled and remote American Soviet competition. One could also of course add to this the possibility of major domestic upheavals. Perhaps even this integration in the neighbouring countries, which by now is also a nuclear power.

To state all of these and to oppose these dilemmas is not a plea for undoing the existing nuclear realities. I am a realist and I do not weep over spilt milk. But it is important to recognize that the interaction of several potentially antagonistic nuclear powers in immediate contiguity to one another. And motivated by serious national grievances in a more complex situation than the earlier American-Soviet strategic competition and that justifies in turn, a broader conclusion that the strategic situation in the Asian part of Eurasia is likely to be more complicated, potentially more dangerous than the one that has existed for the last 50 years in the western periphery of Eurasia. And that the situation will be further complicated by domestic uncertainties to which I have already alluded and which could act as catalyst for escalating instability.

Japan has been and in all probability will remain a good international citizenry. Japan has acted with enormous commitment to peaceful conduct and deserves high recognition for its stance. But I have already outlined the condition in which this would considerably change. And Japanese politics could then become very volatile, very emotional driven by rationalist passion. And these are some signals that in reality should not be entirely discounted.

But what about China? It seems to me that the directions of economic change in China and the political realities of China are not in sink. They do point in different directions. The events of the last two days in Tianamen Square are just but a foreshadow of the kind of domestic problems that could begin to become increasingly a major political reality in China. The Chinese reality in any case is paradoxical for it is communist dictatorship without a communist program. Far from it, this is a communist dictatorship that will discipline an energy that is actively building capitalism. There is fundamental contradiction in that reality. And this is at some point does raise questions regarding legitimacy of the political system. Questions - Would the present generation of leaders seem unwilling to confront?

What about India? How entrenched is democracy in

India? It has been remarkably successful and earned India's respect in the world. And particularly American admiration. But democracy in India existed alongside large-scale illiteracy, low-economic poverty, and passive but deeply entrenched ethnic and religious identities. And will this combination remain non-volatile? And as the population becomes increasingly politically mobilized but insufficiently economically empowered. What will be the impact on India if Sri Lanka fragments or if Pakistan Talibanized? In brief, reality of democracy is not a complete guarantee of its eternity. I think one has to be conscious of that reality and also its implications.

It follows that domestic dilemmas in each to precipitate major discontinuities unleash political passion and thereby further dramatize strategic dilemmas of this part of the world. There is no simple formula for stability in the Asian part of Eurasia. But I can send at least that America should try to contribute to it. And in saying that let me say right on that I see America as involved in Asia as a part of continuing process of trying to create structures and relationship which in time could assimilate the progressive devolution of American pre-eminence. And in that context I am not particularly worried about the India-China-Russia triangle which some have talked about. Because I consider that to be a totally unrealistic geo-strategic alternative - the Chinese do not care for it. If there was such a triangle Chinese will be the dominant in it. And the triangle could not provide either India nor China what both countries need the most which is unlimited, unhindered and massive access to technologies and capital.

In Asia, I see America doing the following. First of all it is important that we maintain our continued alliance with Japan's continued playing role of the good international citizenasy without injecting into Asia. A new reality of the suddenly remlitarized Japan with all the uncertain consequences they would have upon China. And from China on India and thereby enhancing international stability.

Secondly we must continue to seek a deliberate prudential accommodation with China, especially over Taiwan which is a volatile and highly emotionalizing issue. The eventual solution for Taiwan may be some refined formula of one country two systems change rather into one country and several systems. For certainly Taiwan is not likely to adopt estraders similar to that of Hong Kong or Macao. But in any case in the meantime it is important that the US discourage to extend camp separatist tendencies on Taiwan. And also discourage excessively Marshall rhetoric or posturing on the part of China which would contribute to Asian tensions.

Thirdly we should see to promote with China and with Japan some sort of the stable umbrella of phased reunification of Korea. A phased reunification which would permit the continued American presence - first of all in Korea as long as possible and incessantly. And subsequently on some agreed basis in any case in Japan given the first important strategic objective which I have mentioned namely the maintenance of American strategic umbrella over Japan which formulates Japan's constructive international law. This is major and complex undertaking in which again, American involvement is necessary.

Next we need to seek an enhancement of American-Indian cooperation, as indeed both America and India are doing, not because India is a nuclear power but because it is a successful democratic developing country. And Japan and South Korea are compelling a reputation for the proposition that human rights and democracy are somehow not compatible with Asian values.

India is a very imporatnt example and indeed democracy is inherent in Asian values. And in that sense it is a part of the universal aspiration, which in my view is likely to advance India's own economic evolution to a fully free-marketed economy. And that in turn which encourages greater US investment. India needs large foreign investment. Today foreign investment in China is 20 times larger than in

India. American investment in China is 6 times larger than American investment in India. Total FDI in China during the decade amounts to 350 billion dollars and it is one of the major reasons why China today is economically considerably more successful than India. I would define the relationship between America and India as involving sober operation. We should not fast driver illusions about some special strategies on global relationship. Because that is simply unrealistic. I think, instead we should be talking about a sober cooperative relaionship in which we share goals that are important to both of us. Democracy, international cooperation and development of new structures. That is the rife for shared realization in the course of this century of modernity. This is likely to be defined in terms of reality of democratic political system. The consequences of free market economy and an awareness of an objection to respect social justice. That is a very complicated combination. And I do not claim that America lives up as perfectly as India does not but some countries do much less. And that creates a combination for a truly stable relationship of sober cooperation.

Finally I think we ought to explore together the issue whether the time has not come for the shaping of some multi-lateral security structures. I have voted at the beginning of my remarks that the likelihood of conflict in the western periphery of Eurasia is mitigated. But the structures that have emerged in the course of the last 50 years. And I have noted the absence of similar structures in the eastern periphery of Eurasia. And perhaps the time has come to begin the process of constructing Eurasia vide security arrangements.

I have specific suggestions to make in that connection. There exists an organization called Organization for Security and Cooperation in Europe (OSCE). It is an organization which is in fact engaged not only in European states but some central agency states. It is a loose organization and it is certainly not an integrated alliance.

But it is a shared structure, which has in fact engaged in some peacekeeping and peace promotion processes. I think time has come to consider changing the name without changing initials. OSCE in Eurasia is something that I think is needed. And it should embrace Asian countries ready and willing to participate in a larger coveted security process. And with this such a structure one would envisage some standing committee of countries for a variety of reasons are likely to be more directly and more heavily engaged in contributing to continental and trans-continental security. By way of example one could think of a standing committee, which engaged the US, given its involvement in the Far East and Europe at the same time. The European Union has a unit especially since the European union is now engaged in the process for initiating a common security and defense capability.

Russian geographically spans with Europe and Asia. China is a significant power in Far East. Japan is an economic dynamo in the Far East and so is India. Such a relationahip that fosters cooperation and growing sense of responsibility would entail the step forward in the process of widening, and consolidating, institutionalizing not only Asia's security but also Eurasia's security. But such an objective can be sought more effectively if we consciously keep aside the dangerous and potentially self-fulfilling goals towards which there is a tendency today in America and also here and elsewhere.

And there is a tendency to think of China increasingly as a source of threat and instability in the next decades. It may be but need not be and I think how we conduct ourselves is going to influence how China itself conducts itself. We cannot build or seriously discuss security in Asia without Chinese participation. So the first over-simplification, the risks becoming a self-propelling prophecies which must be avoided is that China is definitely to be the source of threat and instability. I think we can try and in any case should to ascertain that this is not so.

And the second threat is from Islam and its fundamentalists. There is a tendency in people to link fundamentalism and Islam. I have heard this many times in America. I heard this quite few times in the course of my three days here in India. While everyone who said it probably then disclaimed the notion. They by saying Fundamentalists' Islam it implies that Islam is fundamentalist. Nonetheless there is an intellectual, psychological predisposition to view Islam as fundamental. Fundamentalism in Islam is an aberration in Islam. It is also minority phenomenon.

But it is far from clear that it is the wave of the future. And in any case, we should not succumb to the automatic conclusion that is instead of acting accordingly. For that increases the probability of that particular intellectual shortcut becoming reality. This is very important because the world of Islam is present here in Asia as well. And the world of Islam has to be incorporated into any structures of international corporation.

Let me conclude by repeating where I started. Eurasia today is the principal arena of power politics. Its stability depends on the inter-play of several major players. From our standpoint that inter-play should seek to create a constructive framework. The emergence of any single power or combination of power as dominant but under-domestic challenge will destabilize Eurasia. As has been the case twice in the last century in the case of Europe. I think we are moving to an age where massive large-scale wars are less likely. But less likely does not mean impossible. And some of the stabilizing forces have to work hard in the Far East and in Asia to achieve peace. They require cooperative response. The response in which America and India can play an active role together. Our statement on relation with China pertains, broadly speaking, to facilitate North East Asia. But then gradually, the resolution of the Korean conundrum and that pertains to the maintenance of the peace talks. And with Taiwan strengthening the eventualities of resolution they have some points in the near future on the unresolved legacies of the Chinese civil war.

And the American–Indian relationship pertains much more to this part of the world.

My talk about this aspect and on the Soviet Union which facilitated the American effort to contain the Soviet Union particularly during the time of the Soviet aggression in Afghanistan. But that era is all over and old.

The world we are living in is fundamental transformation. So far as the information technology is concerned it has brought to the foray many fundamental transformations in many countries. There were qualitative changes in the sect of mankind which while gaining some degress of consolve (phonetic) over the external world to improve the quality of life. And that's how this enormous progress is as a result of industrial relations. And with altogether new acceleration. We are aware Pakistan's continuing long struggle together with its ideals so far as its ideologies are concerned to the outside world. But that era has been changed. And it is setting of new era of knowledge that influences us to change ourselves.

The Soviet Union facilitated the American effort to contain the unrest, particularly in the time during the Soviet aggression in Afghanistan. But that era is over with the times of Gulf war. And our state of relationship with China pertains broadly speaking, is not only in Asia but it pertains to the gradual resolution of the Korean conundrum. And it pertains to the maintenance of East–West relations and the Taiwanese stress sending eventual resolution of some point in this future, of the unresolved legacies of the Chinese civil war.

The American–Indian relationship pertains much more significance in this part of the world under the question of alluding of transfer of oil. American stability, in the adjoining area is also of significance. And India and both the US share this common interest. In most of these systems we assure common interests in the avoidance of nuclear war in this part of the world. Nonethless, all have common interests. Now in the same line all of that I wish to emphasize is about our concept of relations, which do not sub-serve the Union's strategic relations. And by its vacations that are directing against somewhere else. But we are seeking this kind of tendency with China and we are trying to come out with India that there is a normal cooperative relationship in international affairs in which hopefully, low range central global nuclear war is analyzed worthily. There is decline in the overall strategic setting in Asia with the US that can maintain normal cooperative relation with China and it impinges directly on Japanese affairs and contributes to play positive and constructive role by Japan. If the US can maintain normal, peaceful cooperative relation with India why not with others that part of globe? Hopefully it contributes also to have such a normal peace in this part of the world, particularly in so far as some of the immediate neighbours are concerned. And that will ultimately consider still more stable strategic setting in Asia.

I finally conclude by adding that in a global perspective it is true that the strategic situation in Asia is more volatile now than in Europe. Throughout this last century it was complex situation under the Eurasia mega continent that precipitated the global conflicts. These conflicts then directly originated from the western periphery of Eurasia, mainly Europe. Now to the extent that it is foreseen, there is a possibility of many serious conflicts that are more likely to surface in the eastern periphery of the mega continent.

‹2›

Central European Security Policy

András Balogh*

With the collapse of the Warsaw Pact and the disintegration of the Soviet Union, the bipolar system of international relations ceased to exist. This abrupt phenomenon surprised the Western political elites as well as the influential foreign political think tanks, which obviously did not have any practical plan to build up a new international political and security system instead of the accustomed one. Their whole world concept was built on the specific relationship of confrontation and of cooperation with the Russians, who, within a few years, from calculable, well-organized, and formidable giants became incalculable, disorganized and disillusioned dwarfs.

In this period of uncertainties and ambiguities, two progressive security related developments proved to be decisive: one is the stubborn determination of both parts of Germany and Chancellor Kohl's efforts that led to the German unification, the other is the triumph of activism and globalism in the US that strengthened the American leadership in world affairs. Needless to cite the statements and steps of those who wanted to perpetuate the American - Soviet/ Russian dualism or rejected the American involvement in the European developments. By now it is indisputable that any European (and global) security system can only be based on continuous active role of the United States and a strong, stable and unified Germany.

---

* Head, Department of Modern and Contemporary History, ELTE University; Chairman, Committee of International Studies at the Hungarian Academy of Sciences, Hungary.

For Hungary as well as other Central European states any solid and long-term national security should be created in all European frameworks. Central Europe after the dismantlement of the Habsburg Monarchy is a fragmented, vulnerable area; its twentieth century history is a series of devoted but mainly lost battles against invaders; glorious but mainly futile aspirations for democracy, sovereignty and economic welfare. This area has a long history of being a buffer zone or just a zone of interest that the powerful states or alliances were acquiring, ceding or exchanging. But this is only the military strategic dimension. According to Central Europeans, this area inhabited by Poles, Czechs, Slovaks, Hungarians, Slovenes, Croats has always been organic part of western civilization, not less than other Central European countries like Germany and Italy.

Threats and Challenges

Most Central European experts tend to conceive of the security of their countries in a broader sense: among the main challenges against their security they lay greater emphasis on the economic and ethnic factors than on direct military threats. This attitude is rational due to the high costs of a very difficult and too long a period of transition of their economies to an effective market economy. The decisive share of the private sector in the economy, the growing ties with the EU members, the improving infrastructure, the increasing presence of foreign capital, the rapid rise in the industrial export and certain positive macro-economic indices cannot hide the poor economic performance in general: industrial and agricultural output as well us per capita GDP in most Central European countries do not reach the level of late '0-s. Comprehensive and successful economic transformation have been achieved only in three countries, namely in Poland, in Hungary, and in Slovenia.

As to the threats and challenges to the Central European security we have selected two major issues to review. The first is the potential threat coming from the fluid situation in and around Russia, the second is the Yugoslavian crisis, the third is the so-called minority-related conflicts.

Russian Uncertainties

The disintegration of the Soviet Union is a fait accompli and is, at least for the foreseeable future, irreversible. The decision to be separated from Russia seems to be final for all former Soviet republics with the exception of Belarus.

The case of the three Baltic republics is clear, the sovereignty and independence of these countries enjoy massive domestic support and a worldwide recognition. Despite the strong historical, cultural, religious, economic and other links between Russia and Ukraine there is a sufficient base to state that Ukraine will be able to develop its distinct national identity and to overcome the destabilizing cultural and religious antagonisms within the nation and to halt the recent economic deterioration. The Ukrainian independence is the most essential counterweight against any attempt to restore a Russian or Soviet Empire. The Moldavian, the Caucasian and the Central Asian newly independent states, whether they are ruled by former Soviet bureaucrats or not, in all probability, would resist to any attempts to reintegrate them into a Russian or non-Soviet empire. Belarus is, at the moment, an exceptional case. The situation is a quite unusual: the leadership of this new nation is doing everything to make the newly granted interdependence meaningless and irrelevant.

In all the newly independent successor states, there are two factors worthy of special attention that may pave the way to Russian influence. One is the economic hardship; the difficulties caused not only by the transition to a market economy but also by the destruction of old economic ties. The other factor is the presence of large Russian minorities in many of the former Soviet republics. Clearly, some degree of an economic recovery and the democratic treatment of the Russian minorities should be the basic elements of the consolidation of the newly independent states of former Soviet Union.

Russia has lost non-Russian territories of the empire including those areas that their rulers (czars) had conquered centuries ago. Russia has lost its outer empire, i.e. the member states of the perished Warsaw Pact. Russia has lost the influence that it once exercised politically, ideologically and militarily in many parts of the world. This influence, strongly associated with ideological values and requirements, by now, has disappeared in the former Third World as well as in the revolutionary and leftist movements. A nationalist and capitalist Russia cannot be an alternative model for various anti-western political forces.

Russia itself would constitute the greatest danger to Europe and the work through a possible weakening of central authority and through uncontrolled and uncontrollable economic, social and political developments. Contrary to the generally held perceptions, the real threat may come not from a strong fundamentalist leadership (in the context of security, the concrete forms directions, ideologies and slogans of fundamentalism are irrelevant) but from the lack of, or shortcomings of, a stable state structure and from a weakening discipline of the armed forces. The apocalyptic vision of starvation, epidemic and growing criminality cannot entirely be ruled out. And one cannot forget that Russia continues to be a nuclear superpower. The more likely development in Russia is, however, a long and slow process of economic transformation in which former top-level bureaucrats, managers, and criminals will constitute a significant part of the entrepreneurial class presently in formation. Production and consumption would decline or stagnate for a period of time and social differentiation would go ahead. The new Russia would live together with manifest social tensions; its democratic institutions and practices would develop slowly and with the occasional setbacks. Most likely that both (semi) democratic and authoritarian regimes would help the expansion of the market economy.

The Russia described in this scenario would not be one of the two superpowers but definitely a great power with immense human and natural resources, and with a sizeable military strength and influence.

War and Genocide in former Yugoslavia

Besides Russian and related issues, the continuous South Slav crisis has provoked and continues provoking fear and uncertainty.

The Yugoslavian developments tragically revealed that the post-world war II *European security system*, based on a very sophisticated balance of power between the two blocks, no longer exists. More precisely, its important elements survive but these are insufficient for dealing with the entirely new security challenges that Europe is facing. The traditional by-polar system suppressed the nation-state interests, and strengthened block solidarity. The leadership of the superpowers made the territorial integrity of states a sacrosanct doctrine and ruled out any armed conflicts on the European continent. According to commonly voiced opinion of the Cold War era, an armed conflict in Europe would necessarily and immediately have led to global nuclear confrontation. The special status of Yugoslavia should be understood in this context, i.e. after the consolidation of the European blocs, the non-allied Yugoslavia was not a challenge to the bloc logic; it was an organic part of it. The special status of Yugoslavia as well as its integrity was also an important constituent part of the by-polar European and global balance.

As a result of the dismantlement of the by-polar system, Yugoslavia lost its raison d'etre; artificial Yugoslavia was an artificial product of the World War I anti-German and anti-Austro-Hungarian Entente aspirations exploiting the short-lived compromise of Croat and Serb nationalists. This was made manifest by the re-appearance of the same forces that had already abolished Yugoslavia during the Second World War.

Nowadays, many pose the question as to what role certain foreign powers played in encouraging and supporting those who claimed independence for the former member states of Yugoslavia. Foreign forces certainly did have a significant influence. But contrary to many analyses on the topic we are of the opinion that the foreign powers involved did not render substantial support to the secessionists. All that they achieved was the reduction, and later the withdrawal of their support to the centralists in Belgrade. Furthermore, after 1990, the foreign powers did not work for the termination of the Serb domination of Yugoslavia; they only lost their interest to encourage and maintain it in the name of the territorial integrity of Yugoslavia.

After the end of the Cold War, Yugoslavia was no longer a part of a delicate balance of power. Consequently, the Yugoslavian crisis became an almost purely local crisis. The conflicts and wars among the ex-Yugoslavian states and nations no longer had a global dimension. The reactions of the external powers, though certainly did not correspond with certain basic humanitarian principles, were, from the point of view of European security, rational. Their inactivity and later rather limited and hesitant involvement was based on the proven conviction that there was no danger of the spread of the inferno to other regions.

The Yugoslavian crisis has a great many dangerous aspects but, without doubt, the complexity of historical, cultural, religious national and minority related antagonisms of Bosnia have been the most obvious and the most difficult to handle. The European realpolitik has not been able to reach any settlement for four years and without even a fragile peace it has been impossible to persuade all the warring parties to reach some sort of compromise with each other. Finally, the relative calm has been restored by the first US-led out-of-area NATO operation. It was US foreign policy that worked out and implemented the Dayton Agreement. This agreement may easily be criticized for its approval of the de-facto, semi-independence of the three entities that had come into existence partly as a result of aggression and ethnic cleansing. But, to be fair, one has to recognize that in the given conditions this agreement has achieved the cessation of a long-lasting and extremely cruel war, and the further destruction of human life.

The Central European nations have even more directly concerned by the Kosovo conflict. The continuous civil war in Kosovo has resulted in:

1. spreading the tensions in the region, and especially in Albania and in Macedonia,
2. generating ethnic conflicts in the entire region,
3. halting the democratising process in the Balkans,
4. destabilizing the economics of the neighbouring countries,
5. accelerating large-scale exodus of ethnic Albanians,
6. discouraging capital investments to the whole of Central Europe.

From the very beginning it was evident for the Central Europeans that they have not been able to influence the developments, the consequences of which they feared. The Kosovo crisis was an important factor that contributed to the rapid admission of three Central European states (Poland, Hungary and the Czech Republic) to NATO.

Despite the unique character of the South Slav developments, the entire Balkan conflict should be analyzed in a wider international context. An open and extended Balkan conflict would give a chance to certain external destabilizing forces to interfere in the affairs of the Central European region. Unforeseen developments in Russia and in the Islamic world have been seen as security risks to be taken into consideration when formulating a long-term security policy, concerning the tensions in many parts of the former Yugoslavia and of the Balkan area.

Consequently, Central Europeans consider the presence of NATO, and through NATO that of the US peacekeepers, to be a necessary measure to discourage the above-mentioned non-Central European destabilizing forces. The most essential lesson of the Yugoslavian developments is that no credible security system exists in Europe without NATO and that NATO cannot function without a strong US commitment to Europe.

Elements of a European Security System

It is highly necessary to come to some arrangements between the enlarged NATO and those states which do not intend or do not have possibilities to join NATO. Surely, even reformed NATO would never cover the entire continent; and the dangers of a possible new East-West or any other division line should be avoided. One has to face two crucial facts: (1) that Russia is not and will not be a member of the NATO (2) that without Russia a common and comprehensive security system cannot be built. Partnership for Peace programmes and similar future initiatives may help a lot but it is evident that an all-European security institution, probably a stronger OSCE, will have an important function. The good working relationship between NATO and Russia is an essential stabilizing factor in Central and Eastern Europe, and even more significant in the global context. Successful extension of NATO to Central Europe and a strategic partnership between NATO and Russia are the two basic pillars of the European stability. The OSCE has its future role in mediation in long-term conflict resolution efforts and in early warning function.

Regional and sub-regional cooperation in Central Europe can also be elements of the European security. The general impression shared by both foreign observers and the Central European public is that Central Europe does not represent any kind of homogeneity: the population of this relatively small area is divided by traditions, culture, language, religion; and contrary to the West European dominant integrationist trends, the Central Europeans are not capable enough to create firm cooperative structures, they manically talk about European unity but actually they have destroyed even their existing integration forms and, in some cases, their own multinational, federative states.

We are obliged to admit that this image is not merely a fabrication of less informed western scholars or selfish politicians who want to block the enlargement of European institutions. However, the case of the Central European regional cooperation is not entirely hopeless. The historical traditions in Central Europe cannot be identified with the constant triumph of the disruptive and isolationist forces. All of Central Europe's nations, for a thousand years, were organic parts of the same cultural, economic and political heritage. Hungarians, Slovaks, Croats, and Romanians have for centuries lived within the frameworks of the Kingdom of Hungary, and later with Austrians and Czechs in the Habsburg Monarchy. The traditions of the multinational and multi-religious people living together in Central Europe are not shorter or weaker than those in the western half of the continent. The functioning of' the Visegrad Group, the Central European Initiative, the Cespa and many trans-border regional cooperation forms show that the idea of Central European cooperation is present in the region. The reservations and objections against the deepening of the regional cooperation forms cannot be explained by xenophobic nationalisms and anti-neighbour prejudices of the nations of this region. Political leaders in the Central European countries do not intend to create strong regional, political, economic and security institutions of cooperation to avoid the impression that they are thinking of an alternative to the existing Euro-Atlantic institutions. They emphasize that any of the regional or sub-regional frameworks they have established do not have any defence or security aspects. Nevertheless, the very existence of the various regional and sub-regional cooperation forms is a valuable factor of the entire European security architecture.

Last but not least we must recognize the bilateral relations as important elements of a new security system. In Central Europe where the states and the nations do not coincide and in many cases national minorities culturally and linguistically are part of another nation that may be dominant in another country, where in the last hundred years international borders changed frequently, and never as a result of a democratic decision-making, the good neighbourhood is the most essential requirement of regional and the whole European stability. Any lasting reconciliation in the region should be based on two fundamental principles. One is the unconditional recognition of international borders; the other is the unconditional respect for national minority rights including the free use of minority languages in educational and administrative institutions, as well as not only the tolerance but also the encouragement of various national minority entities that express their political interests in accordance with the accepted international norms and practices.

‹3›

The Nature of Democratic Peace
And other Forms of Non-War

*Martin Sherman**

A. Introduction

Among students of international relations, there is a "near consensus" as to the ubiquitous absence of war between democracies.[1] Russett has deemed this relationship to be 'one of the strongest non-trivial and non-tautological generalizations that can be made about international relations'.[2] Indeed, some have gone so far as to claim that this finding is "probably the closest thing that we have to a law in international politics'.[3] However, as Maoz and Russett point out, whether the lack of conflict between democratic states is indeed a law of international politics depends not only on the empirical robustness of this finding, but also on our ability to *account* for it.

It is thus not surprising that in recent years, considerable efforts have been devoted to this end. However, in contrast to the broad consensus as to the finding itself, there seems little agreement as to a generally accepted explanation thereof. Typically, such efforts have either evoked structural constraints on decision makers in democracies, or the externalization of internal norms of compromise and negotiation characteristic in democratic societies to account for the international conduct of libertarian states in general, and for "democratic peace" in particular.[4] Several endeavours have incorporated decision- and

* Department of Political Science, University of Tel Aviv, Israel.

game-theoretic techniques to elucidate the processes and interactions which produce the observed phenomenon of "democratic peace" in the international system.[5]

In the following analysis, I purposefully circumvent discussion of the relative adequacy of the various explanatory approaches to the absence of war between libertarian regimes, and attempt to push the inquiry one stage further, by broaching an additional question which also impinges, albeit indirectly, on issues of causality. Instead of asking: "What are the reasons for 'democratic peace'?" I ask, "What is the nature of 'democratic peace'?" Formulated more specifically, the question becomes:

"Can 'democratic peace' be substantively differentiated from other forms of 'peace' and if so, how? Accordingly, the major thrust of the present investigation will be to address the issue of whether or not "democratic peace" is a *qualitatively* different political condition, based on substantively different motivations, from "peace" that involves non-democratic states?

I approach this endeavour via an elaboration of a rigorously deductive decision-theoretic model developed by Sherman and Doron,[6] in which they show that it is possible to impute differing risk preferences, and hence differing rational actor utility functions, to differing regime types. Their model not only provides a cogent "as if" account for a wide range of empirical findings pertaining to inter-state behaviour, but also a method of integrating the seemingly antithetical regime-insensitive realist and regime-sensitive domestic constraints paradigms of international relations into a single logically consistent conceptual framework. They argue that a link can be forged between the apparent incongruities in these two approaches by means of a decision-theoretic modelling technique, and show that when the element of *uncertainty* is introduced into the decision-making situation in a methodologically rigorous manner, differing domestic constraints can be translated into differing expected utility maximizing (EUM) rational-actor risk preferences, and hence into differing EUM rational actor utility profiles. Consequently, an integrative conceptual scheme is created, in which the *seemingly uniform* realpolitik aspiration of an egotistical pursuit of national interest (i.e. of maximizing expected utility), manifests itself in different policies choices, each of which maximise expected utility for actors of various utility profiles (i.e. for regimes of different domestic structures and hence of differing domestic constraints). Thus an analog model of the international system, comprising duly defined ideal-type libertarian and non-libertarian regimes is constructed, in which the differing degree of political plurality and of accountability of the executive to the citizenry result in risk-averse attributes (i.e. utility curve concave to the X-axis) being assigned to the executive decision making unit in the libertarian regimes, and risk acceptant attributes (i.e. utility curve convex to the X-axis) to the executive decision making unit in the non-libertarian regimes. As indicated earlier, this simple, so-constructed model is shown to be capable of providing a cogent "as-if" explanation for a relatively wide range of empirical findings pertaining to the international system - including the absence (or at least the extreme rarity) of violence between democracies;[7] the apparently exclusive propensity of non-libertarian regimes to initiate preventative wars;[8] the effect of the composition of the political environment on the propensity to war of differing regime types;[9] and the relatively greater sensitivity of democracies to drastic change in their political environment.[10] (A brief synopsis of the model is presented in an appendix to this essay).

By extending the development of this model, I demonstrate that it is possible to arrive at a theoretically formulated distinction between "democratic peace" and other forms of "peace", showing them to be not only qualitatively different, but indeed virtually antithetical conditions - or as Lord Acton may have phrased it - opposing "extremes of political [phenomena], being connected by name alone".[11] Finally I explore the policy-making implications which follow from this distinction both at system and the individual state levels. These implications are of no small import. For if the term "peace" has plural meanings, each comprising radically different political conditions, then both:

(a) the feasibility of its attainment in a given set of circumstances, and

(b) the appropriate nature of the policy by which it might be attained,

are liable to vary greatly depending on which variant of "peace" is referred to. Accordingly, a correct diagnosis of the prevailing conditions and correct definition of the appropriate policy parameters for the attainment of the relevant variant of "peace" assume considerable significance. For the aspiration to an unfeasible "peace" or the adoption of policies inappropriate for the attainment of feasible "peace" are liable to have grave consequences for the insensitive or undiscerning policy maker.

B. Resoluble and Irresoluble Bargaining Structures: An Analysis of Tractable and Intractable Disputes.

We commence the analysis with an elaboration of the model's translation of disparate risk preferences assigned to the different regime types into disparate policy choices. Consider Decision Tree I. below,

Note that in terms of schematic policy options, a decision to choose Option I represents a preference for the maintenance of

DECISION TREE 1

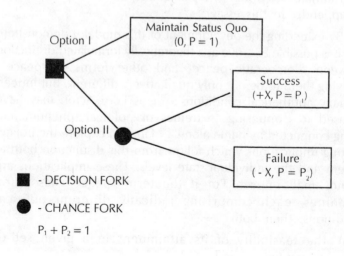

the status quo, while a choice of Option II indicates a preference for a risky attempt to change the status quo by means of force, which may result in high rewards or costly failure. Thus, positive and negative values of X denote, respectively, the gains and the losses involved in a successful and an unsuccessful attempt to force a change in the status quo existing between two states, while p_1 and p_2 represent the respective probabilities of each such outcome.

In the model, the decision situation depicted in Decision Tree 1 is assumed to represent schematically the policy choices available to the executive decision makers in each regime, whenever a potentially violent clash of interests arises between states. (The likelihood of such a situation arising is expressed by the probability, P_c, which is a function of the systemic anarchy i.e. the un-coordinated pursuit of the national interests of the individual sovereign states in the international system).[12]

Now, if for given values of p_1 and p_2, a risk-averse (libertarian) EUM is just indifferent between Option I and Option II, then a risk acceptant (non-libertarian) EUM will have a definite preference for Option II, and vice versa. Thus, ceteris paribus, one can conclude that when confronted with the decision situation in Decision Tree I, the former would have a greater propensity for option I - i.e. to eschew violence and maintain the status quo. Conversely, the latter would have a greater propensity for option II - i.e. to attempt to change the status quo by violence. Note this divergence of preferences prevails even when both protagonists concur entirely as to the significance of the prospective outcomes and the likelihood thereof (i.e. this variance of choice is not to be attributed to mis-perception on the part of one or more of the participants).

Next, consider the range of values of p_1 and p_2 in which a libertarian risk averse EUM will have a definite preference for Option I over Option II, but a non-libertarian risk acceptant EUM will prefer Option II over Option I. This is clearly a plausible scenario and holds for a wide range of values of p_1 and p_2. Indeed, only if there are extreme differences in the values of p_1 and p_2 ($p_1 >> p_2$ or $p_1 << p_2$ i.e. only if either victory or defeat, respectively, are highly likely, can both risk acceptant and risk averse EUMs be expected to choose the same options.[13]

In other words, p_1 and p_2 now take values such that for the former:

$$U(0) - \{ P_1 * U(X) + P_2 * U(-X)\} - \delta_1 > 0$$

while for the latter

$$U(0) - \{ P_1 * U(X) + P_2 * U(-X)\} = \delta_2 < 0$$

Thus δ_1 is a measure of how much a libertarian risk-averse EUM prefers Option I to Option II. In other words such a decision maker will even be prepared to tolerate a certain *deterioration* in the prevailing status quo, say -e, rather than attempt a violent change of the status quo where $-\varepsilon_0 < -\varepsilon < 0$, and

$$U(-\varepsilon_0) = P_1 * U(X) + P_2 * U(-X)$$

As long as $-\varepsilon_0 < -\varepsilon$, a libertarian risk-averse EUM will prefer a certain deterioration of the status quo to an uncertain initiative to change it.

This modification of the decision situation can be depicted in schematic form in Decision Tree 2.

As long as the deterioration of the status quo does not exceed the threshold value of ε_0 (i.e. as long as $-\varepsilon > -\varepsilon_0$), the

DECISION TREE 2

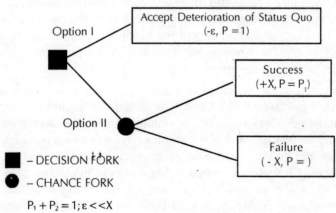

Option I — Accept Deterioration of Status Quo
$(-\varepsilon, P = 1)$

Success
$(+X, P = P_1)$

Option II

Failure
$(-X, P =)$

■ – DECISION FORK

● – CHANCE FORK

$P_1 + P_2 = 1; \varepsilon << X$

preference of a risk-averse libertarian BUM will remain unchanged and he will continue to favour Option I (a certain limited deterioration of the status quo) to Option II (a risky attempt at violent change). Note that this calculation of the threshold value relative to the status quo is very similar to the basic technique for the "indifference premium" calculation in the elementary theory of insurance.[14] Accordingly, e is in fact the "premium" that a risk-averse EUM would be willing to pay in order to eliminate the choice of a risky policy option.

Clearly, a risk-acceptant non-libertarian EUM would only be induced to forego the risky option for a certain *amelioration*, $+\varepsilon > +\varepsilon_0$, of the status quo. Thus instead of a "deterioration threshold" there will be a theoretical "amelioration" threshold", ε_0, such that:

$$U(+\varepsilon_0) = P_1 * U(X) + P_2 * U(-X).$$

below which (i.e. values of $+\varepsilon < +\varepsilon_0$) the risky option will always be preferable to a certain improvement in the status quo.

The existence of such threshold levels defines the "bargaining space" between two regimes which will determine whether or not conflicts are resoluble by non-violent means.

Consider a potential dyadic confrontation between two regimes in our idealized international system. Clearly in such a system, there are three possible types of dyadic conflict configurations:

Democracy vs. Democracy (Dem - Dem dyad);

Dictatorship vs. Democracy (Dict - Dem dyad);

Dictatorship vs. Dictatorship (Dict - Dict dyad).

In a Dem-Dem dyad, whatever the specifics of the general concavity (towards the X-axis) of the respective utility curves of the protagonists, there will *always* be a range defined by the respective deterioration thresholds in which both parties will be willing to make concessions in order to avoid embarking on violence - see Fig 1. Thus a non-violent resolution to the conflict of interests will be arrived at.[15]

The 1995 settlement of the bitter USA-Japan trade dispute would appear to illustrate the principle involved here.

In the case of a Dict-Dem dyad, the relative locations of

Fig. 1 :   Model's Representation of Democratic Peace

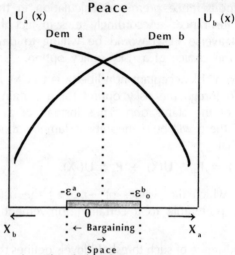

$-\varepsilon^a_0$ = Deterioration Threshold of Democracy *a*

$-\varepsilon^b_0$ = Deterioration Threshold of Democracy *b*

"amelioration" and "deterioration" thresholds respectively will determine whether the bargaining structure is "resoluble" or not. If (as shown in Fig. 2), there is an overlap of the ranges defined by the thresholds - i.e. if the maximum deterioration in the status quo that the libertarian regime is prepared to incur without foregoing its preference for the non-violent Option I, is greater than the minimum amelioration in the status quo which the non-libertarian regime requires for it to forego its preference for the violent Option II - then the dispute will be amenable to non-violent resolution. If there is not such overlap (as shown in Fig 3.), it will not be.

Note however, that in a Dict-Dem dyad, there is no recipe for maintaining peace by some form of reciprocity involving mutual give and take. The only formula by which violence can only be avoided is by the libertarian regime (which will accept

Fig. 2 : A Resoluable Dict-Dem Conflict

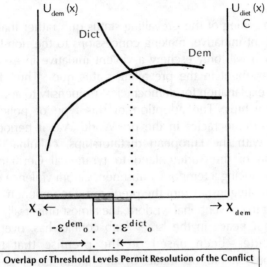

Overlap of Threshold Levels Permit Resolution of the Conflict

$-\varepsilon^{dem}_o$ = Deterioration Threshold of Democracy
$-\varepsilon^{dict}_o$ = Amelioration Threshold of Dictatorship

Fig. 3 : An Iresoluable Dict-Dem Conflict

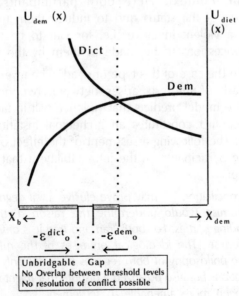

Unbridgable Gap
No Overlap between threshold levels
No resolution of conflict possible

$-\varepsilon^{dem}_o$ = Deterioration Threshold of Democracy
$-\varepsilon^{dict}_o$ = Amelioration Threshold of Dictatorship

some worsening of the prevailing status quo rather than embark on a violent initiative) making concessions to the non-libertarian one (which will only eschew a violent initiative in exchange for an improvement in the prevailing status quo). Thus the model offers an explanation for democracies' propensity to appeasement of dictatorships. The adoption of this type of policy by the European democracies in the pre-World War II period in their dealings with the European dictatorships, culminating in the succession of the Sudetenland to tyrannical Germany in the hope of inducing a temporary abstinence from violence constitute a corroborating instance of the predicted phenomenon. Likewise, according to conventional wisdom, the almost universally accepted formula for peace in the Israel Arab conflict has, over the past five decades, been based on the premise that territorial concessions should be made by libertarian Israel to it's non-libertarian Arab adversaries.

In the case of Dict-Dict dyads no overlap of bargaining positions is feasible (see Fig. 4), at least in an approximately "zero-sum" context. Here both participants require an amelioration of the status quo to induce them to eschew the option of a violent initiative, i.e. for war to be avoided both require concessions to be made to them by the other.

Thus in the case of this type of dyad, whenever a potentially violent clash of interests arises between two non-libertarian regimes, the model predicts that violence will in fact erupt. The Iran-Iraq conflict constitutes an archetypal instance of a Dict-Dict dyad. The following assessment of the effect of the regime-type of the participants on the intractability of that conflict is of significance:

> ... reconciliation ... may prove elusive ... if negotiation or compromise would undermine the raison d'etre of the contending parties. For both Iran and Iraq it is difficult ... to compromise. The ideological premises of the ruling elites and the philosophy of both regimes have not only inhibited negotiations but also polarized a dispute that might otherwise have been more amenable to settlement.[16]

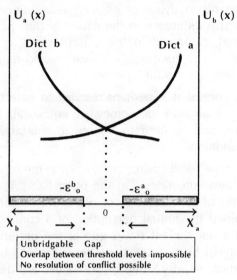

Fig. 4 : Unstable Dict-Dict Dyad

$-\varepsilon^a_0$ = Amelioration Threshold of Democracy *a*
$-\varepsilon^b_0$ = Amelioration Threshold of Democracy *b*

This description appears to illustrate well the volatile quality of the relationships in Dict-Dict dyads suggested by the model. Note the model does not imply perennial and ubiquitous violence between non-libertarian regimes, but that violence will in fact materialize whenever a potentially violent clash of interests (as depicted in Decision Tree 1) arises, and which may be resolved non-violently in dyads of different - i.e. Dem-Dem or Dict-Dem - composition. Thus, the phenomenon of non-violent interactions in Dict-Dict dyads is accounted for by the non- zero value of the systemic constant $1-P_c$ (as defined above). Accordingly, it would be incorrect to interpret the model as presenting violence in a Dict-Dict dyad as deterministically inevitable. Rather it is treated as a stochastic event, the probability of which is dependent of the system-anarchy parameter assigned to the idealized international system.[17]

C. Democratic and the Other Kinds of Non-War

The foregoing analysis of the relationships prevailing between the participants in dyads of differing composition underscores the substantive difference in the nature of the "peace" that can be expected to prevail in the various cases. In particular it emphasizes how a "democratic peace" would differ from other types of "non-democratic" peace.

In this context it is perhaps relevant to note that the word "peace" in itself may be somewhat equivocal, for the same epithet can, and is, used to denote to substantively different political conditions.

On the one hand "peace" may used in the sense of "*mutual harmony*" between states. On the other hand, it may be used in the sense of the "*absence of war*". The former is likely to be maintained by mutual perception of a common interest in preserving a non-violent status quo as the preferred option of all protagonists. By contrast, the latter is likely to be maintained by deterrence, in which one or both sides are dissuaded from embarking on violence as a preferred option, only by the threat of incurring exorbitant cost. This differentiation is pertinent to the subsequent analysis of the differing nature of the "peace" that can be expected to prevail in dyads of differing composition.

Figs 1-4 illustrate the substantive difference in the types of "peace" that can prevail in dyads of differing composition.

Fig 1. depicts the essence of "democratic peace". From the graphic representation is clear that for two participating democracies, there is a range (between $-\varepsilon^a_0$ and $-\varepsilon^b_0$) wherein the status quo can be maintained by a common willingness to make reciprocal concessions (i.e. violence is willingly eschewed by mutual preference). Thus "peace", in a sense which approximates "mutual harmony", can be attained.

The situation is however qualitatively different in a case of a non-democratic participant(s) in the dyad. For example in the case of the Dict-Dem dyad in Fig 2, the clash of interests is indeed resoluble within the range $-\varepsilon^{dem}_0$ $-\varepsilon^{dict}_0$, but not by the willingness of both parties to make reciprocal concessions. Here both parties will eschew violence only if the democratic participant agrees to make concessions to the dictatorial one, large enough to fall in the range $-\varepsilon^{dem}_0 -\varepsilon^{dict}_0$: (smaller concessions will not induce the dictatorship to switch its preference from Option II to Option I in **Decision Tree 1**; while demands for concessions greater than dem will induce the democracy to switch its preference from Option I to Option II.) The only other way to dissuade the dictator from opting for a policy of violent change (Option II) is to alter his perceptions of the potential pay-offs associated with the possible outcomes,[18] so that the expected utility deriving there from is less than that deriving from the alternative of maintaining the status quo. Clearly this ability to inflict greater damage or prevent tempting gains (or to make losses more likely and victory more remote) involves enhancing the deterrent capability of the democracy. Thus unlike the Dem-Dem situation represented in Fig I, in the dyadic configuration depicted in Fig 2, violence can only be averted by *unilateral concession* by the democracy, or by deterring the dictatorship from his predilection for the use of force. These conditions would therefore appear to preclude the attainment of "peace" in the sense of "mutual harmony". Hence, the only version of "peace" that appears feasible under the Dict-Dem conditions in Fig 2 would be "an absence of violence".

The Dict-Dem situation depicted in Fig 3 is again qualitatively different. Here, unlike the case in Fig 2., the structure of the conflict is such that the initial position of the parties permits no non-violent resolution of the conflict even by unilateral concessions on the part of the democratic participant. (Note that there is no overlap of threshold values ε^{dict}_0, ε^{dem}_0 and hence no positive bargaining space.) Thus, if violence is to be averted, this can only be achieved by enhancing the deterrent posture of the democracy. If not, the dictatorship will adopt its preferred option and attempt to impose a change of the status quo by force. In these conditions "peace" of the "mutual harmony" type is unfeasible. Accordingly, if "peace" is to be attained or maintained, this can only be of the "absence of violence" variety, based on the deterrent ability of the democracy.

Fig 4. represents a conflict in a Dict-Dict dyad. Here, as in Fig 3., there is no overlap of the threshold values ε^b_0, ε^a_0, and thus no possibility of conflict resolution either by mutual or by unilateral concessions. Consequently, since for both parties the preferred option is to attempt to forcibly change the status quo, unless either one or both of them enhance their deterrence posture, violence will ensue. Here too, "peace" in the sense of "absence of violence" rather than "mutual harmony" appears to be the only feasible variant.

Table I summarizes the qualitative differences in the substance of "peaceful" relations that can prevail in different dyad-types. It underscores that the substance of the relations prevailing in a "democratic peace" (in a Dem-Dem dyad) differs materially from "non-democratic" variants (in Dict-Dem and Dict-Dict dyads).

TABLE 1

Dyad Type	Bargaining Space	Possible Mechanisms of Violence Avoidance	Nature of the Feasible Peace
Dem-Dem	Always Positive	Reciprocal Concessions	Mutual Harmony "Democratic Peace"
Dict-Dem	Positive	a) Unilateral Democratic concessions	Absence of War
		b) Democratic Deterrence	Absence of War
Dict Dem	Negative	Democratic Deterrence	Absence of War
Dict-Dict	Always Negative	Reciprocal Deterrence	Absence of War

Thus, according to the theoretical developments which derive from the model, it appears that "democratic peace" may be described as a state of "stable equilibrium", which will sustain itself around the prevailing status quo unless some radical form of external disruption is imposed on it, to induce the dyad participants to choose any option other than non-violence as their preferred policy. By contrast, the type of peace prevailing in other dyadic contexts may be designated as a state of "unstable equilibrium" that can only be sustained by some form of external constraints, without which one or both of the dyad participants would choose violence as its preferred option. A graphic representation of this conceptual differentiation is provided in Fig 5.

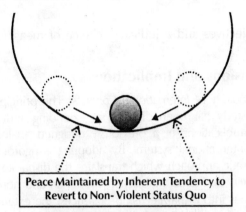

Peace Maintained by Inherent Tendency to Revert to Non- Violent Status Quo

Conceptual Representation of Democratic Peace as Stable Equilibrium

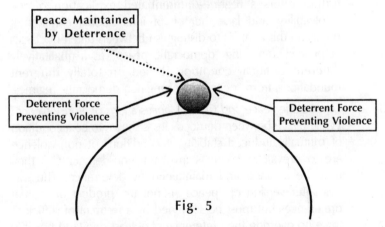

Peace Maintained by Deterrence

Deterrent Force Preventing Violence

Deterrent Force Preventing Violence

Fig. 5

Conceptual Representation of Non-Democratic Peace as Unstable Equilibrium

"Peace", it would thus appear, is a term of distinctly heterogeneous content. The substantive disparity between its multiple meanings are indicative of qualitatively different - indeed virtually antithetical - political realities which should not be overlooked, ignored or misconstrued in any policy endeavour designed to attain or maintain "peace". Indeed, an awareness of these differences is essential for both a prudent definition of feasible objectives and a judicious choice of measures for their achievement.

D. Conclusions and Implications

1) *A Typology of International Conflicts*: The principal thrust of this study has been directed at extending and elaborating the applications of a previously designed analog-model of the international system. By adopting a rigorous decision-theoretic approach which translates the disparate degrees of plurality and accountability in libertarian and non libertarian regimes into disparate risk preferences, the extended model provides a typology of dispute development and outcome, as well as an "as if" mechanisms to account for them. It further offers a regime-differentiated explication of the resolvability, and lack thereof, of international conflicts. It builds on this analysis to distinguish between different classes of peace, identifying "democratic peace" as a qualitatively different political condition, based on totally different foundations, from "peace" involving non-democratic regimes.

2) *Democratic Peace and Other Manifestations of Non Violence*: While peace between democracies is shown to be a condition of mutually induced stability, if conditions of non-violence are to prevail in contexts involving non-democracies they must be attained and maintained by deterrence. Thus, as this latter version of "peace" is not the product of mutual preferences but must be sustained by a restraint of sufficient force, to override the preference of at least one (and possibly both) protagonist(s), it cannot be considered a stable political condition. For if this restraining force were to weaken, allowing the preference(s) of the protagonists to assert itself/themselves, "peace" will be disrupted and violence ensue. It is of significance to note that that this diagnosis of "democratic peace" as a condition of stable political equilibrium, and "other peace" as a condition of unstable political equilibrium, is arrived at neither by:

   (a) ascribing some sort of moral superiority to democracies or to their leaders; nor by

(b) ignoring the fundamental anarchy of the international system, in which every state, regardless of its internal structure, pursues its own egotistical self interests independently of the interests of other states.

Indeed, quite the opposite is true. The behavioural patterns derived are the exclusive product of purely political calculi of decision makers in both democratic and non-democratic regimes.

Moreover, the reciprocity of non-violence that prevails between democracies, is not the result of an assumed lack of conflicting interests in an anarchical environment, but of the mutual preference of democracies to resolve such conflicts of interest, which occur no less frequently between them as they do between other regime types, by means other than violence.

3) *Policies for the Pursuit of "Peace"*: The analysis points to a distinction that has profound consequence for policy makers. For if the objective of any policy is the attainment of peace, the foregoing analysis suggests the success of such policy is contingent on at least two factors: (a) recognition of the type of "peace" that is feasible between the *pertinent protagonists* given the nature of their domestic regimes; and (b) the use of *pertinent policy* instruments for the attainment of the peace deemed to be feasible. Thus if the vision of peace is that of mutual harmony, sustained by a willingness of all participating parties - even in a situation of zero-sum conflicting interests - to make reciprocal concessions rather than to resort to endeavours to acquire gain by force, its attainment is feasible only in a fully democratic (Dem-Dem) environment. In this type of environment, such as exists in North America and Western Europe, disputes may be genuinely resolved by non-violent policies such diplomatic negotiation, or mutually agreed arbitration or mediation.[19] In any other regime-type configuration, accomplishment of such a condition of mutual harmony is unfeasible. In a *heterogeneous* configuration (Dict-Dem), non-violent outcomes to disputes are only attainable either by policies of resolute *democratic*

deterrence (such as the posture adopted by the USA in the Cuban missile crisis) or unilateral *democratic appeasement* (such the repeated concessions made by the western democracies to Nazi Germany in their muted acquiescence to successive violations of the European status quo, from the breach of the Versailles Treaty, through the infringement of the Locarno Pact up to the breaking of the Munich Agreement.[20]

4) *Democracies, Dictatorships and Deterrence*: Note that with respect to both aspects raised in the preceding paragraph, two policy pertinent clarifications are called for, one regarding democratic appeasement posture, the other regarding democratic *deterrence* posture.

(a) With regard to the former, if a policy of "positive inducement" or appeasement of dictators by democracies is not to be merely a stop-gap measure which delays rather than prevents the outbreak of violence (as in the case of the concessions made to the Nazi regime), but is to be considered an effective policy instrument, with a realistic prospect of permanently eliminating the potential for future belligerency, two conditions must be met:

(i) the concessions made by the democracy must be large enough to fully satisfy the dictator's genuine demands; and

(ii) the concessions made by the democracy must not be large enough so as to undermine its own vital interests and impair its future deterrent capabilities.

For if the proffered concessions are less than the dictator's real demands (whether overt or covert), they will do nothing to advance the cause of averting violence. Even if they are accepted, they will only create a new undesirable status quo, involving further dispute the resolution of which will require further democratic concessions, which if not forthcoming will precipitate violence. Thus if appeasement is selected as a policy option, it should be clear that only total fulfillment of all dictatorial demands, including any hidden agendas that may exist (i.e. total democratic capitulation), will render it an option that may have a chance of success in averting the outbreak of violence. (Indeed, history has shown that even this may not suffice.)[21]

(b) However should a democracy decide that it is not prepared to make the pertinent concessions (either because it fears that these will undermine its own vital interests or because it fears that its dictatorial opponent has a "hidden agenda" and after attaining his initial demands will subsequently insist on the fulfillment of additional ones), then violence can only be avoided by a suitable deterrent policy - since no dictatorial concessions will be forthcoming to resolve the dispute in a mutually harmonious fashion In this regard it is crucial for the democratic policy maker to be aware that in the design of his deterrent posture vis-a-vis a dictatorial opponent, the robustness of this posture must exceed that he would consider sufficient to deter himself (or a regime of structure similar to his own) from instigating violence. For as Sherman and Doron point out, any deterrent policy that is just robust enough to successfully deter a (risk-averse) libertarian regime, will definitely fail to do so against a (risk-acceptant) non-libertarian regime.[22] (See point 6 below for the implications this has for the security dilemma.) It is thus essential that in the design of any defence posture, the democratic policy maker avoid making his own value system or priorities on the basis of such a design, or imputing a similar value system or priorities to his dictatorial rival.

5) *Dictatorial Belligerency*: In a *homogeneously dictatorial* configuration (Dict-Dict), disputes seem to irresoluble by bona-fide bi-lateral or even unilateral concessions and the prospect of violence can be avoided only by all dispute-

participants adopting a deterrence posture sufficiently robust to dissuade any one of them from aggression. (As previously pointed out, the model does not imply that every interaction between dictatorships must inevitably degenerate into a potentially violent dispute. It will be recalled that the occurrence of such potentially violent disputes, whose probability of occurrence is defined by the P_c — see section B - is a stochastic function of the system anarchy.)

6) *The Implications for Security dilemma*: The essence of the classic dilemma focuses on the uncertainty in identifying the point at which, in the pursuit of *increased* security, a given state will begin to be perceived as a threat by another, thereby provoking a response on the part of the latter, and thus *decreasing* the security of the former. In its conventional form, this conundrum is usually presented in regime-insensitive manner.[23] However the foregoing analysis would appear to suggest that this is likely to be inappropriately undiscerning and that an element of regime-type differentiation ought to be introduced. Thus building on Sherman and Doron's inference that even under strict *ceteris paribus* condition, a more robust deterrence posture is called for a risk-acceptant dictatorial adversary than for a risk-averse democratic one, it would appear that disparate regimes make disparate attitudes towards the security dilemma necessary. Accordingly, in the case of a dictatorial adversary with its relatively higher propensity to forcible violation of the status quo, considerations of *bolstering deterrence* should be afforded greater weight than the fear of *causing provocation*. Conversely, it seems that this relative emphasis should be reversed in the case of a democratic adversary. For on the one hand, there is less need to invest efforts in dissuading violent initiatives aimed at violating the prevailing status quo, because of such regimes' greater predilection for its preservation. On the other hand, in view of its greater sensitivity to radical changes in its environment,[24]

and its greater propensity to pre-emption,[25] a democratic regime is more likely to perceive a qualitative increase in the military prowess of potential rival as a severe threat to the existing status quo, and respond forcibly to pre-empt it (the Israeli strike against the Iraqi nuclear facility in 1981 being a case in point). Thus, in addressing the security dilemma, it would appear that even under strict *ceteris paribus* conditions, different regime types require that different weights be accorded the countervailing considerations of increasing security on the one hand and the avoiding of provocation of the other.

7) *The Practical Relevance of the Theoretical Analysis*: The set of rules for regime-related patterns of international behaviour derived from the model have much the same relevance for executive decision makers and policy formulators as the principles derived from micro-economic models have for the formulation of marketing (or acquisitions) policy of a commercial corporation. Just as an awareness of the effect of various economic parameters on consumer demand does not supply a unique formula for the setting of an optimal advertising budget, so an awareness the effects of the various regime related political parameters, specified in the models developed in this article, do not provide a precise operational formula for the prescription of optimal foreign policy. However, just as an awareness of the effects of such variables such as elasticity of demand (or supply) and market segmentation and so on, can make for a more informed and effective commercial policy so an awareness of the effect of various behavioural propensities in the international system make for a more informed and effective foreign policy. In this regard, it is perhaps fitting to conclude with a reference to Waltz's recommendations for the future theoretical advancement of international relations:

> To construct a theory we have to abstract from reality, that is, to leave aside most of what we see and experience. Students of international politics have tried to get closer to the reality

of international practice and to increase the empirical content of their studies. Natural Science, in contrast, has advanced over the millennia by moving away from everyday reality and by fulfilling [the] ... aspiration to lower 'the degree of the empiricism involved in solving problems'. 'Natural Scientists look for simplicities: elemental units and elegant theories about them. Students of international politics complicate their studies and claim to locate more and more variables. The subject matters of the social and natural sciences are profoundly different. The difference does not obliterate certain possibilities and necessities.[26]

It should be recalled that not only *natural* scientists but economists (i.e. *social* scientists have constructed successful models of highly complicated market processes by employing simple hypothetical fictions of utility maximising consumers and profit maximizing firms. These models intentionally ignore the myriad complexities and intricacies that are undeniably part of the households of the consumer and boardrooms of the firms, i.e. they do indeed "leave aside most of what we see and experience". However, such abstraction and simplification has done nothing to reduce the power and practical pertinence of the conclusions drawn from these models, or to prevent them becoming the cornerstone of the economic policies of many states and international organizations. *Prime facie* there seems no reason why inter-state behaviour should be intrinsically more abstruse or less amenable to similar avenues of intellectual endeavour.

APPENDIX

Because of the centrality of the Sherman-Doron decision theoretic model to the development of the subsequent analyses, I briefly summarise the features of its major components.

Modelling the International System: Internally Disparate Ideal-Type Sovereignties in Environmental Anarchy.

In accordance with the "as if" analog approach adopted in the development of the model, an "idealized" international system is proposed. The basic units comprising this system are sovereign entities, called 'states'. Since these entities are by definition "sovereign", they are immune to sources of authority external to themselves. Thus, the system which they comprise must also be, by definition, "anarchical", that is devoid of any hierarchical structure regarding the ranking of the authority of units in it.

Now, in conformity with the realpolitik paradigm, these sovereign entities are assumed to behave in a manner commonly (indeed necessarily) ascribed to states in their anarchic milieu i.e. they each strive to pursue their own egotistic national interest without coordination with, or subordination to, the interests of any other state. In a decision-theoretic context, pursuit of this interest is taken to be the aspiration to maximize expected utility from available policy options in which the relevant pay-offs are defined in terms of national power and security.[27]

· Furthermore, all the regimes included in this theoretical system are assumed to be either "in-disputably democratic" or "indisputably dictatorial". To avoid becoming embroiled in a semantic dispute as to what precisely constitutes a "democracy" and a "dictatorship", each of the regimes is defined in terms of a set of five parameters as follows:

i.   The legitimacy of overt, legal political opposition to the incumbent executive authority.

ii. The effective limitations imposed on the power of the executive - i.e. the degree to which there exists effective separation of powers, or alternatively an effective system of checks and balances.

iii. The degree of public participation in the political routine and the extent to which this participation determines the composition of the executive.

iv. Limits on the possible use that can be made of state resources by an incumbent executive to further his own ends (as opposed to those of the state).

v.   The independence of the communication media from control by the incumbent executive.

A regime in which all five parameters are manifested to a maximum degree is defined as "indisputably democratic"; a regime in which they are manifested to a minimum degree is defined as "indisputably dictatorial".

In the model, the problems of operationalizing these parameters (which can all, in principle can be conceived of as quantifiable variables ranging between two polar values) have been purposely avoided. However, this does not detract from the methodological validity of the approach adopted, which draws on diagnosing, identifying and correlating clearly discernible qualitative (or at least "order-of-magnitude") differences in both the dependent variables (international behaviour) and the independent variable (regime types), rather than measuring graduated variation in these variables.

Accordingly, in all the regimes included in the "idealized" international system postulated above, these five parameters are either "maximally" or "minimally" manifested. Thus for example, in these regimes, there is either total government control over the media or total absence of such control. Similarly, there is either total prohibition of overt opposition or complete toleration thereof.

Clearly, in the real-world international system, it is unlikely that the empirical domestic attributes of actual regimes will exhibit all (or any of) these five parameters to their theoretically most extreme degree. However, the design of an international system comprising only two distinct regime types, is a hypothetically fictitious construct and which like concepts of "perfectly competitive markets" and "frictionless surfaces", does not purport to mirror the reality of the empirical world. Rather, it is employed as an analytical tool in an effort to formulate potentially useful, simplified abstractions regarding the phenomena under consideration.

Note that in such an anarchic system, because all units in it are sovereign EUMs, all engaged in an uncoordinated pursuit of their own self interest), there will clearly be a non-zero probability of a clash of interests arising between any two such entities. This probability, which will be a function of the prevailing systemic anarchy, is denoted by Pc, with $0 < Pc < 1$. Note that in an anarchic environment, there is no a *priori* reason to assume that Pc will be a regime sensitive, unless one makes far reaching (and seemingly arbitrary) assumptions (a) as to the linkage between domestic structure and international behaviour, in general; and (b) as to the propensity of certain regime types to *coordinate* or *subordinate*, their interests to those of other states, in particular. Such assumptions would clearly run counter to the assumptions of international anarchy on which the model is based. Therefore, in the model, the likelihood of a clash of interests arising between two states (as distinct from the preferred mode of resolution of such a clash) is independent of the states' internal political structure.[28]

In summary then, the model on which the ensuing theoretical developments is based, consists of a finite number of sovereign entities, whose internal political regime may be one of two antithetical hierarchies, either "democratic" or "dictatorial", duly defined by the maximum or minimum intensities of the five defining parameters. These entities operate in an environment of external anarchy, which is a necessary result of the sovereignty of the component entities. In such an anarchical environment, there is a defined probability of a clash of interests arising between any two such entities, all striving, to maximize their expected utility, which is a function of the levels of power and security they endeavour to attain. This probability is a systemic variable defined by the (necessarily) uncoordinated pursuit of the egotistical sovereign aspirations in an anarchical self-help environment.

Regime Type as a Determinant of Risk Preference

In similar vein to Bueno de Mesquita, the model treats the executive authority of a regime "as if it were a single EUM decision maker".[29] As we have seen, this is in complete conformity with the realpolitik perspective. The domestic constraint component of the model is expressed by demonstrating that different domestic structures in libertarian and non-libertarian regimes generate different levels of accountability, which constitute the differing domestic constraints in these disparate regimes. These differing domestic constraints are shown to translate into differing rational actor risk preferences, and hence differing rational actor utility profiles. Specifically the model assigns risk averse attributes (i.e. utility curve concave to the X-axis - see Fig. I A) to the executive decision making unit in the libertarian regimes, and risk acceptant attributes (i.e. utility curve convex to the X-axis - see Fig 2A) to the executive decision-making unit in the non-libertarian regimes.

Fig. 1A

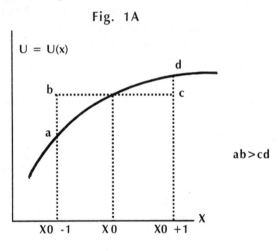

Fig. 2A

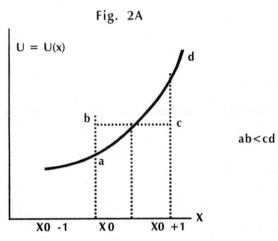

The assignment of these respective risk preferences is based on detailed analytical arguments supported by empirical research data.[30] Consequently the *seemingly uniform* realpolitik aspiration of maximizing expected utility will express itself in *different* policies choices (each of which maximize expected utility for actors of different utility profiles).

This principle may be schematically illustrated by an analysis of decision situation represented in Table A 1:

		OUTCOMES	
_DECISION	I	0	0
OPTIONS	II	+X	−X
PROBABILITIES		P1	P2

Table A1   Decision Making Situation Involving Choice Between Certain and Uncertain Option Initiatives

Note that in terms of schematic policy options, a decision to choose Option I represents a preference for the maintenance of the status quo, while a choice of Option II indicates a preference for a risky attempt to change the status quo by means of force, which may result in high rewards or costly failure. Thus, positive and negative values of X denote, respectively, the gains and the losses involved in a successful and an unsuccessful attempt to force a change in the status quo existing between two states while P_1 and P_2 represent the respective probabilities of each such outcome.

In the model, the decision situation depicted in Table 1A is assumed to represent schematically the policy choices available to the executive decision makers in each regime, whenever a clash of interests arises between states. It will be recalled that the likelihood of such a situation arising is P_c.

Now, when a risk-averse (libertarian) EUM is confronted with the decision situation in Table 1, he would *ceteris paribus* have a greater propensity for Option I, i.e. to eschew violence and maintain the status quo. By contrast, a risk acceptant (non-libertarian) EUM would have a greater propensity for Option II, i.e. to attempt to change the status quo by violence. Thus, if P_1 and P_2 are such that former would just prefer Option I to Option II, while the latter would definitely prefer Option II and visa versa, even when both concur entirely as to the significance of the prospective outcome and the likelihood thereof.

In the model, these hypothetical simplifications and abstractions set out above, which draw on both the realpolitik paradigm of the international system (that assigns EUM-characteristics to all foreign policy formulators) and the domestic constraint paradigm (that imposes different utility curve profiles for policy formulators in different regimes), are integrated into a single analytical framework in a manner which reconciles the apparently contradictory perspectives of the two opposing paradigms. Moreover, as mentioned in the introduction to this essay, this model is capable of accounting for a range of observed empirical phenomena pertaining to the functioning of the international system and the observed relationship between the domestic political structure of the state on the one hand, and its conduct in the international system on the other.

Notes

1. Z. Maoz & B. Russett, *"Alliances, Contiguity, Wealth and Political Stability: Is the Lack of Conflict among Democracies a Statistical Artifact?"* **International Interactions**, Vol. 17, (3), 1992, pp. 245-6.

2 B. Russett, **Controlling the Sword: The Democratic Governance of Nation Security**, Cambridge, Mass.: Harvard Univ. Press, 1990, p.123.

3 See Maoz and Russett, p. 246.

4 Ibid.

5 For a game-theoretic approach, see Bruce Bueno de Mesquita and David Lalman. **War and Reason: Domestic and International Imperatives**. New Haven: Yale University Press, 1992. For a decision-theoretic approach, see Martin Sherman and Gideon

Doron, *"War and Peace as Rational Choice in the Middle East".* **The Journal of Strategic Studies**, Vol. 20(1) 1997, 72-102, and Martin Sherman**, Despots, Democrats and the Determinant of International Conflict,** London: Macmillan, 1998.

6   Sherman and Doron, op. cit

7   See for example, P. Wallensteen, **Structure and War**, (Stockholm, Raban and Sjoren, 1973); R. Rummel, *"Libertarianism and International Violence"*, **Journal of Conflict Resolution** Vol. 27, 1983 pp. 27-71 and, *"Libertarian Propositions on Violence Within and Between Nations: A Test Against Published Research Results"*, **The Journal of Conflic' Resolution**, Vol. 29, 1985, pp. 419-455; S. Chan, *"Mirror Mirror on the Wall - Are Freer Countries More Pacific?'*, **Journal of Conflict Resolution**, Vol. 28, 1984, pp. 617-648; M. Doyle, *"Liberalism and World Politics"*, **American Political Science Review**, Vol. 80, 1986, pp. 1151-1161; F. Fukuyama, *"The End of Ideology"*, **The National Interest**, Vol. 16, 1989 pp. 3-18; Z. Maoz and N. Abdola H. *"Regime Type and International Conflict, 1816-1976'"*, **Journal of Conflict Resolution**, Vol. 33, 1989, pp 3-35; S. Bremer, *"Dangerous Dyads: Conditions Affecting the Likelihood of Interstate War 1816-1965"*, **Journal of Conflict Resolution** Vol. 36, 1992, pp. 309-342; and Maoz and Russet op .cit and, *"Normative and Structural Causes of Democratic Peace, 1946-1986"*, **American Political Science Review** Vol. 87, 1993, pp. 624-638.

8   R. Schweller, *"Domestic Structure and Preventative War: Are Democracies More Pacific?"* **World Politics**, Vol. 44(2), 1992) pp. 235-269.

9   Z. Maoz, **Domestic Sources of Global Change**, Ann Arbor: Michigan University Press, 1996.

10 Ibid.

11 J.E.E Acton, (Baron) Nationality, in **Essays in Freedom and Power**, Boston: Beacon Press. (1948), pp. 166-95. Acton used this turn of phrase to describe the antithetical relationship between two opposing manifestations of nationalism.

12 P_c, is thus an expression of the likelihood of potentially violent clash of interests arising between two sovereign states each pursing their own egotistical national self-interest in an anarchical system.

Note that there is no a *priori* reason to assume that $P_{c'}$ will be regime-sensitive, unless one makes far-reaching a *priori* assumptions as to linkage between domestic structure and international behaviour, in general; and as to the propensity of certain types of regime to *coordinate* with or even *subordinate* their interests to those of other regimes, in particular. Thus, the likelihood that a clash of interests between two states may arise is (in contrast to the preferred mode of resolution of such a clash) independent of the state's internal political structure, Sherman and Doron, p. 89.

13 For a detailed discussion of the effects of the value of P_1 and P_2, and variations therein, see Sherman and Doron, pp. 79-83.

14 See for example H. S. Denenberg, et al. **Risk And Insurance** Englewood Cliffs, N.J.: Prentice-Hall 1974, pp 17-22.

15 The precise details of the solution and which party concedes more and which less will depend on negotiating skills of each and/ or the specific shape of the two parties utility curves. However, the details of this aspect are beyond the scope the present analysis.

16 C. M. Helms, **Iraq: Eastern Flank of the Arab World**, Washington D.C.: The Brookings Institution, 1984.

17 See Sherman and Doron, pp. 89-91.

18 That is, to increase the perceived potential costs and/or to reduce the perceived potential returns entailed in the choice of this option, or to increase the likelihood of incurring costs and/ or reduce the likelihood of procuring gains.

19 See W. J. Dixon *"Democracy and the Management of International Conflict"*, **The Journal of Conflict Resolution,** Vol 37, No. 1. March 1993, pp. 42-68; and *"Democracy and Peaceful Settlement of International Conflict"* **American Political Science Review,** Vol. 88(1), 1994; and G.A. Raymond, *"Democracies, Disputes and Third Party Intermediaries"* **Journal of Conflict Resolution,** Vol. 38(1) pp. 24-42.

20 These were vividly described by Churchill in the following terms:

Look back and see *"what we had successively accepted or thrown away: A Germany disarmed by solemn treaty; a Germany rearmed in violation of a solemn treaty; air superiority or even air parity cast away; the Rhineland forcibly occupied and the Siegfried Line built or building; the Berlin-Rome Axis established;*

Austria devoured and digested by the Reich; Czechoslovakia deserted and ruined by the Munich Pact; its fortress line in German hands; its mighty arsenal of Skoda henceforth making munitions for German armies; ... the services of thirty five Czech divisions against the still unripened German Army cast away - all gone with the wind. (W. S. Churchill, The Second World War: The Gathering Storm, Vol. I, London: Cassel & Co., 1949, pp. 346-47).

21   For example the Italian foreign minister during WW II, Count Ciano, made the following observation at the proclivity of the Nazi regime:

The [German] decision to fight is implacable. .. [the Nazi leadership] rejects any solution -which might give Germany satisfaction and avoid the struggle. I am certain that even if the Germans "were given more than they ask for they will attack Just the same... (Count Galeazzo Ciano, **The Ciano Diaries 1939 -1943,** H. Gibson, ed.. New York: Doubleday, 1946. p. 119).

Neither does this appear to be a case-specific feature of the Nazi tyranny. *Lord* Avon sees very similar traits in the Fascist regime in Rome. He cautioned against making any conciliatory initiatives to Mussolini, warning "that it is dangerous to offer such gestures to dictators', and that "... no amount of promises or understandings or renewed professions of friendship or even humble crawlings on our part will affect Mussolini's course (A. Eden, (Earl of Avon), **The Memoirs of Anthony Eden**; Facing the Dictators, Boston: Houghton Mifflin, 1962.p. 453 & 480). In a more generalized vein, Janice Gross Stein warns that potential aggressors "are as likely to misperceive and misinterpret accommodative signals as they are coercive language. If they interpret conciliatory offers as evidence of weakening resolve, as they frequently do, then deterrence failure can become much more likely". (J. Gross Stein, "Calculation, Miscalculation and Conventional Deterrence II: The View from Jerusalem", **Psychology and Deterrence**, R. Jervis, R.N. Lebow and J. Gross Stein, eds., Baltimore: John Hopkins Univ. Press, 1985, p.87.)

22 Sherman and Doron, pp. 97-8. Note that if a deterrent policy is just sufficiently daunting to dissuade a (risk averse) democracy to eschew a risk attempt to forcibly change that status quo s.t.:

$$U(0)\text{-}E[U(x]= e \to 0, \varepsilon > 0$$

where $U(0)$ is the utility deriving from the maintenance of the status quo and $E[U(x)]$ is the expected utility deriving from a risky attempt to change it by force; then *any* (risk-acceptant) dictatorship will *definitely* opt for the risky option.

23 R. Jervis, *"Cooperation under the Security Dilemma"*, **World Politics,** Vol. 30, No. 2. 1978, pp. 167- 214; J. L. Snyder, *"Perceptions of the Security Dilemma in 1914"*, **Psychology and Deterrence,** R Jervis, R.N. Lebow and J. Gross Stein, ed., London: John Hopkins Univ. Press, 1985, pp. 153-179.

24 Maoz, 1996

25 Sherman and Doron, 1997

26 K. Waltz, **Theory of International Politics**, Reading, Mass.: Wesley Publishing Co., 1979, p.68. (Emphasis added.)

27 Although they are rather lax in distinguishing between the independent variable (utility) and the independent variables (power and security) Bueno de Mesquita and Lalman also cite the pursuit of later as the goal of EUM decision maker in the realpolitik approach (B. Bueno de Mesqita, and D. Lalman **War and Reason: Domestic and International Imperatives**, New Haven: Yale University Press, 1992, p. 12, 17 & 36).

28 See Maoz, p. 1996, for interesting empirical corroboration of this theoretical premise.

29 B. Bueno de Mesquita, **The War Trap**, New Haven: Yale University Press, 1981, p.20).

30 For details see - Sherman and Doron, pp. 79-83.

◀4▶

The Emerging Order for Regional Peace & International Security

*Arya Bhushan Bhardwaj**

The emergence of the New Global Economic System (Economic Globalization) has entirely changed the concept of regional peace and security at the global level. In the last decade of the 20th century, a very powerful international lobby had built a strong public opinion through the electronic and print media that there was a universal need for more and more liberalization in the fields of trade, commerce and industries. This process of globalisation culminated in the formation of the World Trade Organization (WTO). More than a hundred and seventy nation-states have come together in an unprecedented agreement to globalize their approach in the field of economic activities. In other words, we can say that governments of 170 countries mutually agreed to have their common Minister for Economic Affairs, in the form of the WTO, cutting across geo-political boundaries and political ideologies. Apparently, this new phenomenon of Economic Globalization appears to be very lofty in ideology.

The idea of the WTO was floated by rich countries in the guise of so-called universal progress and development. The WTO brought about a diabolical change in global politics. Until the recent past, it used to be the "political powers" that have been influencing the economic policies of a particular nation-state.

---

* Founder Director, Gandhi-in-Action Constructive Workers' Home, New Delhi, India.

The powerful nation states used to influence the economy and politics of the politically and economically weaker nation-states. With the emergence of GATT and WTO, the "Economic Powers" have gained the upper hand by acquiring the power to decide, direct and dictate the "political leadership" of its member countries at the nation-state as well as the overall global level.

The WTO has virtually become the deciding factor as to which economic policy has to be adopted, in order to serve a particular economic interest. Before the emergence of GATT and the WTO, the economic powers at the national level had been influencing the policies and politics of the nation-state from behind the scenes. But now these forces have come to the fore and sidelined the "political powers" by taking over the decision-making authority on the economic policies. The nation-state agencies are being forced to act as a corollary of the WTO in economic matters. For example, it is the WTO that is dictating as to what is to be produced and how much is to be produced, and how much a country can import and how much it can export.

No individual nation, who has signed the GATT agreements, can henceforth decide its economic policies unilaterally, and in isolation. It has to go through the WTO.

The New Global Economic System (NGES) has taken the existing "Political Systems" for a ride. Therefore, it has become imperative that vital issues like "The Emerging Order For Regional Peace and International Security", the "New Economic Order", "The New Information Order", and "The Emerging Social and Cultural Order" be analyzed in the light of the changing global scenario. Existing political systems will hereafter be controlled, influenced, and ultimately forced to accept the policies decided by the "New Global Economic System" (NGES), which is currently being dominated by the "Capitalistic" forces. In this changed environment, a "New Global Political System (NGPS)" has become the dire need of the hour. Whether an international agency like the UNO has the political will power and moral support from its dominant member-nations is a million-dollar question. Would the UNO be able to take on the challenge to work for a NGPS paradigm, which could be more positive and better than the existing political systems? It is a must in order to keep checks and balances on the emerging NGES paradigm.

Let us briefly evaluate the global impacts of the two existing political and economic systems, Democracy (based on capitalistic economy) and Democratic Socialism (based on the communist philosophy of social change). These two systems have been influencing the issues of "Regional Peace and International Security" till the last decade of the twentieth century. These two popular political systems were gradually evolved to replace the centuries-old, redundant political and economic systems such as monarchy, feudalism and colonialism. These three old systems from the Middle Ages had been most barbaric and the worst exploitative systems that human history ever witnessed. Democracy in most of the countries was based on the British Parliamentary System. Democratic Socialism was based on the Marxist theory of an egalitarian society. It also claimed to be better than the Westminster type of Parliamentary System of democracy. The communist system came in to existence after the 1917 revolution in Soviet Russia while democracy was born in Britain in the 18th century and has since been partly in practice in western countries.

At the end of the eighth decade of the 20th century (1989), the USSR got dissolved and all its republics were disintegrated and became independent countries. They were forced to adopt the free-market based capitalist system. Till then, the whole world by and large, remained polarized around these two systems: democracy and democratic socialism. For all diplomatic purposes most of the nation-states were identified as direct or indirect supporters of, either the Eastern Bloc (led by the USSR joined by China) or of the Western Bloc (led by the USA and its allies), baring a few exceptions. The Western Bloc was open and a free world based on democratic values. Under this system, the ordinary people have full freedom and liberty. On the other hand, the Eastern Bloc was named the "Iron Curtain World" where the citizens have no freedom and civil liberties. It remained a hard fact that neither of the two systems could fulfil their commitments and come up to the expectations of the ordinary masses of both the Blocs. In fact, both got into a long-drawn-out Cold War and have been busy in a mad race of building armies and armaments, totally forgetting the promises that their political leadership made to the people.

Let us take a quick look at the twentieth-century social, political and economic outcomes, which have immensely affected the common masses all over the world. In the first decade, M.K. Gandhi and others gave a clarion call to fight at the people's level against the cult of colonialism and feudalism of the rich West (pretending to believe in democracy). The cult of colonialism has been used to enslave and exploit "the poor" all over the world. This struggle for basic human rights began from South Africa in a small but very unusual way, by adopting the innovative human technology of a non-violent struggle, the Satyagraha. This unique movement slowly spread all over the world, particularly in the Afro-Asian countries, which were mostly under colonial rulers.

In the second decade, people had to witness World War I (1912-13), which brought in its wake innumerable deaths, immeasurable destruction of human and material resources, besides leaving behind awful miseries and sufferings to face, for millions in the decades that followed. The horrors of this ugly war brought into being the League of Nations with a hope to establish global peace and security. But not much could be achieved in the direction to build a "Global Order for Peace and Security". In the latter part of this decade emerged the 1917 Revolution in Soviet Russia. It came with a ray of hope of building an egalitarian society based on the Marxist theory of economic equality and social justice.

In the early thirties, M.K. Gandhi gave a new dimension to his non-violent civil disobedience movement through his historic Dandi (salt) March. It not only shook the Indian masses but also drew the attention of the global community. It brought about a global awareness of basic human rights, and gave a new impetus to the struggle of the oppressed and depressed all over the world. The whole world was badly hit by the worst economic recession in the mid-thirties in which the poorest had to suffer the most. Then came the Holocaust of the Nazi Regime followed by World War-II, in the mid 1940s. For the first time in human history, nuclear weapons were used in this war. More than 350,000 innocent people, men, women, young, old and infants, were killed in the two cities of Japan, Hiroshima and Nagasaki. Thousands were left to die a slow death due to delayed radioactive effects, which has been continuing till date. This perhaps was the worst tragedy the millennium was to witness.

The horrors of World War-II again compelled the political leadership all over the world to constitute a broad-based international forum, which could effectively work for "Peace and International Security". Hence, the League of Nations was thus replaced by the formation of United Nation Organization (UNO). It was hoped that this international forum would be able to achieve the goal of peace and security in the world. But unfortunately, it remained a daydream. Despite the endless efforts of the UNO and its various forums like the Security Council, the world has witnessed many dreadful wars in the'50s, '60s, '70s, and '80s, and also in the'90s. Millions of innocent people lost their lives in these purposeless and most unfortunate wars. Besides, the Cold War continued after World War-II, between the two superpowers. It had almost brought the world to the brink of a Third World War. Human and material resources worth billions and billions of dollars had been spent in piling up nuclear as well as traditional weapons at the cost of millions, while millions of people were dying of hunger, poverty and diseases. Even after a decade of the post-Cold War period, there seems to be no end to this mad race. Many people have now started thinking that the UNO has also lost its purpose and direction. It has practically been reduced to a tool in the hands of a few vested interests and the lone superpower, the US. The Secretary General of the United Nations, Kofi Annan, in his Millennium address to the UN General Assembly on September

8, 2000, himself expressed his doubts about the future role of the UNO in the fast changing global scenario.

The twentieth century has been very unique and eventful in many ways. On the one hand, the world has moved far ahead in the direction of so-called "material progress and economic developments". Scientific and technological discoveries and inventions have totally changed the face of our planet Earth. Electronic highways have practically demolished all geo-political boundaries and have reduced the planet to a "Global Village". There has been tremendous progress in the fields of technical education, physical health, communications, information technology and the transportation systems. These material changes have revolutionized the standards of living and quality of life for a few. But on the other hand, unfortunately, there has been an ever-increasing gulf between the "haves" and "have-nots". Almost two-thirds of the people living on this globe are still half-naked, half-fed and half-sheltered.

On the basis of the above discussion, I have to make two observations. These are the outcome of my personal experiences of the past three decades, of my study and research at the micro and the macro-level. These observations are based on the performance of the above-mentioned two main political systems, in relation to the problems of peace and international security. Firstly, I want to say that none of these two political systems (democracy and democratic socialism or communism), that dominated the polity and economy of the 20th century (till the fall of the USSR in 1989), were able to face the real and genuine problems of the teeming millions. They have failed to meet the aspirations of the people at large.

In the USSR and other communist countries, their political system failed due to the wrong policies of its exponents. The political leadership in these countries totally ignored to fulfil the promises that they made to work for economic equality and social justice to the masses. The countries under the Iron Curtain of the communist regime were totally lost in the mad race for building armaments. These countries, under the leadership of the USSR, had fallen into the wrong trap that was intentionally laid down by the leader of the western world, the USA. Common people in the communist world could neither get their personal freedom nor achieve economic equality and social justice. A false fear psychosis was created by the political leadership in the minds of the ignorant people that it was imperative to build armaments in order to meet the potential war threats from the USA. This artificially created fear totally ruined their economy and made the USSR bankrupt. How long could the people stand this type of mental as well as physical torture in a situation of near-starvation? The obvious result had to be the unfortunate fall of the communist era.

The second observation I would like to make is about the so-called democracy and the free market system of the western world. Coincidentally, when the USSR was disintegrating in 1989, I was in the USA on invitation from the University of Texas in Austin to speak on Gandhi and non-violence. When the news of the fall of USSR reached the university campus, I was surprised to hear the immediate reaction of some of the faculty members and the scholars: " We were expecting our system (the American System) to collapse as it has also become redundant. The ordinary people under this capitalist system have also been reduced to the conditions of a slave like people under the communist regime".

The difference was merely situational. Under the Iron Curtain Rule, the people were made slaves by the political system, while under the capitalist regime; the people were forced to become slaves to their artificially created desires and lust for more and more material possessions. The commercial media, the mad race for consumerism and cutthroat competition, was creating the urge for such slavery. Therefore, we can say that in one part of the world the political system was making common people slaves, and in the other part the economic system was responsible for their voluntarily accepted slavery. Qualitatively, there was not much difference in the lives of the ordinary people from the point of view of the wider goal of peace and security, which was never addressed sincerely.

Another important universal phenomenon of the socio-cultural changes in the late 20th century has been the ever-rising trends of hidden violence in the personal life of the individual. It is very often reflected in the society in the form of social and political violence. People are still divided over colour, caste and creed and, of course, by the ill-founded concept of "Majority and Minority" (the founding principle of the Westminster system of parliamentary democracy). Most of the wars that have been fought in the latter half of the 20th century in many parts of the world, have their roots in ethnicity. It is basically a human-attitudinal problem deeply rooted in the human psyche. How can we bring about a fundamental change in the human attitudes at the personal level and the circumstantial changes at the societal level, in order to combat personal and social violence? This change has to come about at the socio-political systems level. Is this an indication towards the limitations and partial failure of the present form of the democratic system dominated by the capitalist forces? Is it not a big challenge before humanity? This, I believe, is the real riddle to be solved in order to build a "New Order for Regional Peace and International Security" in any part of the globe.

M.K. Gandhi, in the beginning of the 20th century had warned the world about the ills and limitations of the parliamentary system of democracy in his controversial book "Hind Swaraj" which he wrote in 1908 in his mother tongue, Gujarati. His own political party, the Indian National Congress disagreed with his theory. He was left alone when India got independence from British Colonialism in 1947. Nehru had tried the Soviet model for development against Gandhi's will and failed miserably. Now we have gone in for economic globalization on the GATT and WTO lines. It is like going from the frying pan to the fire.

We have to look back to Gandhi. After the near failure of both communism and capitalism, we have to look for a third power, which could provide a better and more positive "Humane System" for building a better world - a new system that would be free from any sort of violence at the individual as well as at the social level. Herein lies the relevance of Gandhian thought, which advocated a new socio-political system based on the human values of love and compassion. It could be achieved firstly by invoking the spirit of voluntarism, which is hidden inside every human being, to serve the downtrodden. And secondly, imbibe the life of complementarity in place of competition, to complement the life of the local community or village through social and economic activities, without exploiting one another's skill, and also without the exploitation of Mother Earth, for satisfying the greed of material powers and consumerism. This pattern of life at the local and global level can build "Regional Peace and International Security" at the global level.

With the fall of the USSR and the end of the Cold War, the situation in the Asia-Pacific has taken on new dimensions. The US administration's foreign policy of keeping strong army bases in the Asia-Pacific region has slowly been changing. Asia-Pacific countries are emerging as Regional superpowers, economically as well as militarily. Take the example of Japan - it has challenged the superpowers like America in the field of economic prosperity. Similarly small countries like Korea, Taiwan, Singapore, Malaysia, and Hong Kong, have developed their economies in a marvelous way and have become prosperous. India has also made its place in the IT (information technology) sector.

The place and role of China has also been acquiring more and more importance in the Asia-Pacific region, in the fast changing global scenario. After the fall of the USSR, China is coming up as a superpower parallel to the USA. The question of peace and security of the Asia Pacific Region now very much depends on the role of China. Old diplomatic tricks are not going to work any more. The traditional theory of "Divide and Rule" is becoming redundant although this theory is still in practice and the so-called superpowers are still trying to use these age-old tactics in order to establish their hegemony over the economically weaker and developing countries of the Asia-Pacific. But it has to be discarded. The socio-political situation is changing fast. We must bring about drastic changes in our pattern of traditional negative thinking. Asia-Pacific countries should not follow the western system of development and defence as it has brought the world to a point of nuclear holocaust.

To conclude, I have the following suggestions to help build a new Asia-Pacific Region for permanent Peace and Security:

1. All disputes in the Asia-Pacific region must be solved across the table without involving outside forces and intermediaries.

2. Countries of the Asia-Pacific may start a process of having a common Minister for Defence and Minister for External Affairs, as 170 countries have accepted the WTO as their common Minister for Economic Affairs.

3. Providing merely the "Vote Power" to the voter will not strengthen the roots of democracy at the local level. We must think of providing "Note Power" to the voter. That means making a voter an equal partner in the Gross National Production (GNP), so that the national wealth can be shared equitably. This will reduce the gap between the haves and have-nots, which is root cause of hidden social violence. The decision-making power should also be vested in the local democratic institutions as had been visualized by M.K. Gandhi in his concept of "Village Republics".

4. Wherever there are violent struggles for local autonomy in the Asia-Pacific Region, local people should be allowed to decide about their future instead of forcing them to accept the status-quo position like the situation in Kashmir, Sri Lanka, Tibet and other parts of the region.

5. The Indian government should start normalizing its relations with the neighbouring countries. Recently, there have been sincere efforts at the people's level to normalize relations

between India and Pakistan from both sides. These efforts must continue and moral pressure on both the governments must be put. The top leadership must refrain from creating a war-like situation.

6. All countries of the Asia-Pacific region must refrain from involving MNCs in their process of economic development. More and more efforts must be made to develop local natural resources with the help of local technology and human resources based on a decentralized system of production and distribution.

7. All heads of the Asia-Pacific region should meet once a year in order to develop more and more mutual understanding and avoid confrontations on issues of mutual interests.

8. Last but not the least: a five-year moratorium should voluntarily be enforced on the military budgets in the region and the money thus saved should be spent on improving the lot of the poorest of the poor.

‹5›

A New Era of North-South Korean Reconciliation and Co-operation

Yong-Ok Park *

The North-South Korean Summit in Pyongyang in June 2000 was truly a turning point in the inter-Korean relations. The Summit left behind a tremendous impact on every aspect of North and South Korean societies after 50 years of division and fierce competition. In South Korea there have been growing perceptions that a new era of reconciliation and cooperation has finally dawned. Even though there are on-going debates about the real intention of the Pyongyang regime behind the dramatic developments in recent months, many in South Korea and elsewhere seem to feel that the Koreas are finally entering a long-overdue peace process. All these highly visible achievements in inter-Korean relations are, I strongly argue, primarily the result of our consistent policy of comprehensive engagement toward North Korea, or what is more commonly known as the "Sunshine Policy." Indeed, I believe a peace process has started on the Korean peninsula, and our goal for considerable period of time will be building peace on the Korean peninsula. Unification can come only after this period of a peaceful coexistence.

More than ever before, tension reduction and building a new peace regime on the Korean peninsula are gradually

* Senior Research Advisor, Korea Institute for Defense Analyses, Seoul, Korea

drawing attention of many security analysts and ordinary people alike. Currently there are more than four on-going meetings between the North and the South, including high-level talks, defense ministerial talks, the Red-Cross talks, and family reunion talks. At the first-ever defense ministers' talks on September 24-26 of this year, for example, the two sides began to discuss measures that are highly symbolic in bringing reconciliation and cooperation in the military field. They made a joint press release, in which they agreed to resolve military issues that may arise in ensuring the visits, exchanges and cooperation between the civilians, and they agreed to setting up a working-level military commission to facilitate the opening up of the Kyong-ui (Seoul-Shinuiju) Railway and an adjacent highway, all in the spirit of the June 15 Joint Declaration.

The current ROK Government of President Kim Dae-jung has been very active and consistent in pursuing its policy of comprehensive engagement toward North Korea. It has set the objective of its policy on the improvement of relations with the North through peace, reconciliation and cooperation. In other words, the ROK Government wants to achieve four objectives, which include (1) a peaceful management of the current military standoff between the two Koreas; (2) pursuit of reconciliation and cooperation rather than a premature, hasty unification, (3) encouraging and inducing North Korea's reform and openness; and (4) opening a new era of peace and stability on the Korean peninsula.

The ROK Government has made consistent efforts to dismantle the Cold-War structure on the Korean peninsula and to lay ground for a peaceful unification through a peaceful coexistence with North Korea. Here, dismantling the Cold-War structure on the Korean peninsula means: (1) easing hostile relations between the two Koreas; (2) normalizing US-DPRK, Japan-DPRK relations; (3) creating an environment conducive to Pyongyang's reform and openness; (4) abolishing weapons of mass destruction (WMDs) on the Korean peninsula; and (5) replacing the Armistice Agreement of 1953 with a permanent peace treaty between the North and the South.

Also, it has consistently held on to the three principles of its North Korea policy: first, the ROK Government will never tolerate any military provocation from the North that would destroy peace; second, the ROK Government has no intention whatsoever of unifying the peninsula by absorbing the North; and third, the ROK Government will actively promote reconciliation and cooperation on the peninsula. So far, the ROK Government's comprehensive engagement policy toward the North has proved successful in bringing reconciliation and cooperation in various sectors.

Yet, despite the current euphoric mood of reconciliation and cooperation on the Korean peninsula, North Korea is continuing its military activities. I am going to give you some examples. The summer training was conducted in North Korea at the highest level in ten years. Forward deployment of mechanized units and restructuring of artillery units are just a few indications that Pyongyang has increased, not decreased, their military readiness. North Korea is continuing to build up its forces, producing and deploying long-range artillery pieces and constructing underground tunnels to store missiles. And North Korea is making every effort to tighten their military discipline after the inter-Korean summit.

Rationale for the ROK-US Alliance and Security Cooperation with Neighbouring Countries

As we enter a new era of reconciliation and cooperation with North Korea, we will face many opportunities as well as many challenges. The peace process on the Korean peninsula will be basically revolving around the two actors, North and South Korea. And the ROK-US alliance will continue to play an important role in securing our peace and integration with the North. This peace process, however, should be supported by all four surrounding powers, namely the United States, Japan, China and Russia. This has been our policy towards these neighbouring countries and we will continue to implement this policy as we proceed in building a peace regime on the Korean peninsula. And we· will continue to enhance transparency in our dealings with North Korea.

In this context, the future multilateral security dialogue and cooperation among the regional actors will complement, but not replace, our traditional bilateral alliance with the United States. For example, President Kim Dae-jung has made it clear over and over again that we want continued US military presence even after unification with the North. And he made this point very clearly to the North Korean leader, Kim Jung II, who shared his view during their recent summit meeting in Pyongyang. Without doubt the roles and missions of the US troops that will remain stationed on the Korean peninsula will adapt to changing security environment in Northeast Asia. But the alliance that has proved so beneficial to our two countries should and will remain robust and will continue to play an extremely important role of reducing tensions in the region in the years to come.

‹6›

Indian Diplomacy & the Emerging World Order
Options, Opportunities and Constraints

*Arun Kumar Singh**

The events which shaped the present course, content and contour of international politics since 'the end of the Cold War' have posed challenges to and created opportunities for the nations of the world - big or small, rich or poor, weak or strong - to redefine and reorient their foreign policy goals and objectives in order to protect and promote their national interest(s) in the changing international scenario. The termination and the end of the East-West confrontation which was the hallmark of the post Second World War, Cold War period was viewed as an event to herald an era of peace and prosperity. It was hoped that the world would become a saner and safer place based on the principles of coexistence. It was also hoped that a nation, particularly a smaller nation would be able to achieve its foreign policy goals and objectives, which it could not do, due to the constraints of the Cold War world politics. That the strings - political, strategic, economic and technological -attached to a nation's behaviour in its relations with other nations would be loosened in the post Cold War period.

The New World Order:

The events which followed the demise of communist regimes in East Europe, the reunification of East and West Germany and

* Reader, Dept. of Political Science, Arunachal University, Itanagar, Arunachal Pradesh, India.

the disintegration of the 'mighty" Soviet Union made us believe that a new world order is emerging or at best a new world system is about to emerge. The concerted efforts of the world community in expelling Iraqi forces from Kuwait in 1991, further bolstered this belief.

Fukuyama's The End of History? :

Francis Fukuyama, the Deputy Director to the US State Department's planning, in his pioneer but the most controversial essay 'The End of the History?" published in the National Interest, Summer, 1989, remarked "In watching the flow of events over the past decade or so, it is hard to avoid the feeling that something very fundamental has happened in world history".[1] This 'something very fundamental" is explained by him and to quote "The twentieth century saw the developed world descend into a paroxysm of ideological violence, as liberalism contended first with the remnants of absolutism, then bolshevism and fascism, and finally an updated Marxism that threatened to lead to the ultimate apocalypse of nuclear war. But the century that began full of self confidence in the ultimate triumph of Western liberal democracy seems at its close to be returning full circle to where it started: not to an 'end of ideology' or a convergence between capitalism and socialism, as earlier predicted, but to an unabashed victory of economic and political liberalism".[2]

The essence of 'the End of History" thesis is that with the end of the hostile, mutually destructive and the confrontationist Cold War ideological rivalry there has been a triumph of liberal democracy and this combined with open market economies has become the 'only model a state would follow and would prevail everywhere"[3] that any government that did not follow or failed to follow the path of liberal democracy and market economies would be consigned to the 'ash heap of history". With the end of communism, there exists no conceptual or ideological alternative. Moreover, the forces of globalization are irresistible and 'world is moving towards a 'global village" where the values of liberal democracy would rule the roost. Economic reforms would propel political reforms. Free trade, markets, capital and technological flows would accelerate the processes and forces of democratization in every country of the world.[4] The 'end of the history' paradigm was based on the assumption that the end of the Cold War has resulted in the end of the major conflict or conflictual points in global politics and the emergence of a harmonious world. As Fukuyama remarked "we may be witnessing ... the end of history as such : that is, the end point of mankind's ideological evolution and the universalization of western liberal democracy as the final form of human government"[5] The future would be devoted not to great exhilarating struggles over ideas but rather to resolving mundane economic and technical problems.[6]

The Features/elements of the New World order:

The disbanding of the Warsaw Pact and the disintegration of the Soviet brought an end to the Cold War. It helped create a sense of optimism, albeit a short lived one, which the era of struggle was over and the period of peace and prosperity was to begin. The changes and the events which followed the demise of a formidable and a monolith communist system seemed to offer a hope for the beginning or emergence of a 'new world order' based on and characterized by international law, great power cooperation and greater and more effective role for international organizations.

Mikhail Gorbachev, while addressing a meeting of the World Media Asia in Moscow, on 11 April 1990, commented "we are only at the beginning of the process of shaping a New World order". But, it was only in the aftermath of the Iraqi invasion of Kuwait of 2 August 1990, the terminology 'new world order" gained popular and global attention. President George Bush, speaking before a joint session of both houses of Congress, on 11 September, 1990, observed that ". . . a new world order can emerge; a new era free from the threat of terror, stronger in the pursuit of justice and more secure in the quest for peace, an era in which the nations of the world, East and West, north and South, can prosper and live in harmony.

A hundred generations have searched for this elusive path to peace, thousand wars raged across the span of human endeavour. Today, that new world is struggling to be born, a world quite different from the one we have known, a world where the rule of law supplants the rule of the jungle, a world in which nations recognize the shared responsibility for freedom and justice a world where the strong respect the rights of the weak".[8]

In the new world order, the international institutions, particularly United Nations, will be called upon to play a more active (proactive) and important role in global governance and management of relations between the nations. Freed from the constraints of the Cold War politics, the Security Council will become the custodian of international peace and security and will be able to discharge its duties as per the provision of the UN charter.

Unipolar:

Another remarkable feature of the emerging or the new world order is the dominance and preponderance of one power or a single actor in the international politics. Francis Fukuyama's 'the End of History?' was, in fact, aimed at eulogizing the triumph of American supremacy in world politics. The United States in the absence of the USSR, emerged as the sole superpower and the sole" arbiter of world politics. It is the US, which would define and determine the course and direction of world politics. No other country would now present a military challenge to the United States, which also seemed to emerge as the institutionalized stabilizer of the globalized world economy. Culturally, too, the world seemed to be attracted to the American society and way of life the best example is McDonaldization of world economy and culture. It was going to be a world as designed and desired by the United States without conflict and challenge.

The US led UN military operations in the Gulf and the NATO actions and Kosovo were the clear signs of the emergence of US led world system. The United Nations functioned as per the whims and dictates of the United States. Whether it was WTO or CTBT, or Haiti or Somalia, the American hand and head were visible everywhere. The Cold War period marked by a bipolar world system was now extinct and the new world order has been witnessing the emergence of a unipolar world system dominated politically, economically, technologically, militarily and culturally by the United States of America. The entire world would come under the sphere of influence of American diplomacy.

Multipolar:

Henry Kissinger in his celebrated work 'Diplomacy' has argued that during the Cold War period there was intense ideological conflict and only one country, the United States "'possessed the full panoply of means - political, economic, and military" - to withstand the challenge of the communist world and to defend the noncommunist system. But in the post Cold War period, the relative military power of the United States will decline and there will be domestic pressure to shift resources from military and defense to other priorities. "The international system of the twenty first century will be marked by the emergence of six major powers - the United States, Europe, China, Japan, Russia and probably India as well as a multiplicity of medium sized and smaller countries'.[9] The international relations will become truly global. "The New World system will be marked by a seeming contradiction: on the one hand fragmentation; on the other growing globalization".[10] The diffusion of military, economic, and technological power will result in multipolarity or polycentrism of world politics. These tendencies will be more pronounced in economic fields where American predominance is already declining.

Multicivilizational:

However, the "Clash of Civilizations" paradigm of Samuel P. Huntington first appeared in Foreign Affairs (1993), has been the most debated, discussed and controversial aspect characterizing the nature and trends of international politics in the post Cold War period. Huntington writes "In this new world, local politics is the politics of ethnicity, global politics is the politics of civilizations. The rivalry of the superpowers is replaced by the clash of civilizations. In this new world the most pervasive, important and dangerous conflicts will not be between social classes, rich and poor or other economically defined groups, but between peoples belonging different cultural identitites".[11]

According to Huntington it is culture and cultural identities reflect civilizational identities which would determine 'the pattern' of cohesion, disintegration, and conflict in the post Cold War world. A civilization based world order is emerging. The most important distinctions among countries today are not ideological, political, economic. They are cultural. The root cause of conflict in today's world will lie not only in clash of interests but in assertion and advancement of identity based on civilizations. Conflicts are likely to be between states and groups from different civilizations. And examples are galore - the breakup of the Soviet Union and Yugoslavia and conflicts taking place in former territories, the rise of religious fundamentalism, the struggles within Russia, the trade conflicts between the United States and Japan, the resistance of Islamic States to Western pressure on Iraq, Iran, Bosnia, the efforts of Islamic and Confuscian states to acquire nuclear weapons, etc.[12] Huntington's 'clash of civilizations' paradigm discounts the Fukuyama's thesis that the collapse of Soviet communism means the end of history and victory of liberal democracy throughout the world as "there are many forms of authoritarianism, nationalism, corporatism and market communism (as in China) that are alive and well in today's world, . . . and in the modern world, religion perhaps is the central force that motivates and mobilizes people'.[13]

The Reality:

The debate still continues whether a new world order as envisaged by George Bush and confirmed by Bill Clinton has become a reality in place of the post Second World War Cold War international system. The events since the Gulf war suggest that the post Cold War international politics still remains undefined due to its fluidity and unpredictability. The argument that the end of Cold War has led to the end of ideology and thus the end of history and that the world would be more safe and peaceful in the absence of major ideological confrontations did not seem to hold good for long. It has been a sudden and a well-intentioned thesis put forward by Francis Fukuyama to herald the victory of western, particularly American liberal democracy and market economics. The rising trend of ethnic conflicts within the nations - Yugoslavia, Rwanda, Burundi, Somalia, Sierraleon to mention a few - have posed a serious threat to international stability and 'order' The economic crisis which emerged in the late 1990s in the East and South East Asia was a major set back to the argument that everything is perfect with market economies and it is the invisible hands which would decide the future course of global economy.

Resistance and challenge to the western liberal democracy has come not only from the ethnic strife and some evil leaders like Saddam Hussein but also from the countries like China which still holds on to the communist political system. Today China is perceived as the most formidable challenger to the American/Western interests or 'hegemony'.

The argument that the post-Cold War world is gravitating towards a unipolar world. It is also discounted by many — including Kissinger and Huntington as discussed earlier. The Gulf War and the NATO's action in Bosnia and Kosovo did suggest this. But the reality is that a diffusion of power is taking place in international politics. The United States does not command the similar military and, most importantly, economic superiority and supremacy, today, as it did when the world system was bipolar. Challenges to its power have emerged from the European Union, Japan and more importantly China. The Non-Aligned Movement (NAM) is in disarray and directionless but it still continues to exist and has the capacity to influence the course of international politics particularly at a time when new challenges have emerged in the forms of global terrorism, human rights, environmental issues and issues related to globalization. The world order, which is emerging, is likely to be multipolar and polycentric though the United States will continue to be a decisive player in international politics.

Whether the new world order will be based on civilizational patterns are a matter of academic discourse and interest. The root of all conflict will be the clash of interests, which might be cloaked under the garb of clash of civilizations. Martin Wight is right when he says that underneath the skin of ideology is a hard core of great power national interest.

Challenges and Opportunities before India's Diplomacy:

The end of the Cold War and the consequent disappearance of a bipolar system provided opportunities and challenges to the Indian foreign policy makers to redefine and reorient the course of Indian diplomacy in order to readjust its relationship with the nations of the world in the changed global political, economic and security scenario. The strings and constraints of the Cold War world order have disappeared. It has provided Indian diplomacy flexibility and maneuverability to conduct India's relations in such a manner that the country's national interests are maximized and realized.

In the early days of Cold War period i.e. in the 1950s and the 1960s diplomacy was aimed at creating a world opinion against the forces of colonialism, racism and imperialism. India played a leading role in the decolonization process and was the leader of the Afro-Asian resurgence against the racist and the imperialist forces. The formation of NAM was the singular achievement as it was done when the choice before the newly independent nations was either limited or nonexistent in a bipolar world system. It was Indian leadership, which magnificently and decisively carved out a place for the people of Asia and Africa in the world politics. Despite being poor and non-industrialized and also the constraints posed by its neighbours, India managed to emerge as a significant player in world politics.

India played a significant role in the United Nations particularly: field of peace keeping operations, disarmament and decolonization movements. Indian diplomacy was successful in   projecting the Third World views at the international forums on the political, economic and security matters. As leader of the Third World, India played a prominent role in de-escalation of Cold War tensions.

The formidable challenge before Indian diplomacy during the Cold War was how to manage and protect its national interests -political, economic and security - without diluting and endangering its image of a non-aligned nation. The wars with Pakistan, and China and some international developments particularly in Central America, Africa, and Asia did compel our foreign policy makers and diplomats to move closer to the Soviet Union. Though the end of the Cold War has removed compulsions and constraints on Indian diplomacy, new challenges have emerged. The rise of the United States as the sole superpower and the demise of the Soviet Union has left us with no option but to redefine and reorient our foreign policy goals and principles which has brought us closer to the US, Kashmir, Comprehensive Test Ban Treaty, global terrorism, cross-border terrorism, are a few areas where Indian diplomacy has come to play an important role. In the absence of the Soviet Veto at the Security Council, India faced a formidable challenge on the question of Kashmir. There was a fear that the United States and its allies would put pressure on India on the Kashmir issue to force it to toe the American line on international issues. Indian diplomacy, so far, has succeeded in mobilizing world opinion in India's favour but at some cost. India was pushed to sign the WTO and now it is being pressurized to do the same in case of CTBT.

Indian diplomacy faced major challenges in the aftermath

of the Pokhran nuclear tests in May 1998. But today the world has come to understand the compulsions and circumstances, which forced India to go nuclear. The US design to monopolize the nuclear regime with the help of a few select powers had always been opposed by India. Moreover, growing nuclear capability of China and clandestine nuclear programme of Pakistan left India with no option. How Indian diplomacy is able to reconcile the US stand on CTBT and Indians response to it will be the acid test of our nuclear diplomacy.

The menace of Islamic and cross-border terrorism particularly in Kashmir posed a challenge to India's diplomacy. Today India's diplomacy aims at generating and mobilizing world opinion against global terrorism and the forces, which are behind such acts of terrorism. Terrorism, particularly Islamic terrorism, has become a serious threat to international peace and security. Countries such as India, China, Russia, Central Asia and even the United States have been the victims of the acts of terrorism.

In order to be more effective, the Security Council needs to be restructured, democratized and made more representative. India's diplomacy aims at this. The success of our diplomacy will be determined by the fact that whether India becomes the part of the permanent member of the Security Council. For this India needs to adopt a multilateral approach to wrest the initiative from not only big powers but also from the non-aligned nations. One hopes that India has learnt lessons from its debacle at the UN when it lost to Japan for non-permanent seat at the Security Council.[15]

Besides, the emerging trend of globalism and globalization has compelled us to review and reorient our foreign policies to facilitate India's integration with the global market economy. A multilateral approach is required to deal effectively with the IMF, World Bank and the WTO. The attempts on the part of the developed nations to attach non economic issues like environment and human rights with trade has posed considerable challenge to India's economic diplomacy.

A multilateral approach to a multipolar world requires that India play an important role in the Non-Aligned Movement and help it take up the new challenges of the New World order. Besides India's diplomacy needs to be oriented to deal effectively with the regional groupings particularly the European Union, the ASEAN and the SAARC.

The interests of India will be best served only if we are able to create environment of peace and cordiality in our neighbourhood. In this regard, India's diplomacy aims at consolidating ties with China, and the SAARC nations. India-China cordiality is important not only to thwart US hegemony, particularly in Asia, but also to seek the Chinese support on the question of Kashmir and India's pursuit for the permanent seat at the United Nations.[16]

Conclusion:

In the changed international environment where a new world order of nations will continue to compete politically, economically and strategically a nation like India needs a well defined and pragmatic diplomatic initiatives of cooperation and competition with other nations, to be in a position to counter the impact of hegemonistic world system. Nehruvian foreign policy was formulated in the context of the Cold War and a bipolar world system and the optimum diplomatic strategy for India to that situation was non-alignment. "Today, any Indian foreign policy formulation will have to start with an over-all Indo-centric assessment of evolving a global strategic environment and an appropriate policy framework to advance Indian interests and security in that environment."[17] This calls for a 'multi-disciplinary', multilateral and integrated diplomatic approach to the global environment "involving the inputs from the fields of economics, technology, politics and international relations as well as an understanding of the perceptions and aims of major global actors".[18] India can play a major role in the promotion of peace, security, cooperation, human welfare and in the creation 'of a world free from poverty, disease, inequality and discrimination if our diplomacy succeeds in wresting the opportunities and facing the challenges of the emerging world order. It requires freeing ourselves from the Nehruvian mindset and adoption of more realistic diplomatic postures at regional and global level. And diplomacy will succeed only when we succeed in enhancing our economic, political and strategic capabilities. Time has come to think and act globally.

Notes

1. Adam Roberts, "A New Age in International Relations", *International Affairs*, Vol.67, No. 3, July 1991, P.518.

2. Ibid.

3. Charles William Maynes, "Squandering Triumph: The West Botched the Post-Cold War World", *Foreign Affairs*, January/February, 1999, P. 15.

4. Ibid. P. 16.

5. Samuel P. Huntington, The Clash of Civilizations and The Remaking of World Order (Penguin Books India Ltd., New Delhi 1997) P. 31.

6. Ibid.

7. Adam Roberts, No. 1, P. 519.

8. Ibid.

9. Henry Kissinger, Diplomacy, (published by Simon and Schuster, New York, 1994) PP. 23-24.

10. Ibid. P.23.

11. Samuel P. Huntington. No. 5., P. 28.

12. Ibid.

13. Samuel P. Huntington, "If Not Civilizations, What? Paradigms of the Post Cold War World". *Foreign Affairs*, November/December 1993, PP. 187-188.

14. Ibid. P.191.

15. C. Raja Mohan, "Lessons From the Debacle at the U.N.", *The Hindu*, Oct. 22, 1996.

16. K.K. Katyal, "Stabilizing Ties with China", *The Hindu*, Feb. 7, 1994.

17. K. Subrahmanyam, "Indian Foreign Policy: Caught in a Nehruvian Time Warp" *The Times of India*, November 7, 1995.

18. Ibid.

‹7›

Sources of Insecurity in South Asia
Emerging Trends

Vijay Kumar *

The end of the cold war gave rise to the phrase 'peace dividend' to which many hopes were attached.[1] Sadly, the expected returns have not materialized for South Asia nor for the rest of the world. We have not seen massive funds freed up from military spending and diverted towards problems of environment and development. Rather, the number and intensity of conflicts in South Asia and around the globe appear higher then ever. Geo-politically, South Asia remains a volatile region in the late 90's and promises to continue as such in the 21st millennium. Unlike in the West, where the collapse of the Soviet Empire brought feelings of vindication mixed with strong hopes of a world more amendable to democracy and peace, in the South Asia region there was a strong feeling of vulnerability by a variety of regional, environmental, economic factors.

This vulnerability is evident in various challenges to peace and democracy that surface through nuclear arms race, inflation, riots, nationalism, sub-nationalism, ethnic, religious conflicts. More often than not the common underlying basic factor is 'insecurity' prompted by the perceived threat of poverty or the prospect of marginalization, isolation and fragility through diminishing access to resources.

---

* Professor, Department of Political Science, T.M. Bhagalpur University, Bhagalpur, Bihar, India.

This paper aims to examine and evaluate the new threats to South Asian peace-emerging in the form of 'human security' risks in the present geopolitical, historical and economic setting of the subcontinent. To my mind, these risks threaten South Asian peace much more than traditional boundary and national interest disputes between some of the component states like India on the one hand and Pakistan, Bangladesh, Sri Lanka and Nepal on the other. No doubt, frictions and conflicts between the states are bound to persist for some time into the 21st millennium but these areas within nations are going to divide them internally to the advantage of inimical powers in the region and outside the region.

The Setting

South Asia comprises three densely populated large states – India, Pakistan and Bangladesh, two island communities – Sri Lanka and Maldives, and two landlocked Himalayan states – Nepal and Bhutan. All are member so the nonaligned movement and the Group of 77 and four – India, Bangladesh, Sri Lanka and Maldives – are also members of the Commonwealth (Pakistan has recently been expelled). All South Asian countries are distinguished for being in the Least Developed Countries (LDCs) category of the United Nations.[2]

Conventionally, the strategic location of South Asia makes the region an area of pivotal importance in the World system. Given its proximity to the gulf and its border with Iran, Pakistan is as much as part of South-West Asia as it is of south Asia. Besides, it has strong islamic ties with important Muslim nations of the Gulf Region. IT is also a neighbour of Afghanistan, historically, guarding the invasion routes from Central Asia to the Indo-Gangetic plains of India. India, on the other hand, is not only important in terms of population and geographic location but also as a potentially huge market in the global market economy, rapidly growing technological power, a long term leader among developing nations. Sri Lanka, extending South into the Indian ocean crosses some of the world's important shipping lanes, while Bangladesh lies adjacent to the ethnically volatile eastern areas of India. Nepal, linked with both China and India by all weather motorable road sits as an uneasy buffer between them occupying a strategic position in the South Asian subcontinent. Besides Bangladesh, Pakistan and Sri Lanka look to South Asia and South East Asia for trade and cultural ties. Naturally, politically hegemonic powers, including United States and China are expected to have deep rooted, long-term interest in the region.

❑ History, particularly recent history, has shown that South Asia cannot been seen in isolation from its neighbouring regions. China has come to play a role of some significance in the destiny of South Asia. Its effective military presence in Tibet and Sinkiang has its impact on the countries of South Asia. Apart from its armed conflict with India along the far flung frontier, China has kept up active cooperation with Pakistan which has both bilateral as well as regional, if not global implications. This cooperation has helped to encourage at times, the belligerence of Pakistan's rulers towards India. Besides, Chinese activities in Nepal, Sri Lanka and Bhutan have nurtured anti-Indian elements in those countries. A partial survey indicated that historical animosities and religious and socio-political differences have blocked regional cooperation among South Asian countries despite such an organization as SAARC. A regional arms race, involving not only conventional weapons but nuclear arms as well, imposes severe costs for these poor societies and pose obstacles to economic growth and social justice. China factor, thus, remains important in determining peace in South Asia.

❑ Economic problems in the form of slowdown in industrial and agricultural growth, rising current account deficit and increase in public debt have constrained the governments from spending on their social sectors as these are the first to receive severe expenditure cuts. The economic prospects for the region seem gloomy unless the countries step up public and private expenditure on human development which is at the core of all growth oriented strategies. In case they fail to do this, they will indulge in conventional wars with neighbours – if for no other reason than only to divert popular attention from internal problems.

❑ The routes taken towards political, social and economic development by the nations of South Asia have diverged widely. Three major religious systems – Hinduism, Buddhism and Islam – each one dominant in one or more of the nations account for part, often a major part, of the political culture of the nation concerned. These religious systems, alongwith other important aspects of the social systems – for example, the caste system, which is inherent in Hinduism – provide a traditional divisive force for the political system to contain. As such each of the states of South Asia faces five critical areas of political development.[3]

* nation building
* state building
* participation
* economy building, and
* distribution

All of India's neighbours have regimes which are bent upon destroying democracy and are today battling against democratic forces within their respective countries. State building process has not yet penetrated all levels of groups and individuals and brought into an integration network into a secular community. As such, nation-building process which is assumed to be a shift of loyalty and commitment to the terminal community, i.e. The nation, from the primordial foci of allegiance like tribe, clan, village, locality, petty group, caste, ascriptive community is yet to be achieved. Citizen building efforts of participation of the citizens and their mobilization for decision making is a far cry. And economy-building which is a process of distribution and redistribution of national wealth, services, opportunity and welfare, while employing the political power of the community and the state, has suffered due to globalisation efforts and shift to the market economy which requires the state to remain only an umpire between the economic conglomerates and the society at large. These factors make the states of South Asia uneasy which tells deeply on their foreign policy priorities.

❑ Today, when globalization, transnationalization and consumerism have unleashed forces which pose a serious challenge to national sovereignty, indigenous value system and social structures, the task of keeping South Asia zone of peace and prosperity is quite bleak. Clive Bell announced the end of ideology, history and political boundaries cannot be so easily overthrown. When nations replace ideology by opportunism and stop creating history, the consequent vaccum is inevitably filled by the insatiable consumerist craving and mindless pursuit of mammon. To quote only one instance in this regard would be enough. In Pakistan, the alarming disparity between the rich and poor is mind boggling. 66 per cent of all industrial projects, 97 per cent of all insurance funds and 80 funds and 80 per cent of all bank deposits are in the hands of some 20 families, if feldman is to be believed.[4]

In the light of the above settings, conflicts, which have their own specific causes, identities and characteristics, cannot be ruled out in the region. Some broad categories of the origins of potential and current conflicts are as follows:

A failed process of integration in the creation of nation state (Sri Lanka, Pakistan, India). The absence of a national unifying factor, such as a social class or an enlightened leadership, slows down the process, producing dangerous setbacks. We should remember that it took several countries and numerous civil wars for Europe to reach the nation-state phase and the end if Empires.

* A colonial legacy or a difficult decolonization process, linked mostly with the drawing of borders by colonial powers (India, Pakistan, China, Nepal).

* Regional movements or social revolts infected by terrorist virus to become protracted conflicts receiving training, arms and funds from across the borders (India, Pakistan, Sri Lanka).

* Conflicts based in ethnic tensions (Sri Lanka, Pakistan, India). Strong differences and traditional enemity between ethnic groups are compounded by historical factors and bad management. Power has been monopolized by a specific ethnic group, that refuses to share power for various reasons including fear of revenge.

* Conflicts of a religious character.

* Conflicts based in socio-economic and political tensions.

* The classic war of aggression prompted by the "esprit de grandeur" or the recover lost prestige in previous attempts.

The reasons for the above assumed areas of conflict are not very far to seek. While the entire world has recognised the primacy of economics over politics. South Asia still has to go a long way to reconcile its divergent political perceptions, ethnic and religious tensions and feeling of mutual distrust. The above assumptions are reinforced by the political behaviour and attitudes of the nations of this region.

The Emerging Scenario

Besides these there are certain major trends in the South Asian region which are quite discrenible. They equally threaten creation of peace in the region. The arms race goes unbated. While the global arms expenditure may gone down reasonably in South Asia it has actually shot up.

The Human Development Report, Asia, 1999 points out that the defence spending of Pakistan and India have increased by 14 and 8.5 per cent respectively. The report has also revealed that this extra expenditure has not only resulted in billowing the regions poverty it has also given rise to extreme income inequalities. The richest one-fifth of South Asia's population earn almost 40 per cent of the region's income and the poorest one-fifth earns less than 10 per cent. Some of the people have become rich in recent times through corruption which is at its highest in Pakistan costing $ 100 billion or 5 per cent of its GDP a year. Bangladesh and India too have rising share of corruption in the economy, claiming a huge proportion of their official costs.

This region is home to more than 560 million poor people, with 300 million people having little to eat. There are 380 million people who are illiterate and 200 million people who have no access to safe drinking water. It is an home to 800 million people who have no access even to basic sanitation facilities. The truth of these factors are only substantiated by the findings of late Mahbub-ul-Haq's Karachi based Human Development Centre which holds that South Asia is the home to the largest number of the poor and illiterate in the world, exceeding that of Sub-Saharan Africa.

These figures really baffle one when one contrasts them with the rich resources available in the region, both human and material. The region has about 20 per cent of the world population with the fourth largest pool of techno-scientific personnel, it has 22 per cent of world's fossil and fuel resources, 460 cubic kilometres of renewable water resources, 86 million hectares of forest cover, 250 million hectares of farm land, very rich and diversified mineral, floral and faunal resources and abundance of milk.

The breakdown of the post-war world order has stimulated an inevitable rethinking of the interplay between international, regional and national peace, security and development. Poverty, food insecurity, competition over scarce resources, environmental degradation, transnational movements of population, drugs and arms, ethnic and religious conflicts now pose more serious problems to South Asian peace and security. The political behaviour of some of the nations caught in the grip of "old vested interests" and "emerging demands for social security" may well be trying to protect the old vested interests by adopting threatening gestures to their neighbours, but the gimmick is not going to work for long. The question of human security is gaining precedence and cannot be relegated to the background for long.

Throughout the world, traditional measures for protecting national security, however it may be defined, are failing to prevent tragic violations of the most basic aspects of human security. Territorial sovereignty and militancy capacity are scarcely relevant when human security concerns such as ethnicity, religion, region, space, environment, governance, economy and human rights turn into flashpoints of violent conflict. A preoccupation with state-centered security devours great quantities of scarce financial and human resources through spending on armed forces personnel, militancy hardware and weapons systems. Such misallocations reduce the capacity of the South Asian countries to invest resources in addressing human security problems within their own countries. In the 21st millennium, excessive spending on conventional security measures would indirectly worsen the human security situation, contributing to potential conflicts.

Human-Centered Development and Security

What precisely does human security mean ? It is clear that the traditional concept of security as prevention of foreign aggression and preparedness to protect national boundaries is undergoing a fundamental transformation. Security of people is now the dominant concern and it is increasingly interpreted as:

* Security of people, not just of territory;
* Security of individuals, not just of nations;
* Security through development, not through arms;
* Security of all the people everywhere – in their homes, in their streets, in their communities and in their environment.

Human security implies, as a minimum, a number of interwoven dimensions centered on human dignity.[6] Broadly, therefore, it means:

- ❏ Personal and physical security: the rights of individuals and communities to preserve their own life and health and to dwell in a safe and sustainable environment.

- ❏ Economic security: access to employment and to the resources necessary to maintain one's existence, with adequate measures taken to reduce maldistribution and artificial scarcity and to permit improvements in the material quality of community life.

- ❏ Social security: providing protection from discrimination based on age, gender, ethnicity or social status, combined with access to 'safety nets', knowledge and information as well as freedom to associate.

- ❏ Political security: guaranteeing the right to representation , autonomy (freedom), participation and dissent, combined with empowerment to make choices and a reasonable probability of effecting change.

- ❏ The above political dimension includes legal-juridicial security: individual and collective access to justice and protection from abuse.

- ❏ Ethnic and cultural security: a social climate in which population feels secure in expressing their cultural identity.

Summing up

A preoccupation with state-centered security has long been at the heart of foreign policy makers in South Asian countries. However, traditional measures for protecting national security are failing to prevent tragic violations of the most basic aspects of human security. The moral imperative to justify a nation's decision to resort to force is the preservation of state stability and interest – in other words, maintaining the rule of law and legitimacy. In case of human security, the moral imperative for action would be preservation of human dignity in all its dimensions. No doubt, the crude fact of international life is that in an international system, where a nation's own strength is the only guarantee for its security, where the nature of politics is that of "politics without government", one has to develop and sharpen the might of his own government. " Veer Vogya Vasundhara" is the only valid dictum. But taking care of the human security dimension raises the strength of the nation without making exaggerated demands on the exchequer as it goes toward meeting crucial objectives of both sustainable development and global security.

Notes and References

1. Eileen Conway, 'Focus', *IDRC Report*, Vol.22, No.3, October 1994.

2. Rasheeduddin Khan, "Problems of Nation Building", *World Focus*, Vol.4, No. 11-12, Nov-Dec, 1983,p.11.

3. Craig Baxter, et.al., *Government and Politics in South Asia*, Lahore: Vanguard Books, 1988, p.3.

4. Quoted in D.C. Jha, "International Peace: Conflicts and Harmony...", *Souvenir*, National Seminar on Education and Peace, T.M. Bhagalpur University, Sept. '99.

5. Editorial, Gloomy Scene, *Hindustan Times* (Patna), 18.8.99.

6. I.L. Head, *On a hinge of History: The mutual vulnerability of South and North*, Toronto: University of Toronto Press, 1991. Also see, Mahbub-ul-Haq, "Development Cooperation for Global Human Security", in *SGI Quarterly*, No. 10, Oct. 1997, pp. 2-7.

‹8›

National Security Policy
The Basis for National Resurgence

Bharat Karnad*

1. A Grand Geo-Strategy:

Countries are known by the enemies they keep and the country's fixation with Pakistan has only reduced India to a Sub-Continental State to Islamabad's benefit. The Lahore Bus Diplomacy and attempts to de-fixate Indian policy by emphasizing the Chinese threat, for instance, served the purpose of reorienting the people's strategic world-view. What the BJP Government needs to do is follow-up with the declaration of "a Monroe Doctrine" for India whereby the entire swathe of land and sea -Southern Asia, the extended Indian Ocean region and, on the landward side, the Persian Gulf to Myanmar and South East Asia by way of Central Asia - is identified as an exclusive semi-hemispheric enclave in which no interference of any kind by any outside power will be countenanced. It should be announced that, in this geographical zone, India, in cooperation with the regional states, will be responsible for ensuring peace, harmony, and security and for the protection of open seas and the sea lines of communications.

If such a doctrine seems a bit unrealistic and over-ambitious, then one need only recall what the US President Monroe in 1815 (or thereabouts) enunciated in his doctrine which carved out the America as a distinct geopolitical entity, which was sought

---

* Research Professor, Centre for Policy Research, New Delhi, India.

to be sequestered from the aggressive designs of European powers. The US had no military strength worth talking about and almost no ocean-going navy to enforce the provisions of this doctrine, but the US had clearly put down the stakes and by the end of the 19th century was in a position to defend that doctrine with armed force. An Indian Monroe Doctrine need not name any country as a threat nor need the idea be immediately defensible (in terms of armed force). What it will do is mark out India's sphere of influence for the future.

2. Realizing a Sub-continental Security System and a Regional Order for Peace:

The Grand Strategic "Monroe" - type of Doctrine for India requires the Government to acquire a sense of grandeur. For a start, Pakistan has to be drawn into a sub-continental security arrangement. For this to accrue, the Indian nuclear deterrent should be conspicuously "out of area" in its orientation. Meaning, that nuclearized Prithvi short range surface to surface missile batteries should not only NOT be ever deployed on the border with Pakistan, but Islamabad should be given verifiable proof-perhaps satellite - derived data - of this on an on-going basis, to erode, over time, the suspicions Pakistanis naturally harbor toward India. It will also mean not reacting in any way to whatever deployment the Pakistanis choose for their ex-Chinese and ex-North Korean missiles. Pakistan simply cannot contemplate a nuclear war because any which way they estimate its likely results, while India will suffer grave damage, their country, Pakistan, will become extinct. There can be no greater dampener of aggressive-minded Pak nuclear policies. Trade and economic ties should be prompted and pushed, so that the inter-linkages of this kind also strengthen the process of rapprochement.

In due time, military-to-military links should be forged, and for this purpose collaboration in designing and developing conventional military weapons systems ought to be explored. Military supplies and sales to Pakistan too should be pursued and in time, with the rise in mutual confidence and trust, even cooperation in the nuclear field should not be ruled out. The idea being that the Indian and Pakistani military capabilities will in time become complementary with Pakistan, perhaps, concentrating on short to medium range forces and India on strategic-long range capabilities. This is the sort of thing that Jinnah and later Ayub Khan had visualized. This is moreover a way to distance Pakistan from China.

Co-opting Pakistan into such a security system will register immense domestic gains for the BJP. The Indian Muslim masses will have to radically alter their view of a Party, which not merely befriends Pakistan but involves it as an equal partner in policing the region. Close and intimate relations with Pakistan will prevent their being strung out between the loyalty to their country and their pan-Islamic feelings and their concern for kith and kin across the border. BJP will then be identified as the Party that was the bridge between the Indian and Pakistani peoples and as the originator of enduring peace in South Asia.

A subcontinent that is secure and at peace with itself up the prospects for an Indian-led South Asian security apparatus to include countries in the Indian Ocean Littoral, some of the Trucial States in the Gulf, in Central Asia and will open in South East Asia. This system should be anchored in two friendly States - Israel on the one side and Vietnam on the other with India as the manpower and military -capabilities pivot, able to switch and deploy forces from one flank to the other as crises or contingencies demand. Vietnam is of critical importance because it is the one country that China fears and respects and a militarily well armed and fighting-fit Vietnam will keep China on its toes and less eager to sally west of the Malacca Straits. Vietnam's Cam Ranh Bay is Asia's finest deep-water port. A bilateral agreement to have it host, on a permanent basis, an Indian Navy flotilla monitoring Chinese naval and air activity in the South China Sea and otherwise getting a continuous electronic and other fix on the most probable adversary, could be the cutting edge of such a cooperative effort. On passing nuclear tipped missiles, of the kind Beijing has transferred to Pakistan, to Vietnam conforms to the "Laws of Hamurabi" - an eye for an eye, a tooth for a tooth. It is the Indian unwillingness to play hardball, which motivates adversarial countries to take liberties with India's national (security) interests. International politics is an intolerant and unforgiving game and India should stop looking on it as a Boy Scout outing where moral protestations are of no value. Any thing to discomfit an enemy is an advisable thing to do, as Kautilya had counseled, especially as these same "enemies" (US, China) have long prospered strategically by hemming India in this manner (by cultivating Pakistan).

Intensive military, political and economic relations with certain key States - Mauritius, Oman, CIS, Myanmar, Sri Lanka, ASEAN members and Vietnam, are a key to the working of this regional system of security. However, India should be wary about building bridges with China. The objective vis a vis this country in the Grand Strategic Game Plan should be to somehow bring about the status quo ante in Tibet, circa 1950 and the occupation of that independent country by the Chinese PLA. As long as Tibet was a buffer state, relations between India and China were without incident. It is this state of affairs that needs to be realized. The 1954 Nehru- Zhou-En-Lai accord affords the perfect platform for a change in India's China policy. That agreement said that India recognized the Chinese region of Tibet as long as it was "autonomous".

3. Appreciation of the Military Power of the State:

There has to be an absolute conviction about the unmatched political utility of the military power of the State and where it stands in relation to the civilizational and economic powers. The relative values can be expressed schematically by a series of concentric circles, the center of which is the military power of the State. This power is contained within a large circle representing the economic power, which, in turn is encased within a still larger circle signifying the civilizational power of the state. For a country to aspire to excelling in the economic and civilizational spheres without firming up the center is to proceed on the basis of a hollow core. Military weakness wedded to political timidity is a recipe to render India vulnerable to predatory actions of foreign nations singly or jointly engaged in furtherance of their respective national interests to whittle away at the inherent Indian advantages and influence in economic and civilizational terms.

India has always been radiating cultural influences westward into the Middle East, northward into Central Asia, into the Java Sea in the south-east and eastward as far as the Sea of Japan, for millennia. But lacking a strong sense of nationhood and strong Indian military capabilities, India, at least in the modern era, has been perennially a "nation of subjugations" with its civilizational impact muted. This traditional systemic weakness of India can be changed now and in the future with the acquisition of a significant nuclear deterrent, comprising sizable numbers of high-yield megaton thermonuclear weapons riding intercontinental range delivery vehicles - missiles and aircraft. Faced with a 'nuclear-weapons-wise' and a determined India, no country anywhere will risk provoking India in any way. This was the philosophic bedrock on which de Gaulle built up an independent-minded France. For example, when he proposed an independent French nuclear force, President Charles de Gaulle put it bluntly: **"Preparons-nous a tirer dans tous les azimuts s'il y va de la vie de la France."** ("Let us prepare to fire in any direction if it is necessary for the survival of France.")

Historically, Nation States (Bismarck's Germany, the British Empire, and Communist China) have become Great Powers mainly on the basis of military clout. This is so because military capability (1) generates the national self-confidence to shape the larger environment according to one's national values, precepts and ideology within the country and respect in the world outside, (2) provides the political and diplomatic leverage for the purpose and otherwise helps in advancing national interests, (3) creates economic opportunities and enhances trade in the global marketplace, and (4) expands the space in which cultural and civilizational effervesance takes place. (The universal culture and values today, for example, are American in origin and the US, not coincidentally, is the preeminent military power.)

4. A Globe-girdling Deterrent:

Nuclear Weapons have the core function of deterring a nuclear attack. But a thermonuclear arsenal, symbolic of potency and of national grit and resolve, have the far more political benefit of deflecting unwanted international attention and pressures. Moreover, such an arsenal is emblematic of strategic independence - the ability autonomously to pursue one's national interests in the maximum ways possible. No such latitude is available to lesser powers or States with more limited nuclear forces. This is what has to be borne in mind in structuring a thermonuclear force.

Analyzing the various countries in terms of the power characteristics (physical size, geographical centrality, population, natural resources, trade and economic potential, ambits naturally restricted to at most the European continent, are in the P-5, and India is not. The BJP Government should fully appreciate the leverage the country now has owing to its, albeit partially developed, nuclear weapons and long range missile capabilities. Having gone overtly nuclear, it would be counter-productive to agree to any limits on the realization of a considerable thermonuclear deterrent the equal of at least China's. This will require the Government to back off on the CTBT. The PM's statement that India might consider joining this flawed treaty only if the US and Russia unconditionally ratify the CTBT, still does not provide adequate defense against it in case the Clinton Administration somehow manages to get the treaty ratified by the US Senate, and then compels the Russian Government to do the same in the Duma. The fact is, signing and ratifying this treaty will put India on a slippery slope towards acceptance of the NPT regime. Unless India carries out a series of explosions to test high yield thermonuclear weapon designs and devices before considering signing it. It would thereafter be desirable for the BJP Government to get passed a Constitutional Amendment requiring two-thirds of both houses of Parliament to ratify any international treaties in the future. The absence of such a mechanism in effect means that any Government can sign any treaty and commit this country to treaty obligations, which might be harmful to Indian national interests.

The alleged American argument that Washington needs an Indian signature on CTBT to get it ratified by its own Senate is suspicious, at best. Because then the US Senate will feel free to impose conditions on its ratification vitiating the effects of the CTBT. In this regard, the American case that New Delhi will lose nothing by signing and that it need not proceed with "ratifying" or with "depositing the instruments" in Geneva, which is when the treaty becomes valid for India, is another path that will lead India into an obvious trap. There is simply no reason for GOI to panic on this matter and to rush into anything. Considering the reluctance of the US Senate, the Russian Duma and the Chinese Government, the CTBT may not come into effect at all - which will be all for the best. In which case, why limit India's options in any way by signing on to a bogus treaty, thereby committing this country to this and any other treaty with similar aims and objectives that could be rifled up with the demise of the present CTBT?

The FMCT in embryo is unfair, iniquitous, and impracticable and should be so denounced. It should be made known that it is something that India will simply not adhere to for any reason, short of the country's reaching its strategic goal of a "nuclear weapons State" with a weapons inventory in excess of 500 nuclear weapons and a fissile material stockpile equivalent of thousand weapons plus.

There is a lesson here somewhere for the GOI, against its indulging in diplomatic giveaways. There was no compelling reason for promising a moratorium on testing or for indicating readiness to consider CTBT and join in negotiating an FMCT in the wake of the May 1998 tests. These are matters of hard negotiations. Having unilaterally given way on these issues, India is being pressurized to cede even more ground. This is a natural thing to happen in international relations where concessions are wrung out of the weak by the strong. The best counter-strategy, under the circumstances, would have been to give away nothing, take extreme positions than concede a centimeter at a time in return for real and substantive policy benefits. India should stop being the sucker. There has been enough provocation for GOI to withdraw from these earlier positions on CTBT and FMCT. It should do so and adopt a far more uncompromising stand. It will fetch better results.

As the P-5 are unwilling to accept India as a nuclear weapons State under the NPT dispensation, India, in turn, should make it clear, that it is under no obligation whatsoever to obey the strictures of the NPT, CTBT and least of all the FMCT. India should show it means business by conducting additional tests to inspire absolute confidence in the User Services about the thermonuclear weapons designs of yields in the range of One MT (megaton) to Five MT. Such multi-megaton thermonuclear tests should be speedily sanctioned and proceeded with, without delay. Likewise, the PSLV technologies should be transmuted expeditiously into a full- fledged ICBM, flight-tested to extreme ranges of 15,000-20,000 kms over the southern Indian Ocean and continental Antarctica. In addition, the ISRO technology for putting special satellite packages into separate orbits from an Indian satellite should be appropriately configured into MIRV (Multiple Independently targetable Reentry Vehicle) technology. MIRV-ing Indian missiles will enable Indian ICBMs to carry a number of warheads to distinct and separate targets to anywhere on earth. This is the basis of a globe-girdling nuclear deterrent that India can and should rightfully have.

In India, the supposedly dominant school of strategic thought wrongly and unfortunately equates a minimal deterrent with moderation. As the experience of the P-5 shows, any country crossing the nuclear Rubicon had better acquire the maximum clout with the maximum "vector distance" pretty fast if it is not to face the possibility of a preemptive strike. Such a surgical strike is now far more probable than ever before simply because the advanced informatics technology derived weaponry in the hands of the US (as evidenced in Allied operations in Iraq and now Kosovo) can today conventionally take out, with surgical precision, even deployed nuclear weapons systems, leave alone the nuclear infrastructure. There is therefore that much less opprobrium attached to forcefully neutralizing a problematic nascent nuclear power without the reach to threaten countries that can unleash such attacks from beyond the range of the targeted power.

The globe-girdling deterrent - it may still be called a "minimum credible deterrent" because the 500 plus Hydrogen weapons with India are numbers-wise minuscule compared to the arsenals of the US and Russia, numbering in the tens of thousands of nuclear weapons - is a strategic necessity for a more compelling reason. In the post-Cold War era, there is no strategic counterpoise to the US. It is a situation that favours Washington to act arbitrarily and with punitive-mindedness. It can decide, as in Kosovo, how, when and why to intervene in the internal affairs of other countries. And it has now expanded the NATO Doctrine to facilitate Western intervention without so much as a bow towards the United Nations. With the UN going the way of the League of Nations in the inter-war years when Italy invaded Abyssinia and the League did nothing, the UN too cannot any more prevent US/Western/NATO interference in third countries. In other words, there is no real protection for a country like India, which is not an American camp follower. At any time it chooses, Washington can decree a military action over Kashmir or whatever and India will be able to do nothing. The only sure and certain protection for India is a Thermonuclear Deterrent boasting of sufficient numbers of high yield weapons/warheads carried by ICBMs/Mirv-ed Missiles to defeat any anti-ballistic missile shield. Short of the ability to inflict grievous harm to continental United States, India will always remain a potential prey for predatory US, China or any other Big State exercising power without scruples or restraint.

In order to obtain a Deterrent in short order, after a few more Agni-II test-firings this missile type should be productionized and the Agni-III (of 3,000-5,000 kms range) should be serially test-launched in quick time parallel with the design, development, testing and deployment of the PSLV-ICBM. The ICBMs need not have great accuracy, because as long as it carries hydrogen warheads able to bust whole cities, it will be deterrent enough. The IAF's Sukhoi-30 MKI contingent should likewise be immediately readied as a medium-intermediate range manned delivery platform with a provision to extend its strike range (to hit Beijing, for instance) by acquiring aerial tankers.

5. Getting over the Inordinate Fear of Economic Sanctions/Trade Embargos:

All this nuclear build-up activity presupposes that the BJP Government will keep its nerve, and will have the guts and the gumption (of the sort that China routinely displays usually from a weak position) to stand up to the P-5 countries, and particularly the US, and tell them just where to get off. The fact is US/West have already done their worst during the last year, in terms of economic sanctions, and the country has not merely survived but in this period grown by 5% plus. Any intensification of this economic trade and embargo regime will only hurt those among them that want to risk alienating the only Big Emerging Market (BEM) outside of Brazil and China. Then again, India is democratically vibrant, optically stable and a militarily responsible power to boot, - attributes not shared with Brazil or China. Compare India's current economic standing with that of Brazil which has entered the American umbra after it recently accepted a $ 41 billion bailout. Or with that of China, which is increasingly on the outs with Washington, its economy is slowing down, and it is ceasing to be the preferred destination for free-moving international venture and industrial capital.

The unsubstantiated fear of economic sanctions which is the greatest obstacle to realizing a "credible" deterrent. The source of this fear is the Finance Ministry which, as it was said of a conservative American politician, "knows the price of every thing, but the value of noting." It certainly does not seem to understand the value of military power and even less of a strong and independent nuclear force. The Finance Ministry is the great stumbling block and aids and comforts the enemy by beefing up the lie that India cannot survive another round of American/ Western economic and trade sanctions. Those persons propagating such nonsense should be banished and punished and a more dedicated lost brought in to manage the economy and to generate the resources or both "guns and butter". As has been pointed out, the nuclear weapons and missile programmes have come on stream at a time when the defense budget is hovering at a miserable 2.3% of the GNP. So being able to afford a more muscular military and a hefty nuclear deterrent is not in doubt. All it requires is for the vested bureaucratic and private sector interests who have fattened on the lisence-permit raj, to curb their obstructionist attitudes and practices. But this will require the Prime Minister to lay down the law and to entertain no negativist nonsense from any quarter.

The meta-solution lies in accelerating the economic reforms and liberalization programme. The vast and expanding Indian economy and the usually innovative Indian entrepreneurs should be given their head to make money for themselves and to create employment and wealth for the country. Export-led growth will become the economic engine for dealing with most of the pressing economic ills plaguing the country. But the socialist mentality of government as the employer of last resort will have to be discarded. Plugging the PSUs into the international market is a nostrum that should be followed without let or hindrance. This policy should include the defense PSUs, which should be encouraged to export and sell abroad both to amortize the public investments in them and to force them to produce better quality military goods. Opening up the defense exports market will do wonders for the entire military industrial complex by actively encouraging the meshing of the private sector and public sector in this high value sphere.

6. Technology denial/control Regimes are Good; these Promote Self-reliance:

Certain sections in this country have sedulously nurtured the idea that India cannot do without American and Western "dual use" technologies. Washington uses this idea in its "carrot and stick" policy to pressurize India on the nuclear weaponization and other fronts. The fact is India has been under a technology denial regime for nearly two decades now (i.e., ever since the 1968 NPT got on stream without India's signature). What it has done is push India into relying on its own incomparable human and industrial resources to produce substitute/replacement technologies. Indeed, if anything the Western technology-denial policies are a boon. Most of the critical strategic technologies that have gone into the nuclear, missile, computing, satellites, electronic sensor programmes and systems, have been developed indigenously, affording this country a unique kind of functional freedom and room for maneuver. Imagine the straits this country would have been in had the US sold the Cray XMP-14 super computers in the mid-80s. There would have been NO Param or any of the other two Super Computing systems that are as good as any in the world and a whole lot cheaper and India would have relied permanently on a foreign source to meet our high speed computing needs. The upshot was that Cray Computers of Minnesota has gone into liquidation even as Indian Super computers daily find a new market in the world.

The fact is that in the critical technology-sphere, external help will stop well short of frontline levels of technology for twin fears: the fear of creating (1) a competitor, and (2) an autonomously acting player on the world scene. Once these factors are digested, then the conclusion is that even if India were to fall in line with the Western dictates, we will not be permitted to have access to the latest American technologies. So what is the point of succumbing to technology as temptation when such a course has more minuses than pluses?

7. Timeliness of Policy or knowing when to jettison old Postures:

India suffers from many liabilities, not the least among these is the tendency to stick rigidly to a policy prescription long after it has become turned unprofitable and obsolete, and long after the objective conditions have changed. In the Fifties, the Nehruvian espousal of Disarmament was a realpolitik device to put the nuclear weapons States on the moral defensive and to ensure that it was not used against countries like India, which did not have these weapons. But in the wake of the 1964 Chinese N-explosion, the situation had altered dramatically and India should have lost no time in quickly gearing up to produce nuclear weapons. It continued to mouth Disarmament-related banalities and failed to take the appropriate weaponizing decision. After the 1974 test, again GOI stopped from going ahead and weaponizing for fear of Western economic sanctions but also of transgressing Nehruvian injunctions. Once again the chance was lost to correct a grievously tilting strategic imbalance vis a vis China, and as it turned out the P-5. Similarly, in the economic sphere, the emphasis on the command economy was merited in the immediate post-independence phase because the private sector did not have the will or the wherewithal to invest massively in infrastructure - steel mills, hydroelectric projects, basic pharmaceuticals, cement factories, etc. But the GOI did not have the wit to realize that the returns of this policy were diminishing by the mid-70s. Liberalizing the, by then, fairly matured economy and freeing it of unnecessary red tape and regulations would have led to a sustained economic growth for 20 years now. Instead, India stayed mired in the "Hindu rate Growth" of 3-3.5%. In the 90s, with the NPT-CTBT regimes putting their full weight on India, New Delhi took the easy way out and did nothing on resumption of testing and, worse, froze the Agni missile development at the technology demonstrator stage.

It is as much a part of good governance for leaders to know when a policy track has outlived it usefulness and to move on to newer policy actions and measures. Innovative and iconoclastic thinking is a must for a country to stay ahead in a dog-eat-dog world.

8. A Genuinely Third World Orientation to Indian Policy:

One of the biggest virtues of Nehruvian foreign policy was that it conceived of a Bloc of developing countries, which would become a major international actor. The trouble was this emphasis on the Third World remained restricted to the level of rhetoric and the occasional international meet India hosted or participated in abroad. So India never managed to generate the loyalty to itself in the Third World despite its signal successes in spearheading the decolonization in the post World War Two period and in combating racism in the Third Committee of the UN. The clearest evidence of The Indian policy bias may be seen in the weightage accorded postings and promotions by the Indian Foreign Office and Indian diplomats. Every body strives to get a cushy European or a US posting and the high policies are usually geared to dealing with Washington, Tokyo and the European capitals. Those pulling duty or specializing in Developing Countries and Third World problems rarely climb to the top at the Foreign Office and rarely get a hearing.

One of the spillover effects of realizing a regional security system will be the shifting of political weight to policies dealing with Third World countries as the policy thrust. The rewards (promotions) system will soon begin to reflect this change in policy priorities.

‹9›

Korean Peace Process and Emerging Regional Order in East-Asia

Changsu Kim*
Taeho Kim**

1. Korean Peace Process: Reconciliation and Cooperation

In the wake of the North-South Summit in Pyongyang in June 2000 there have been growing perceptions in South Korea that a new era of reconciliation and cooperation has finally dawned. Amid debates about the real intention of the Pyongyang regime behind the dramatic developments, that is fundamental strategic change vs. tactical change, many in South Korea and elsewhere is wondering whether a peace process has indeed begun on the Korean peninsula. Many security analysts in South Korea and the United States are predicting that the future of the ROK-US alliance and the US military presence on the Korean peninsula will be one of their most important security issues in the not-too-distant future.

More than ever before, tension reduction and building a new peace regime on the Korean peninsula are gradually drawing attention of many security analysts and ordinary people alike. At the 'first ever' defense minister talks on September 24-26 of this year, for example, the two sides began to discuss measures

---

* Korea Institute for Defense Analyses, Korea.
** Korea Institute for Defense Analyses, Korea.

that are highly symbolic in bringing reconciliation and cooperation in the military field. They agreed on setting up a working-level military commission to facilitate the opening up of the Kyong-ui Railway and an adjacent highway and explored some elementary military confidence- building measures (CBMs), in the spirit of the June 15 Joint Declaration.

In retrospect, the previous governments of South Korea have successfully deterred military threats from the North and yet have negotiated with Pyongyang with little success to bring reconciliation and cooperation. The current ROK government has set the objective of its policy toward North Korea on the improvement of relations with the North through peace, reconciliation and cooperation. It has made consistent effort to dismantle the Cold War structure on the Korean Peninsula and to lay ground for a peaceful unification through peaceful coexistence between the North and the South. Also, it has consistently held on to the three principles of its North Korea policy: first, the South will not tolerate any military provocation from the North; second, the South will not harm the North or try to achieve unification by forcibly absorbing the North; and third, the two sides should peacefully co-exist through reconciliation and cooperation, that is, to abide by the Basic Agreement of 1992. So far, the ROK government's comprehensive engagement policy toward the North, or what is more commonly known as the "Sunshine Policy,"[1] has proved successful in bringing reconciliation and cooperation in various sectors.

II. Future Tasks of the ROK-US Security Alliance

For the past 50 years the objective of the robust military alliance between the ROK and the US has been to deter North

---

[1] For a summary of the ROK government's position on how to dismantle the Cold war structure on the Korean Peninsula, see Lim Dong-Won, "How to End Cold War on the Korean Peninsula," speech delivered at a working breakfast meeting hosted by the Korea Development Institute (KDI), April 23, 1999 in Northeast Asia Peace and Security Network, Special Report, June 15, 1999.

Korea's military provocation and, if deterrence fails, defeat it. The alliance has benefited both countries in their pursuits of stability, economic prosperity and democratization. As North and South Korea continue to move ahead in their reconciliation and cooperation, and as the US and the DPRK normalize their relations, the traditional security alliance between Seoul and Washington will adapt to this unprecedented sea change in their security environment.

The major tasks of the future ROK-US security system that purports to dismantle the Cold-War structure and establish a peaceful unification on the Korean peninsula will thus include the following: How should the ROK-US alliance develop in order to support and facilitate the process of a peaceful unification?[2] What would be the most desirable options in our pursuits of resolving various issues related to the future of the US Forces in Korea, most notably changes in its roles and missions and the level of its presence? Because changes in the ROK-US alliance and the roles and missions of the USFK require the understanding and cooperation on the part of other neighboring countries, how can the ROK and US search for a new paradigm of regional security cooperation for peace and unification of the Korean Peninsula?

Without doubt these major tasks of the ROK-US security alliance all point to one sublime goal of a peaceful unification of the North and South. Peaceful unification would be possible on the Korean Peninsula only if another war is deterred and prevented, if crises in the North are managed in a rapid and effective way, and if the blessing of the neighboring countries is obtained. If any of these were missing, the unification process of the North and South would be a difficult one entailing tremendous sacrifice and opportunity cost. These three aspects

---

[2] Joint research was done at KIDA and RAND in 1993-94 at the direction of the then Minister of National Defense and Secretary of Defense. See Jonathan D. Pollack, Young Koo Cha et at A New Alliance for the Next Century! The future of US-Korean Security Cooperation, RAND, 1995.

of a peaceful unification did exist in the past, but their characteristics and intensity will change as we enter the 21st century. The fierce aspects will probably remain unchanged, but their mix or combination will definitely change. In other words, the three aspects will carry different weights and importance if we can conceptually differentiate the process of peaceful unification into three phases, initial, middle, and final. In the initial phase the deterrence aspect of the alliance system is far more important than the other two, followed by the crisis management aspect and the regional cooperation aspect, respectively. In the middle phase the deterrence aspect would weaken relative to the other two that would gain more importance. But as we enter the final phase of the peaceful unification process, the first two aspects would greatly lose their importance and the third aspect of regional cooperation would gain more prominence.

The ROK-US security alliance in the 21st century needs to develop into one that best prepares for an uncertain future rather than specific threats. Some measures that will ensure a safe path to the new security system include: adjusting the alliance to better fit the changing security environment of Northeast Asia; expanding the role of the USFK in maintaining stability and peace of the region while adjusting the level of its military presence; and expanding ROK contributions to the regional security as its national power grows.

To be more specific, there are many concrete tasks the ROK and US should confront and fulfill as they endeavor to further develop their security system to facilitate a peaceful unification of North and South Korea. First, if the two allies can agree on the direction of their security alliance in the peaceful unification process and post unification, they should coordinate their positions and prepare some detailed directives concerning the five sub-fields of their security cooperation in the next century. They include options and paths of the alliance; changes in the ROK-US combined command system, changing roles and missions of the USFK; burden-sharing in combined defense; and the relationship of the bilateral alliance and an emerging multilateral regional cooperative system.

Second, the ROK and US should respond effectively to an extreme nationalism and a new isolationism as they approach the unification of the two Koreas. They need to consult far in advance on the likely advent and expansion of anti-American and anti-Korean sentiments in their respective nations that may result in greater calls for relocations of the US bases inland the withdrawal of the US Forces From South Korea.

Third, they need to examine in detail the security implications of their insufficient defense budgets, decreasing levels of readiness of their forces, and the expansion and modernization of Japanese and Chinese forces. In particular, if the current economic and financial difficulties facing the ROK were to last longer than expected, there would emerge many obstacles in the ROK-US military cooperation. Reductions and postponements in weapons acquisition would hamper effective operation of the combined defense, which in turn might challenge the current framework of military cooperation of the two nations.

To summarize, the major tasks of the ROK-US security system in the 21st century should be centered on supporting and securing a peaceful unification of the two Koreas. First, the two nations should consult and prepare a mid- /long-term blue prints for their alliance and security system in general. The core of their developing alliance is to make transition to a regional security alliance from the existing threat-driven alliance, and then to a profit-generating alliance. At the same time, they should resume discussions on sub-fields. Second, they should work on preparations for possible changes in the USFK role and other issues in order to shape an environment favorable to continued forward presence of the US forces. Finally, they should also promote multilateral security and military cooperation in Northeast Asia as a means to safeguarding the peaceful unification on the Korean Peninsula. The two nations have different roles to play in promoting mutual understanding and building confidence among the regional countries, as they relate to the future US military presence, the relations of a Unified Korea with its neighbors, the control of weapons of mass destruction, etc.

III Changing Roles and Missions of the USFK?

The East Asian Strategic Report of 1998 sets out the basic direction for the roles and missions of the future US forces in Korea. It maintains some 100,000 troops are present in East Asia for a very long period of time while expanding their regional security roles, and it predicts a continued US alliance with a unified Korea and some military presence post-unification. This blueprint reflects US perceptions of the strategic importance of the Korean peninsula even after North Korean threats disappear and unification is achieved. It also reflects the US intention to maintain its vested interests in the strategically important Korean Peninsula post-unification.

The roles and missions of future US forces in Korea will be to a certain extent dependent upon the modality and timing of the unification of the two Koreas. Korean unification can be largely divided into two categories, sudden unification resulting from contingencies in the North and a protracted unification in which the two Koreas go through the phase of accommodation and integration before reaching unification. The restructuring of the USFK will differ in the two different categories. For instance, how UN forces including American forces manage contingencies and restore order in North Korea will likely define the ROK-US relations and will have great impact on the roles and missions of the US forces that may or may not be stationed post-unification.[3]

The changing roles and missions of the USFK and its level of presence will also be determined in the greater context of the size, force structure, and roles and missions of the US armed forces that will most likely remain forward-deployed or forward-present in the Asia-Pacific. The US DoD has made effort to build a diverse and flexible force presence for common security

---

[3] Pollack and Lee examine four probable scenarios of the North-South Korean relationship, that is, integration and peaceful unification, collapse and absorption, unification through conflict, disequilibrium and potential external intervention. See Jonathan D. Pollack and Chung Min Lee, *Preparing for Korean Unification: Scenarios and Implications*, RAND. 1999.

in the Asia-Pacific by maintaining bilateral alliances and promoting multilateral security cooperation in the name of security pluralism.[4] A total of some 100,000 US troops, it recommends, will remain stationed for a considerably long period of time utilizing the diversity, flexibility and complimentary facets of their force structure in the region. This represents the basic principle in its policy of military presence in the Asia-Pacific and can be applied in the unification of the North and South. If the size of US forces stationed in the region declines, the roles and missions of the USFK will be greatly restricted, no matter how flexible and complementary the US utilizes its forces stationed in the region. In this case the USFK will likely play roles and missions in response to crises in other parts of the regions.[5]

The next thing to consider is the linkage of the USFK and USFJ in the process of Korean unification. US force structure may vary in the Asia-Pacific according to conflict scenarios, and the linkage of the USFK and USFJ will be considered in this context.[6] In particular, during the early part of the next century the linkage will be greatly affected by the US-China relations and the US-Japan-China trilateral relations. The rationale of the USFJ providing rear-area support to the USFK is easily acceptable when there are strong needs for deterrence against North Korea's military threats and or crisis management in the event of contingencies in the North. The same rationale, however, will lose its validity when North Korea's military threats

---

[4] William S. Cohen, *The United States Security Strategy for the East Asia-Pacific Region*, 1998.

[5] For an argument for continued US military presence in Korea, Kuwait and Saudi Arabia, see Michael O'Hanlon. *How to Be a Cheap Hawk: The 1999 and 2000 Defense Budgets*, Brookings. 1999. Also see the same author's article entitled "Keep US Forces in Korea after Reunification." *The Korean Journal of Defense Analysis*, Vol. X, No. I (Summer 1998). pp. 5-20.

[6] See John Y. Schrader and James A. Winneteld. *Understanding the Evolving U.S. Pacific Rim Security: A Scenario-Based Analysis*, RAND (R-4065-PACOM), 1992, pp. 41-54.

have decreased completely or disappeared. In this case, US troops may remain in Japan while they may be gradually reduced in Korea. And US troops may remain stationed in Japan and Korea to respond to threats and contingencies outside the Korean Peninsula.

In sum, the roles and missions of the US forces in Korea may invariably change as we go through a peace process, i.e. peaceful unification in the 21st century. It is quite conceivable that the current Army-centered USFK may see growing proportions of its Navy, Air Force and information-collecting units.[7] The US troops that may remain stationed in the Korean peninsula around the time of unification will likely play the roles of maintaining regional, not peninsular, peace and stability. In addition, they will also likely conduct humanitarian assistance, disaster relief, anti-terror, anti-pollution and anti-drug trafficking operations, anti- and counter-proliferation of WMDs, and other MOOTWs.

IV Emerging Regional Order in East Asia

Predicting East Asia's future strategic environment is a problematic, daunting, hazardous task at the current state of social science theories and empirical knowledge to say the least. One of the most prominent challenges is to ascertain future relationships among the major powers in the region and their interactions with other regional actors as all of them are, to a varying extent, in transition and the global, regional, and domestic environments in which the changes occur are also undergoing transformation as well.

On the other hand, the recent past and the ongoing trends and developments in East Asia and beyond are fundamental,

---

[7] For a recent exposition on this, see Payne P. Hughes, "United States Maritime Strategy and Naval Power in East Asia in the 21st Century," Paper presented at the Sixth International Sea Power Symposium, Hilton Hotel, Seoul, August 5-7, 1999. Hughes predicts there will be more naval forces than air force units stationing in the post-Korean unification era amid a moderate reduction of the US Navy in the West Pacific

sustaining, and impregnated ones to warrant educated guesses and reasoned speculations for the unfolding future strategic configuration in East Asia. In particular, some fundamental policy dilemmas inherent in the three-way relationships among the United States, China, and Japan remain unsettled. Barring unforeseen developments and future shocks, it stands to reason that their continuing dilemmas would likely carry the existing strategic configuration in East Asia into the early next century.

For one thing, one of the principal foreign-policy challenges for the US in the 1990s has been to provide China with a tacit recognition for its rising status and importance and to assuage its deep-seated suspicion that the post-Cold War US-Japan alliance is targeted at China, while at the same time offering security commitment and credibility to Japan by strengthening alliance relationship with the latter. How could the U.S. cope with this continuing dilemma without fundamentally altering its current policy course toward Japan or toward China?

For another, in light of China's policy conundrum in its relations with the US, i.e., the US remains the most important country in its economic development and foreign policy but, at the same time, poses the greatest threat to the continued communist rule in China and to the prospects for reunification with Taiwan, are there any viable options for China to get out of this dilemma?

For still another, while US alliance exists, ties with Japan and Korea remain strong and are likely to do so in the foreseeable future, will they continue to be robust enough to withstand future regional challenges and crisis, of which the "rise of China" looms largest? Should not Japan and Korea need to pursue hedging strategies now and in the future, as all rational actors would do ?

This brief discussion argues that beneath the facade of relative stability in Northeast Asia lies profound uncertainty over the region's future in general and over China's in particular, and that for East Asian states including South Korea (or unified Korea) how best to balance the leading US and the rising China. This is likely to become the primary security challenge in the foreseeable future.

V Diverging US and Chinese Interests over Korea

In light of individual regional states' shared perceptions on regional uncertainties, one useful way to assess future East Asian stability is to inquire about the health of US-China relations, the two most powerful actors in East Asia as well as on the Korean peninsula. Ideally, an amicable relationship between the US and China, especially renewed security cooperation, would contribute to regional stability, the attainment of their respective objectives in East Asia, and peninsular stability.

In reality and contrary to the popular belief, however, the prospects for an improved US-China relationship remain quite cloudy, if not bleak, for the foreseeable future. Few of their outstanding issues, including the Taiwan issue, human rights, trade, nuclear espionage, and nonproliferation, show signs of early or conclusive resolution. On the contrary, there seem to exist some fundamental differences between the two countries in terms of political systems, social values, and strategic objectives. Given also the ongoing leadership transition and internal political dynamics in Beijing and Washington, compromise on these differences will also be difficult to achieve in the near future.

Viewed in this light, the Korean peninsula also occupies a central place in their crowded bilateral and regional agendas. Notwithstanding the long list of their outstanding disputes at both bilateral and regional levels as noted above, on the other hand, China and the US have time and again argued-at the official and declaratory level, at least — that they share a set of common interests over the Korean peninsula — namely peninsular stability, North-South Korean dialogue, and peaceful reunification.

In light of their vast differences in strategic visions, political systems, social values, and strategic objectives, let alone their diverging interests over bilateral and regional issues, it is far more logical and — we would argue — more empirically valid to make a case that the US and China will likely remain divergent over peninsular issues as well. Beneath the facade of the "strategic constructive relationship," moreover, their interests could be significantly in conflict with one another when confronted with some concrete issues and longer-term agendas. Prominent examples include, but are not limited to, a North Korean contingency, future status of the USFK, the question of WMDs in North Korea, and military capability and strategic orientation of a unified Korea.

VI Seoul Between Eagle and Dragon

China's more confrontational posture toward the US and Japan is likely to continue for years to come. In particular, a sustained confrontation between the regional superpower and the global superpower could sharply exacerbate their potential and real differences over a host of peninsular and regional issues. In particular, China's growing influence over, and interdependence with Korea amid the continuing rivalry between the US and China could well make untenable the proposition that both countries can jointly cooperate in resolving a plateful of concrete policy issues and longer-term questions on the peninsula. Korea's balancing act between its alliance with the US and its cooperation with China, in short, could well turn out to be the most prominent security challenge in the twenty-first century.

In order to avoid the possibly stark strategic decision, Korea should be able to "walk on two legs" — to paraphrase the Maoist slogan — by maintaining a strong security relationship with the United States, while charting out a long-term, comprehensive strategy toward China, which envisions post-unification relations between itself on the one hand and the US and China on the other.

Korea's economic cooperation, augmented by increased diplomatic and cultural contacts, is essential for the expansion of their bilateral ties. Military-to-military relationships need to be set up as well. Given the current and expected influence of the PLA in China's domestic and external policies, it seems only prudent for the ROK to gradually foster personal ties and eventually institutional relations with the Chinese military. In addition, Korea needs to formulate in due time a panoply of security- and confidence-building measures (SCBMs) specifically designed to address Chinese potential concerns, including a unified Korea's intention to promote friendly relations with China, the creation of a buffer zone in and joint development of Sino-Korean border areas, and the establishment of a three-way security dialogue among China, the United States and unified Korea.

For its part, the US should continue to pursue the strategy of "comprehensive engagement," especially in areas of mutual benefit (e.g., Chinese economic reform and trade). Additionally, US China policy must be firmly linked to its overall Asia policy, carefully weighing the costs and benefits of the former to the latter. Conflict between the two policies would require a strong political will and leadership in official Washington. Finally but not lastly, the US must differentiate national interests from universal values, strategic flexibility from policy reversals, and long-term goals from short-term gains. But if and when the above efforts yield no reciprocity from the Chinese side, the US must consider possible alternatives to the present strategy of comprehensive engagement, with consequences difficult to predict.

All in all, to advance the longer-term goal of a stable and prosperous East Asia not only should the US and East Asian nations recognize China's differing yet often legitimate security requirements, but also make genuine efforts to build confidence with China, which is a time-consuming yet least threatening way to make China more transparent. The paths China and US choose will continue to influence both East Asia's future economic and security trajectories and the individual states' strategic soul-searching.

‹10›

Religious Harmony and World Peace:
A Gandhian Critique

*A.K. Chirappanath**

The greatest problem the world faces today is that the people are losing their sense of values in the society. Mahatma Gandhi beautifully summarized the social problems of today in "Seven Social Evils".[1]

1. Politics without Principles
2. Wealth without Work.
3. Commerce without Morality.
4. Education without Character.
5. Pleasure without Conscience.
6. Science without Humanity.
7. Worship without Sacrifice.

Today, man in society is valued on the basis of "What he has"; "What he is" is of no matter to anyone. This shows that our value system has undergone a big change or rather a perversion. Values based on religion, spirituality, morality etc., are totally discarded in our society. Material economic welfare has become the only concern for our leaders and people. The values of Truth, Love and Non-violence have been reduced to some concepts found in some fictional stories of olden days. In short, religion is totally losing its grip on the society.

---

* Professor and Director, School of Gandhian Studies, Mahatma Gandhi University, Kottayam, Kerala, India.

The Crusades and Muslim invasions are clear instances of wars fought in the name of religions. The frequent Hindu-Muslim riots in various pockets of India are also instances of collisions in the name of religion. These instances lead us to conclude that different religions are the causes for tension in society. But this is indeed a hasty conclusion or generalization.

Any organized religion established to act as a decisive unifying force has the uncanny potential for taking a dogmatic and divisive course. The splinter groups of the parent religion usually find themselves locked in interminable and internecine verbal warfare, fighting over rituals, ways of worship and other inanities. No religion is an exception to this.

The Mahayana and Hinayana Schools of Buddhism, the Sanatanis and Aryasamajis of Hinduism, the Shi'ahs and Sunnis of Islam, the Catholics and Protestants of Christianity, the Digambaris and Swetambaris of Jainism etc. are clear examples of division and discord inside the same religion.

In the above account, there are two issues. The earlier part presents cases of interfaith tensions, i.e., between *different religions*. The latter part gives us cases of intra-faith tensions, i.e. between groups of people of the *same religion*.

Now what exactly is the cause of this problem? If the fights were restricted to the first group, we could have concluded that the differences among religions are the main cause for the inter-religious tensions. When it is found among different groups of the same religion, we cannot agree with the conclusion that the differences found among the various religions are the main cause for religious tensions. What else is the main cause for this?

It is in this connection that studies in interfaith relations, intra-religious dialogue, Gandhian perspectives on religion, etc. become of utmost importance. Before entering into the complex issues of inter-religious relations and intra-religious dialogue, it is absolutely necessary to have a correct understanding of religion itself. What is religion? What is its purpose or goal? What are the means suggested for the realization of the goal? These are some very common but important questions, which have to be examined in some depth.

What is Religion?

In traditional language, religion (re+ ligare = re + tying) etymologically means relation of the self/individual with God. Man, who happened to cut himself away from God, is helped through religion to retie or relate with God to attain the purpose of recreation, i.e., salvation. Another etymological explanation of religion relates the word with "re-eligere" meaning "re-choosing." Man, who chose against God, is helped through religion to re- choose God for his eternal salvation. Acceptance of God is generally considered to be an essential element of any religion. (True, Buddhism and Jainism are not considered theistic religions. But then Buddha and the Theerthankaras have occupied the place of gods.)

This idea of religion as the relation of the self with God without specifying the nature of the relation among the individuals and in the society has not been acceptable to many. In fact, religion cannot be a personal affair that goes on between the individual and God in the temples or churches alone. Gandhiji said, religion should pervade every action of ours. It should transcend and harmonize particular religions.[2] Religions have vertical and horizontal dimensions. In other words, religions have to control the vertical relations with God and the horizontal relations with the others.

Accordingly, religion can be defined as peace within oneself, with others and with God. This definition seems to have special significance with regard to the three universal religions i.e., Christianity, Islam and Hinduism. At the very birth of Christ the angels sang, "Glory to God in the Highest and *peace* to men on earth".[3] And Christ sent his disciples all over the world to take to the people his message of universal *peace* and brotherhood. Accordingly, the Christians exchange peace during their prayer services. The very word "Islam" means peace and hence a Muslim must greet his brother with *Salam Alakum* meaning "*Peace* be with you". . . In Hinduism, the Hindu prayers are always concluded with a triple invocation for peace, i.e., *Om Shanti, Shanti, Shanti'*." It is paradoxical indeed that they cannot co-exist in peace.[4] Yet, their goal is the establishment of universal peace.

Coming to the goal of religions it is interesting to note that there is a striking resemblance and unity with all religions. All religions are concerned to solve the problem of life and lead man to a liberated stage from his bonded situation. A recent publication entitled *Salvation in World Religions* with contributions by practitioners and experts of each religion, is indeed a revelation to students of world religions. All religions in unequivocal terms and in one voice have articulated the great truth that their main and sole concern is to help man reach salvation. The idea has been expressed in different terms such as Liberation, Mukti, Heaven, Kaivalya, Nirvana, Linganga Samarasya, etc. This is a concrete manifestation of the universal salvific will of God through cosmic revelation.[5]

In the means suggested to attain the goal, there is not much difference either. Christians are asked to observe the Ten Commandments to attain salvation. The Muslims are given the five Pillars of Islam to reach Heaven. The Hindus have the *Dharmasasthras* to escape the Rebirth cycle and to attain *Mukti*. The Lingayats have the *Panchacara* (5 Rules of conduct) and Ashtauarana (8 protecting shields). *Samyagcaritra* (Right conduct) is prescribed by the Jains for self-Realization. The *Ashtangika Marga* (Eight-fold path) is suggested by the Buddhists for *Nirvana*. In brief, all these prescriptions amount to the Biblical teaching - "Do to others as you want them to do to you." The Ten Commandments and the laws of all prophets of all religions can be summed up in one word, "Love" . . . "Love God above all things and love your neighbour as thyself." In no religious scriptures can we find a teaching to hate anybody or to harm anybody. Hence it is a fact that there is a basic unity among all religions.[6]

But this does not mean that all religions are the same and that there are no differences among religions at all.

Though religion has been explained in terms of a peaceful life with all, all religions do not prescribe the same type of behaviour. How can the same type of life and behaviour be enforced on all people? This is not possible and not necessary either. Still we know that all religions serve the same purpose. But what is this same purpose? Does this mean unity? Is the behaviour alone important? Certainly not. Each religion is different from others. Beliefs and doctrines are different. Forms of worship are different; codes of conduct are different. If so, then how can they bring about human solidarity and communal harmony? If the behaviour unifies, the other differences are unimportant and they will not cause any diversification. But this will lead only to uniformity, and not to unity and harmony. For a variety of reasons, the structural pattern will be different. Then, where is the desired unity and harmony? The principle that unites and controls our life and action, that brings about harmony among people must be fundamentally the same. Then alone will the sources of conflict cease to exist. Such principles can bring about unity among people and harmony among communities manifesting themselves in diversity. This requires a true understanding of religion, which is indeed difficult, but not impossible.[7]

It is here that Gandhiji appears to be worth studying. His approach to religion seems quite feasible to anyone truly religious. According to Gandhiji's understanding of religion, the differences need not divide mankind but only enrich him. Hence, if religions are to play any role in promoting harmony and unity among various communities we have to understand religions as Gandhiji understood them and gave them expressions through his life and thought.[8]

Gandhiji's Views on Communal Problems

Gandhiji was very concerned with riots that resulted in the loss of life and property. One can debate whether the real issues were political and social or religious. Whatever be one's views, the religious differences are certainly an important cause for communal tension. Gandhiji treated these problems as religious problems. We shall now see his specific contributions in this regard.[9]

His Basic Vision of Life

Mahatma Gandhi, leader of the Indian Freedom struggle and the Father of Modern India, had a unique vision of life. Unfortunately, his basic vision of life is often discarded or distorted. The massive and unprecedented advance of industrialization, and urbanization with its atmospheric pollution, ecological imbalances and environmental disturbances, has led some economists to see Gandhi as an economist of prophetic vision who realized that *Small is Beautiful*.

The corrupt practices prevalent in the liberal parliamentary democratic systems, based on party politics, has led some political scientists to look for an alternative system in Gandhiji's *Hind Swaraj*. For them, Gandhi is a great political scientist who foresaw the maladies of the above system and suggested communitarian democracy (*Panchayat Raj*) for the realization of God's Kingdom (*Rama Rajya*). Considering the great threat of unemployment, Gandhi is seen by many as the great educationist who proposed "Basic Education Through a Vocation" (Nai Talim). For social workers, Gandhiji is the best model of selfless service to mankind. But the unfortunate thing is that almost all have conveniently overlooked, if not deliberately forgotten, the very basis of it all - his religion.

It is from his religion that Gandhiji evolved all his philosophy of social, economic, political, educational and other thoughts. "My politics and other activities of mine are derived from my religion."[10] He was a man of God who lived an intensely religious inner life, from which his outward activities derived their strength and meaning. It was in religion that he found his true being. In short, his basic vision of life was deeply religious.

His Religious Philosophy

There is a distinctive character to Gandhiji's idea of religion.

Every evening after the prayer meeting he used to discuss problems - social, political, economic, as well as religious - with the members of the prayer-group. For Gandhiji, life was one. It was not divided into watertight compartments like social, political, economic, moral, religious etc. Man is all of these, everywhere and each and every moment of his life. A truly religious man has to be religious everywhere and at all times and he cannot put up with injustice anywhere. Thus, his entire conception of life and religions was an integrated one. "Religion must pervade every one of our actions".[11] You must watch my life - how I live, eat, sit, talk, and behave in general. The sum total of all of these in me is my religion.[12] That is why he called his religion ethical religion.[13]

Religion and Morality

It is clear that he saw a good and moral life as the expression of religion. However, he did not deny or reject the commonly accepted elements of religion, i.e., (1) Creed (2) Cult and (3) Code of conduct. In fact, he was ready to tolerate any creed or religion, even if it is unreasonable, provided it was not immoral. Similarly, he fought those religious doctrines, which were in conflict with morality. The same holds true with the cult. He did not object to any form of worship, which was not immoral. He believed that creed and cult are meant for the promotion of good conduct. If not, they are no good for any religion.

For Gandhiji, religion and morality are intimately interrelated. They are inseparably bound to each other. He compared religion and morality to water and seed sown in the soil.[14] The essence of religion is morality. Often he considered them identical. When morality incarnates itself in all living man, it becomes religion, because it binds, it holds, it sustains him in the hours of his trials. To judge whether a doctrine is religious or not, the criterion he used was morality. He did not consider a man religious, if he violated moral laws. As soon as one loses the moral basis he ceases to be religious, according to Gandhi. Hence he called his faith "Ethical Religion"

Religion and Prayer

He considered prayer an integral part of religion. Prayer purifies and reforms man for a better life. Therefore, he defined prayer as the intense longing of the soul for greater purity."[15] For him it was the most potent instrument and the greatest weapon for safeguarding spiritual life. He was convinced that prayer was more indispensable for the soul than food for the body. So if anybody does not pray, his life will be dull and empty and he will not have any inward peace. He was so devoted to prayer that he could well claim that no act of his was done without prayer.[16]

"Begin therefore your day with prayer and make it so soulful that it may remain with you until the evening. Close the day with prayer so that you may have a peaceful night free from dreams and nightmares. Do not worry about the form of prayer. Let it be any form, it should be such as can be put into communion with Divine. Only, whatever be the form, let not the spirit wander while the words of prayer run on out of your mouth."[17] Gandhiji used to have two prayer-sessions a day.

Prayer is the best source for peace with oneself, with the world and with God. In the eternal struggle going on in man's heart between the powers of darkness and light, he who has not the sheet anchor of prayer to rely upon will be a victim to the powers of darkness. The man who goes about the affairs of the world without a prayerful heart, will be miserable, and will also make the world miserable. Apart from its bearing on man's condition after death, prayer has incalculable value for man in this world of the living. As Alfred Tennyson puts:

> *"More things are wrought by prayer*
> *Than this world dreams of"*[18]

Prayer is the only means of bringing about peace in our daily life.

"It is only after I have prayed here every day that I feel the bliss of having tasted the amrit(nectar) of knowledge. For that, the man who wishes to be a real human being, *dal* and *roti* are not his food. They count but little for him. His real food is prayer."[19] Gandhi was convinced of the fact that prayer is more essential for the well being of the soul, than is food for the maintenance of the body.

Divine Paternity and Human Fraternity

Another basic theme of the religious philosophy of Gandhi is the fatherhood of God and the brotherhood of man.[20] God's paternity and man's fraternity are the basis for Gandhiji's social concern and humanitarian activities. We all come from God, Our father. We are marching towards Him as brothers and sisters. It is in this that he finds the fundamental unity of religions. He went further, however. He wanted to identify not merely with human beings, but with all forms of life. All come from the same God. Thus he extended brother-hood to all living beings.

"We are all children of the same Father, whom the Hindu, the Muslim and the Christians know by different names . . . The Allah of Islam is the same as the God of the Christians and the Iswara of the Hindus. Man has tried in his humble way to describe Mighty God by giving Him attributes, though He is above all attributes. Indescribable, Inconceivable and Immeasurable. Living faith in this God means acceptance of the brotherhood of mankind. It also means equal respect for all religions."[21]

Unity of All Religions

Nobody can deny the fact we are living in a world of religious pluralism or diversity. Underlying this diversity there is a oneness. Underneath these many religions there is *one Religion*. There are differences but in the final analysis, these are insignificant. Convinced of this, Gandhiji had great reverence for all religions and admired their noble manifestations. All religions revealed the Eternal Truth (God) and showed man the path of liberation. Only their descriptions varied. If there is religious strife, religionists, and not religions, are responsible. Therefore, he exhorted people to live the religion to which they belonged, in truth and spirit.[22]

This in turn will bring about better relations and harmony among religions.

The Mahatma clearly saw the need of the time - respect for one another among the devotees of different religions. What is required is not the dead level of uniformity, but unity in diversity. Religion can be expressed in a variety of forms. The various forms will persist to the end of the time. Wise men will ignore this crust and see the soul beneath the crust. God is one and is identical with Truth. Truth (God) cannot be the exclusive property of any single religion.

Different religions are but different flowers of the same garden, or branches of the same tree. "Just as a tree has a million leaves, similarly, though God is one, there are as many religions as there are men and women though all are rooted in one God. Each mind has a different conception of God from that of the other."[23] However, Gandhiji did not aim at any fusion of religions. He sincerely believed that each religion has something unique to contribute to mankind in its cultural background.

To discover the underlying unity in diversity, Gandhiji has a master key - Truth and Non-violence. Through the perfect observance of Truth and Non- violence together with other Ashram (monastic) vows, a person can easily realize the basic unity of all religions. Self-imposed discipline alone can lead one to this realization.

Truth - Search of all Religions

The basic quest of all religions is to seek, find and realize the Eternal Truth. They all share the same Truth (God). Perhaps because of this, Gandhiji said, "All religions of the world are true, more or less." The "More or less" is because religion as conceived by man can never be perfect, perfection being the exclusive attribute of God alone. If all faiths outlined by man are imperfect, the question of comparative merit does not arise, says Gandhiji. All faiths aim at revealing Truth (God). Truth is like the fire at the heart of a many-faced jewel. Each angle shows a different aspect and a different colour.[24]

Imperfect as we are, we can see Truth only in fragments and act according to our limited vision. Only God knows the reality. Therefore, we must not be like the "frog in the well" which imagines that the world extends only up to the walls of the well. In other words, we must not think that our religion alone is true and others are all false. A reverent study of other religions would show that they are also true like our own, though all are necessarily imperfect. Therefore, we must extend the same respect to all faiths. When such an attitude becomes the law of life, the conflicts based on religious differences will disappear from the face of the earth.[25]

Equality of all Religions

Just as he believed in the unity and Truth of all religions, GandhiJi also believed in the equality of all religions.[26] All religions have the same source, goal and concern. They are all imperfect too. Therefore, they are equal on many grounds. When he says that all religions are true and equal, he does not necessarily mean that "they are equally true" in religious terms or they are absolutely true. Another person's religion is true for him, as much as mine is true for me. We are not to sit on the royal throne and pass judgement on them. "Judge not, that ye be not judged".[27]

We know that no two bodies are identical, nor two leaves of a tree. There is bound to be some difference. Similarly, each one prays to God according to the light he has received. How then can one pass judgement as to "who prays better"? For Gandhi, "If I am a seeker of Truth, it is sufficient for me."

Since there is only one God and there is identity in the essential moral principles of all religions, in theory there can be only one religion. But in fact, there are many religions because men, who are imperfect by nature, interpret these moral principles according to their own temperament, environment and culture. "In theory, since there is only one God, there can be only one religion. But in practice, no two persons I have known have had the identical conception of God. Therefore, there will, perhaps, always be different religions answering to different temperaments and climatic conditions.[28] The duty towards self and the relationship with one's neighbour is the same in all religions.[29] And what distinguished religions one from the other, are the external practice, their liturgy and their formulae of prayers. He compares different religions to different roads leading to the same God. "Religions are different roads converging to the same point. What does it matter that we take different roads so long as we reach the same goal?[30] Thus, Gandhi concludes that all religions are equal.

The acceptance of the doctrine of equality of religions does not do away with the distinction between religion and irreligion. He says that no man can live without religion. Some people may claim that they are agnostics and atheists and that they have nothing to do with religion. He compares them to a man who breathes but has no nose. According to him, man by nature is religious, and he has to follow some religion. That will lead him to God who rules his every breath.[31] Often what the atheists reject is the corrupt and perverted forms of religions, not the true religion.

God's Will for Universal Salvation

It is God's will that all His creation be saved. That God is the saviour of all is clearly told in the creation account of Genesis.[32] Even after man's disobedience to God, we see God's plan remaining unchanged. "The faithfulness of God endures forever" (Ps. 117) in spite of man's infidelity. God has only one destiny for all men - their salvation. God's plan and His call are dynamic and effective. This means that God reveals Himself to each man's conscience to work out his salvation by himself.

God can reveal more to each person through Nature. The unfailing alternation of the seedtime and harvest, cold and heat, summer and winter, day and night is God's own appeal to men for our recognition of His love and His offer of salvation. The dynamism of Biblical Thought excluded any real separation of the natural and the supernatural, the sacred and the secular.

The prophets of various religions are another manifestation of the universal salvific will of God. They teach people the

Dhannapatha (way of righteousness) in their own countries and cultures."[33]

All these manifestations/revelations show that God sees that the way of salvation is open to all. All the same, this way is a narrow path and not humanly attractive.

Necessity of Religion

God is the author of all religions. He manifests Himself or reveals Himself to men in apparently diverse forms to control, reform and leads men to their destiny. Therefore, religion is absolutely necessary for man. In Gandhiji's opinion, no one can live without religion.[34]

Even the agnostics or atheists who say they have nothing to do with religion, admit this moral order because they associate something good with its observance and something bad with its non-observance. After giving the example of Bradlaugh, the well-known atheist, Gandhi concludes "that even a man who disowns religion cannot and does not live without religion."[35] To prove the necessity of religion in the life of a religious man he examines his own life and says: "I could not live for a single second without religion . . . I go further and say that every activity of a man of religion must be derived from his religion, because religion means being bound to God, that is to say God rules you every breath."[36]

Respect for All Religions

Since all religions have a basic unity, and they share the same Truth and are equal, we must cultivate the same respect for all religions. This is possible only if we study all religions with **"equimindedness."** We should have no desire to criticize any aspects of other religions simply because they are not ours. We must have the humility to confess that we do not understand everything of a religion. Every religion has four elements: these are mythical, mystical, ethical and theological. It is natural that the mythical and mystical elements often present difficulties in understanding them by means of reason.

Still, there are many things, which one can learn from other religions. Therefore, Gandhiji exhorted the people of different religions; "I would advise the Hindus and the Sikhs to read the Quran as they read the Gita and the Granth Sahib. The Muslims should read the Gita and the Granth Sahib with the same reference with which they read the Quran. They should understand the meaning of what they read and have equal regard for all religions. This is my life-long practice and ideal."[37]   On another occasion he advised the Hindus, "Leave the Christian alone for the moment. I shall say to the Hindus that your lives will be incomplete unless you reverently study the teachings of Jesus."[38] To the Missionaries he said, "You, the missionaries, come to India thinking that you come to a land of heathens, of idolaters, of men who do not know God, . . . He (an Indian) is as much a seeker after Truth as you and I are, possibly more so . . . I tell you, there are many poor huts belonging to the untouchables where you will certainly find God. They do not reason but they persist in their belief that God is. They depend upon God for His assistance and find it too . . . I place these facts before you in all humility for the simple reason that you may know this land better, the land to which you have come to serve."[39]

His Approach to Conflicting Beliefs

As early as 1909, in *Hind Swaraj*, Gandhi dealt with the problem of conflicting beliefs. His imaginary reader asks, "How can India be one nation? Hindus and Muslims are old enemies. Muslims turn to the West for Worship, while Hindus to the east. Hindus respect the cow; Muslims kill her. Hindus believe in *ahimsa*. Muslims, do not . . . How can India be one nation when there are all these differences."[40]

Gandhi approached the problem in more than one way. One way of removing conflict is to replace the worst interpretation of a religion by its best interpretation - the best interpretation bring that which is accepted by a good follower of the religion. For example according to him to say that Hinduism regards cows as superior to man, or that it accepts distinctions of high and low is to caricature Hinduism. If interpretations in terms of the worst aspect of a religion is replaced by interpretation in terms of its best aspects, then it will be found that all great religions spring from the same source and the fundamentals are common to them all.[41]

This is indeed a salutary piece of advice, very often forgotten in practice. Another way is to replace the misunderstanding of a belief by correct understanding. For example it is a misunderstanding to think that Buddha did not believe in God. "In my humble opinion such a belief contradicts the very central fact of Buddha's teaching. In my humble opinion the confusion has arisen over his rejection, and just rejection, of all base things that passed in his generation under the name of God.[42] In a similar way Gandhi reinterprets the belief that *nirvana* means complete extinction.

In summary, Gandhi held to a "doctrine of the equality of religions" "We recognize that all these faiths are true and divinely inspired, and all have suffered through the necessarily imperfect handling of imperfect men."[43]

The problem of **creedal** differences among religions can be best overcome by appealing to the manner of life that goes with belief. Is there any religion higher than the Truth and any practice higher than love? Is this not a sufficient basis for ritual co-operation and reason to ignore the apparently conflicting elements?

The important point of Gandhi's religious philosophy is that not only does it say that all religions are true, but it also says that all religions are false. Gandhiji's view differs from the traditional understanding. Gandhi tried to give a new understanding of religion. Because of the political and social struggles in the country, one can say that he held these particular views about religion, because of the needs of these struggles. They do not, therefore, represent a theoretically viable view of religion. It is necessary, therefore, to say that the view of religion that Gandhiji put forward is not without plausible theoretic support.[44]

Religion and Secularism

If Gandhi's views are accepted then we have a solution to a problem, which often dogs our political and social life - the interference of religious beliefs in the solution of the political and social problems. One view is that the only way of overcoming this difficulty is to accept a secular approach to these problems and think of religion as a strictly personal matter. Gandhi's approach to the problem is quite different. For Gandhi, religion is not restricted to some one aspect of life, but pervades all its aspects. And yet, Gandhi succeeds in solving the problem for which secularism is supposed to be the only answer because his conception of religion and secularism is quite different.

His religion is not static and obscurantist beyond the reach of reason; it is dynamic and rational and progressive. It is something that grows with the times. If religion is to be all that Gandhi wants it to be, it is not necessary to cut it off from the political and social aspects of life. What is necessary is to cut off a rigid relationship between religion and particular social and political arrangements, but not from social and political arrangements in general. But is this not as good as cutting off religion from these issues? No, because even when the relationship allows flexibility, religion performs a significant role. No longer does religion require the following of a particular code. It requires a constant moral quest. Insofar as Gandhi does so, his solution is qualitatively different from secularism; and it avoids the theoretical difficulty with which secularism is faced. What is the role of religion that is strictly personal? What is this business between a man and his maker, which does not manifest itself in all aspects of a man's life ?[45]

In this connection, it is interesting to note the specific Indian understanding of the concept of secularism. Today, many identify secularism with irreligion and atheism. In the historical background of its origin in Europe, secularism was separation of religion from state. In America, if I rightly understood, secularism is the indifferent attitude (no-concern) of the State to religion. In the U.S.S.R., secularism was understood as irreligion and atheism. But India has developed a different concept or definition of secularism based on the religious philosophy of Gandhiji.

The 42nd amendment of the Indian Constitution makes India a secular republic. Secularism generally means that the State does not recognise any religion as its own. An indifference if not apathy, is maintained by the state with regard to religion. In India, people are exhorted to respect all religions. The Government treats them all equally. *Sarva Dharma Sama Bhavana* (equality of religions) is a vow to be taken and observed by people, for a better world and world peace.

References

1. Gandhi M. K., Social Service, Work and Reform, Navajeevan, Ahmedabad, p.

2. *Harijan* (10 Feb 40), 445

3. Luke 2:14

4. Chirappanath, Editorial, *Indian Missiological Review* 3, No.4 (Oct 82), 319. The journal is cited hereafter as IMR.

5. Chirappanath, "God's Plan of Salvation through Cosmic Revelation," IMR (Oct 1981),298-303.

6. There is considerable debate over these issues. Some Muslims say belief in Allah leads to Paradise. Some Christians find salvation in Christ. The Ten Commandments are in the Hebrew Scriptures. The Jewish Bible. Ed.

7. Chirappanth, p. 83 in *Religions in National Integration* ed. Thomas Manickarn: Bangalore: Dhamiaram, 1984.

8. Ibid.

9. Ibid.

10. *Harijan* (2Mar 84), 23.

11. Ibid. (10 Feb 40), 445.

12. Ibid. (22 Sep 40), 321.

13. Gandhi, *Ethical Religion'*, Ahmedabad: Navajivan, p. 12

14. Gandhi, *Ethical Religion*, p.49.

15. *Young India* (24 Mar 40), 1. (Hereafter YI)

16. YI (25 Sep 24), 313.

17. *Prayer*, Ahmedabad: Navajivan 1977, p.9.

18. Alfred Tennyson, Morte d'Arthur
19. Prayer, op. cit., p.l0
20. Gandhi, *All Men Are Brothers*: Ahmedabad: Navajivan, 1960, Gandhi, *All Religions Are true*; Bombay: Pearl 1962, p.9.
21. *All Religions*, p. cit., p.vii
22. Chirappanath, *Religions*, op.cit., p.88.
23. All Religions, op. cit., p.vi
24. Ibid., p.v
25. Ibid., p.4
26. Ibid.,p.l0
27. Matthew 7:1.
28. *All Religions*, op. cit., p. 10.
29. Ethical Religion, p. 5.
30. Gandhi, *Hind Swaraj*, Madras: Ganesh, 1908, p. 50.
31. Yl (23 Jan 30), 25, and, Harijan (2 Mar 34) 23.
32. Chirappanath, *God's Plan*, op. cit., p.298.
33. Ibid.
34. Yl (23 Jan 30), 25.
35. Ibid.
36. Gandhi, *Harijan* (2 Mar 34), 23.
37. Gandhi, All Religions, op. cit., p. 26.
38. Chirappanath, "Gandhiji's great Challenge", IMR, I. No. 1 (1979), 47.
39. Ibid.
40. Gandhi, *Collected Works*, New Delhi: Government of India, 1958-, X:28
41. Chirappanath, Religion, op. cit., p.92.
42. Ibid.
43. K. L. Seshagiri Rao, *Mahatma Gandhi and Comparative Religion*, New Delhi: Motilal Banarsidass, 1978, p. 145.
44. K.J. Shah, *Religion and Secularism in India*, Dharward: Karnatak University, unpublished.
45. Ibid

‹11›

The Emerging Order for Regional Peace and International Security

Debasis Bagchi*

The early man saw a boulder or a branch of a tree falling on some other branches or twigs and causing some sparks. The sparks, though tiny, with the fanning from the breeze pretty soon caused a mighty conflagration. Large forests turned into an inferno engulfing everything within which was simply reduced to ashes. When man learned to harness fire he could use it in various ways. While a ring of fire ensured him protection from the wild animals or from the members of another clan prying away something from his territory, he also learned to use this formidable power for acts of usurping or destruction. So easily do we conclude that the gigantic dinosaurs could not survive long as they had a very small portion of gray matter in comparison to their huge bodies. Yet they roamed over the surface of the earth for 135 long million years before they became extinct and that too, more likely, due to the elements' razes, rather than in efforts of dominating over the others of their tribes. However the homo sapiens, the children of the other day, in a very short span of their standing erect, and so called civilized existence over a few millennia past, have already masterminded two World Wars wreaking havoc on fellow humans not in thousands but simply in millions (an estimated 55 million human lives Were lost in World War-II). The dropping

*   Inspector General of Police (Enforcement), Delhi Vidyut Board, Delhi, India.

of the two small atom bombs sent a chill down the spine of the civilized society. Yet who decided and used them were very advanced (sic) nations of the World. And they conveniently used logic for doing so. When Ernest Rutherford, a pioneer of modern atomic science was unraveling the mighty power of the atom, Reginald Revans, a scholar then young, withdrew from his team. In 1989, then a nonagenarian, Revans told us that he had shuddered to toy with its destructive properties. Even about 35 years back, when China was through with her successful tests and added a few such weapons in the arsenal, and in a debate on the floor of Parliament the then Indian Premier was pressed hard by about 80 Members of Parliament to draw India forthwith into this race, the very idea had shaken us. Bertrund Russel had discussed these topics in his book 'Has man a future'. One missile destroyer was equal to one hundred thousand tractors ! Freed from foreign yoke not even two decades back, for India, a developing country, then putting in the best of her efforts to providing food, clothing and shelter to the teeming millions, the very idea had shaken her to the roots. A few wise ones also suggested to the Government to take shelter under a nuclear umbrella.

Years have passed. Much water has flown down the Nile, the Danube, the Ganges, and the Mississippi, we have seen birth of nations and countries gaining independence, we have as well seen how countries have been torn to pieces. We had never been satisfied with the crucifixion of one Jesus. We have taken the lives of many Joans of Arc (1412-1431), Atahualpa (1502-1533), Galileo Galilei (1564-1642), Mahatma Gandhi (1869-1948), Martin Luther King Jr. (1929-1968). Assassinations run galore and have become the order of the day. Massacring millions of fellow humans do not touch our hearts today.

Even President Bill Clinton admitted and stated at the White House (April 6, 1999) on the hate crimes related to the late happenings in the World today, "And if you look at the whole history of this violence we see in Kosovo, what we went through in Bosnia (both in erstwhile Yugoslavia), this, the fifth anniversary of the awful Rwandan genocide, that I regret so much the World was not organized enough to move quickly enough to deal with it before hundreds of thousands of lives were lost- with the oppression of women in Afghanistan, with the lingering bitterness in the Middle East- you see all these things. When you strip it all away, down deep inside there is this idea that you cannot organize personal life or social life unless some group feels better about itself only when they are oppressing someone else. Or people at least believe that they ought to have the right to violence against someone else solely because of who they are, not because of what they do . . ."

Now that we have seen certain people were not tolerated for their views and certain people - men, women and children alike -were not spared their lives because of "who they were" we may also see what has been the thinking to mitigate the problems of the innumerable ones who are living next door. The Vedas had proclaimed "Sanno dwipade, sanno astu catuspade"- Let us share our wealth among the bipeds, let us share our wealth among the quadrupeds - verily because they realized how essential it was to provide succour all around us so as to be mutually benefited from the same.

The seers in Vedas went even one step further. They had talked of the necessity of keeping the air pure, the water unpolluted, nurturing the seasonally growing plants like the cereals, the large trees to provide us shelter, fruits and other implements of our daily needs including the bark which gave us clothing and definitely the domesticated animals which nourished our lives.

One of the most pressing tasks before the international community in the 21st century is "to save succeeding generations from the scourge of war". This laudable commitment has in fact been enshrined in the Charter of the United Nations. Even at the inception of the United Nations the problem of peace was stirring the minds of all the stalwarts in the Comity of Nations and was considered the basic challenge for mankind. The same has perhaps remained not less pronounced even after more than half a century of existence of this world body known as the United Nations. The statesmen in their prudence, as they had been well aware of their ghoulish experience, took steps from time to time to avert the recurrence of another World War, two of which have eaten into the vitals of civilized society. In the years past, especially after the cold war days, there has been a significant rise in civil wars, insurgencies and armed conflicts in different parts of the world. We have seen that some of the countries have been torn to pieces and innumerable precious human lives have been lost just on flimsy pretexts.

When it was set up, the main task of the UN was to implement the principle of self-determination, help colonized countries to attain independence and socio-economic transformation of lives of people, mainly in the developing world. The other priority area is peace, security and disarmament. For the UN, preventive diplomacy is necessary to deal with potential conflict situation. UN peacekeeping has assumed a vital role in inter-state relations and efforts for greater co-ordination.

National sovereignty being the bedrock of the international system, the UN, even in its peace keeping efforts, is not in a position to impose itself onto a country, if it is unwilling to accept its intervention. For this particular reasons the soldiers of the UN peacekeeping force watched helplessly when the civilians were massacred in Srebenica and Rwanda. In the very recent past a large number of peace keeping force including more than 200 Indian Soldiers could be taken hostage by the Revolutionary United Front in Sierra Leone, because the rules of engagement prevented the UN from taking on the insurgents in a meaningful manner. A specially constituted panel has stressed that the "Peace Keepers must be capable of defending themselves . . . and the mission's mandate, with robust rules of engagement, against those who renege on their commitments to peace accords or otherwise seek to undermine it by violence". The committee showed its concern in cases where one party to a peace agreement has been observed to violate its terms "continued equal treatment of all parties by the UN may amount to complicity with evil." There is also a danger that peace keeping operations could get politicized if any one party is targeted for differential treatment.

It is also to be noted in this context as one author (Simon Jenkins) has very rightly observed: "Armies cannot impose peace on civil wars unless they mean to impose subsequent rule. Almost every instance of outside military intervention in a civil war over the past half century has postponed, rather than hastened, a stable political settlement with the possible exception of the Soviet Union in Hungary in 1956."

Our experience over the past five decades leads us to believe that unless the UN sorts out the basic areas of its thrust it may not be able to serve mankind the way it should. The UN must support democracy and openness of society for these are values that are critical to good governance. The organization has an important role to play to prevent poverty and hunger. Connected closely with this is freedom and human rights, which may be best addressed when people have full stomachs.

Theo-Ben Guirab of Namibia, the present president of the UN General Assembly, maintains that, 'The UN must be an instrument for empowerment and also to propagate human values. It must find a way for restructuring of minds in favour of change. It is peace that is important, equality that is important. The UN must be instrumental in ensuring peaceful co-existence and the Millennium Summit would afford World leaders an opportunity in the 21st Century to aspire towards a future with peace. Without peace development is not possible."

When neighbours do not share common ideas of peaceful co-existence as against war their precious resources are diverted even for a nuclear arms race, whereas much of these differences can be solved across the table if there is earnestness and sincerity. It is time that the UN transforms itself to a decision-making forum of a lady representative body of 6 billion people around the globe. Until the developing countries of the world get an equitable weightage in carrying their say in this august body all the laudable pronouncements from its pulpit will remain a distant dream.

It was at such a juncture that the cycle of the 20th century was over and with the advent of 21st century, a new millennium of recorded human history has started. In the fitness of things, in quick succession two meaningful meets have taken place in the precincts of the United Nations headquarters. The first one is the Millennium Spiritual meet attended by 1500 delegates representing 73 faiths followed by the Summit of the Heads of State.

As wars waged for territory and dominion continued unabated proving the efforts of the UN abortive, a realization has slowly dawned on its office-bearers that certain threats to humankind like natural disasters, epidemics, ecological degradation, drug trafficking, terrorism and so forth may not and cannot be addressed unless a sincere move is rooted in life-enhancing values shared by humankind as a whole.

The millions of individuals around the world who yearn for lasting peace among peoples and nations welcomed the UN's four day long Millennium World Peace Summit held in the UN Headquarters, where spiritual leaders from the 'Anglican to Zorastrian' faiths spoke on the human values: love, tolerance, forgiveness, reconciliation, justice. From this august forum for the first-time they stressed the need to ensure that the ethical and spiritual core of every religion can and must provide the basis to banish fear and want, and the debilitating scourge of intolerance from the hearts of people every where.

The inter-faith meeting, perhaps for the first time, gave credence to India's basic pronouncement in the *Rigveda : Ekam sad viprah bahudha vadanti* - the truth is one, the wise call it by many names. The meet utilized the opportunity to overcome the barriers of hatred and exclusivism, fanaticism and fundamentalism and agreed to respect all the great religious traditions of the world. The leaders of the faiths also deliberated that this was time that they endeavour to involve in the alleviation and ultimate abolition of poverty and deprivation of hunger and malnutrition from the earth. The deliberation assumes all the more significance as much blood has been shed in the recent past in the name of religion, caste, creed and even ethnic groups. Natural environment also needs to be respected and kept free from pollutions, so that for the folly of some irresponsible members of the human race the posterity does not suffer immeasurably. For if it does the loss in this case will be irreparable. The true spirit of the meet came out succinctly when one speaker said "I am all for conversion, but not from one organised religion to another, but conversion from bondage to liberation, from misery to happiness and from cruelty to compassion. That is what the UN should ensure.

The basic issues reiterated in the UN Millennium Summit of 185 Nations were democracy, peace, development and a crusade against terrorism. The Prime Minister of India said, "We cannot have development without peace between nations and democracy within them. Peace, democracy and development secure one another." He quoted the seers' saying, "May peace, harmony, good health and auspiciousness prevail the world over. "India, the world's largest democracy has been a nation wronged: a stable, liberal country, whose sincere overtures of friendship were deliberately spurned; one which has had to witness the killing of 30,000 of its citizens on senseless acts of terrorism actively promoted by a neighbour· and which could no longer regard this nation's peace posturing with any degree of trust. The Indian ethos stemmed from a universalist worldview resting on its ancient wisdom. Such a perpetual propagandist of disarmament may also, however, unavoidably be drawn into the nuclear race to be strong to defend peace."

In the 8th September, 2000 Summit speech the Indian Prime Minister actually laid bare the crux of the formidable challenges facing India, in particular, and the World body, in its entirety today: ". . . Of the many other threats to peace, democracy and development, none has become as dangerous as international terrorism, with its links to religious extremism, drug trafficking and the commerce in illicit arms. Plural and open democracies are the target of the scourge of terrorism that strikes at the very root of tolerance, the mainstay of civil society in a free world.

"For more than a decade now India has been a victim of cross-border terrorism that has claimed thousands of innocent lives . . . India calls for united global action against these dangers . . ."

"Those who have stifled democracy at home, speak of freedom from this forum. Those who have engaged in the clandestine acquisition of nuclear weapons and delivery systems talk of ridding South Asia of these.

The world must see the reality as it is. The acid test of sincerity of purpose is not words, but deeds. Terrorism and dialogue do not go together . . . Countries should cooperate and work closely to prevent, combat and eradicate the illicit trade in small arms and light weapons by adopting an International Programme of Action of Agreed Measures...."

Via drug trafficking some Mafiosi have started invading many hitherto untrodden territories. Laundering much of $400 -$500 billion annual turnovers from illegal drug trade, the tentacles of this hideous monster have spread over millions of unsuspecting victims. A mere 243 drug addicts, in a recently concluded study of the ACPO Working Group, have been found to be responsible for 500,000 crimes over a period of 11 years. Some countries like India sandwiched between the growing and trading countries, are suffering the brunt of terrorism, being easy targets as transit countries. For want of adequate measures the menace is spreading like wildfire. The drug business reinvesting its profit is acquiring an increasingly powerful position in legitimate business. Within another 3 years' time, the capital value of drug related funds would approximately equal $ 15000 billion exceeding the current annual GDP of the USA. Only through a serious concerted strike at its roots by bilateral, multilateral and international efforts can the scourge be arrested.

The recent collapse of the communist block and the capitalist unification of the planet around the neo-liberal beliefs has opened new pastures for drug production which has increased and diversified, and for drug-trafficking on a global scale, which brings together criminal organizations from around the world.

A UNESCO seminar held in Tashkent (Uzbekistan) reckoned how over the last few years Central Asia has become a drug trafficking corridor. The UN Drug Control Programme's representative in Central Asia has watched the narcotics industry take on huge and alarming proportions ever since the fall of the Soviet Union, and reported:

"Afghanistan, the world's single largest producer of illicit opiate drugs, shares its border with three Central Asian states - Tajikistan, Uzbekistan and Turkmenistan. In 1997, Afghanistan produced 2,800 tonnes of raw opium, or 58% of the world's illicit supply. According to UNDCP estimates, upto' 65% of Afghanistan's narcotics exports, or upto 80 tonnes of heroin equivalent, may be passing through central Asian states annually on their way to markets in Western Europe and elsewhere."

Control of the industry is clearly in the hands of Mafia. "The mafia of the former Soviet Union, including Russia, Central Asia and the Caucasus, is one of the largest and perhaps, the most powerful in the world," says Dr. Kadyr Z. Alimov, Uzbek economist and researcher. The organization "consists of more than 5000 groups and more than three million people. It operates in all 15 former Soviet republics and even has its own land, sea and air forces' He also mentions, "As a result of government corruption producers are now informed about anti-drug enforcement operations well in advance so they are able to conceal their raw materials before hand." As these states are struggling economically, and their populations are feeling the squeeze of poverty drug traffickers can move their cargoes easily without detection, by paying the country folk a pittance.

Maratkali Nukenov, the vice-president of Kazakhstan's national security committee claims that his services have identified 125 organized crime groups operating in Central Asia, 30 of which were involved in drug trafficking in Kazakhstan alone.

Alimov has shuddered to inform that, "Although some among Central Asia's politicians would like to halt the drug problem, they are frustrated at every turn. The drug mafia is too powerful, too rich, too smart. Borders are too porous, and there is too little cooperation between the police and the various states in the region, or with Interpol. The "narcomafia" in Central Asia is here to stay."

In Myanmar, the cultivation of drug producing plants is growing unabated and the processed product is passing through India as well.

From the late 1970s, under the sponsorship of the UN, the governments of Thailand, Myanmar, and other Southeast Asian countries, have launched severe campaigns to eliminate drug producing and processing bases and the lairs of drug dealers' groups. Serious measures have also been taken to control the channels of drug production, import, and transportation. The government of Hong Kong has also mobilized much of its police force, cracked numerous drug dealing cases related to the Golden Triangle and arrested a large number of specialized drug dealers. Such actions have directly hit the conventional routes of drug trafficking in the Golden Triangle areas.

But the drug-dealing groups have changed their strategies and turned their attention to mainland China. From the 80s, the smuggling of drugs created its own environment in China. From 1990 to 1991 there was an increase of 200% at 7000 kgs, which went up to 10,000 kgs in 1992. A 1997 report indicated that a new Golden Channel was opened up in South China. Stringent measures have enabled the authorities to track down in China a large number of cases in the first half of 1997 alone which exceeded the total of all the cases tracked so far in all of the previous years. The drug related crimes have also increased there simultaneously.

India, already armed with two stringent statutes » viz, the Narcotic Drug and Psychotropic Substances Act, 1985 and PITNDPS Act, 1988, has been struggling hard with a multi-pronged and multi-agency drive under its nodal outfit Narcotic Control Bureau to tackle the drug problem seriously. Huge areas of land formerly used for growing the Poppy or Cannabis plants are being systematically cleared, properties forfeited and detentions ordered. In the current year, 543 kgs of Heroin and 987 kgs of Opium have been seized and 4810 persons have been arrested (upto 31.7.2000 provisionally). Close cooperation with various International agencies through resident Drug Liaison Officers of USA, UK, Germany , Canada, INTERPOL and World Customs

Organizations ,is being continued to dealing with the menace.

Over the last few decades, there has been an unprecedented interest shown by criminals in drug trafficking, particularly for the immense potential of narco-trade. From the producer to the ultimate user at every intermediate stage the value, of narcotic drugs and psychotropic substances, increases by leaps and bounds and opens the gate of a veritable gold mine for the dealers. The huge sums of money thus generated are known as "dirty" money. It is of little use to the sophisticated criminals because it raises the suspicions of law enforcement agencies and leaves a trail of incriminating evidence. So to disguise the billions of illegally earned or hoarded dollars, deutschemark or yen and to use them without detection the criminals "clean" the "dirty" profits. This is done through money laundering. The laundered money disguises the illegal profits without compromising the criminals who wish to benefit from the proceeds. It is a dynamic three-stage process in which the funds are first moved from the direct association with the crime, that is, the sale of drugs, and then the trail is disguised in the second stage to foil pursuit. In the third stage the money is made available to the criminals once again, now with the occupational and geographic origins hidden from preying eyes. With the globalization of the world economy these funds are transferred quickly across international borders. Due to a very fast development in financial information, technology and, communication, money moves anywhere in the world with speed and ease. Over the last decade of the Twentieth Century international finance has become totally linked to computers. The era has ushered in electronic banking and trading, cashless transactions and computerized clearing and has created the so-called "Megabyte-money" (in the form of symbols on a computer screen) that exists on terminals from New York to Tokyo- thus across the globe. This is operated 24 hours a day, seven days a week and is being shifted by the criminal's dozens of times to prevent the law enforcement agencies from tracking it down. One current report estimates that at least the drug traffickers launder $ 200 billion every year. The international trade in drugs being valued at more than twice that figure, this estimate appears to be a conservative one. Further to facilitate the laundering the organized criminals, in this field; float a large number of "anonymous" corporations, whose number is reported to be more then 1 million worldwide.

Bank secrecy and financial havens initially worked for a legitimate purpose and had a commercial justification. With the passage of time they offered unlimited protection to criminals who abuse their intent for the purpose of doing their clandestine business at any cost.

The illicit proceeds from drugs are invested in such sectors of the economy where the assets can later be used as laundering machines. These are pumped into business involving high volumes of cash, such as restaurants, casinos, cinemas and even banks.

The UN Under-Secretary-General, Pinto Ariacchi, Executive Director of the Office for Drug Control and Crime Prevention rightly observed, "By bringing entrepreneurs, linked in 'uncivil society' into the legal system, fresh strains of adventurism and anarchy are placed in the economic market. Their presence has the potential to trigger an explosive worldwide financial breakdown that so many people fear."

In an article on "Transnational criminal organizations and drug trafficking", P. Williams and C. Florez have dealt with the subject in depth. They have found that transnational criminal organization, particularly drug-trafficking organizations, operate unrestricted across international borders. They are very similar in kind to legitimate transnational corporations in structure, strength, size, geographical range and scope of their operations. Above all other features they engage in unregulated forms of capitalist enterprise.

In the last two decades, drug traffickers have moved from domestic-based enterprises into large-scale criminal organization that "treat national borders as nothing more than minor inconveniences to their criminal enterprises". The transnational criminal organizations have a home base in one State but operate across national borders and engage in criminal activities in one or more host States. They engage in unregulated forms of capitalist enterprise, involving either illicit products or the illicit smuggling of licit products, or both. In effect, gangster capitalism is simply unregulated capitalism taken to excess.

Transnational criminal organizations obtain access through circumvention rather than consent, and systematically evade efforts to detect, monitor, intercept and disrupt their activities.

Understanding transnational criminal organizations and their role in drug trafficking has been hindered by two different tendencies. The first is the growing journalistic focus on the global Mafia or what is sometimes termed global organized crime. Although there are linkages and alliances of convenience among some transnational criminal groups, there is no monolithic global criminal organization. There are many organizations that engage in cross-border criminal activities and sometimes cooperate and sometimes compete with each other. Treating these groups as an amorphous but unified entity is a form of distorted sensationalism that hindered a differentiated assessment of transnational criminal organizations, and understanding of their strengths and weaknesses, and an evaluation of the linkages among them. In practice, these linkages range from simple exchanges of drugs for money to full-fledged strategic alliances, joint ventures and partnerships. To acknowledge such connections, however, is a far cry from embracing a concept of global organized crime that is helpful neither at the analytical nor the policy level.

A second obstacle to understanding transnational criminal organizations is that organized crime has traditionally been a domestic phenomenon to be examined and understood at the local and national levels. Moreover, some criminologists dismiss the transnational emphasis as reminiscent of discredited alien conspiracy theories that explained organized crime in the United States as a transplanted rather than indigenous phenomenon. Underestimating the importance of transnational criminal organizations, however, is as damaging as treating these organizations as a global monolith, and ignores the new opportunities for criminal activity.

Among the criminal organizations that operate across national borders are the Sicilian Mafia, Chinese Triads, Japanese Yakuza, Colombian cartels, Nigerian drug-trafficking groups, Jamaican posses, and criminal organizations in the Russian Federation. Some of these groups, especially the Asian criminal organizations, have a long history, but have become increasingly transnational in the scope of their operations. Others have emerged more recently in response to a range of economic and political pressure and opportunities — especially those associated with the emergence of the global narcotics industry. That industry encompasses producing countries such as Afghanistan, Myanmar and Peru, transit countries such as Mexico, Thailand and Turkey, processing countries such as Colombia or Pakistan, and service countries such as Panama. Major cities or territories such as Bangkok, Hong Kong, Houston, Istanbul or New York, act as both consumer and distribution centers. The various components of the industry, however, are linked together by transnational criminal organizations.

This is not to suggest that the drug-trafficking industry and the activities of transnational criminal organizations are synonymous. In fact, transnational criminal organizations vary in several important ways, including the extent of their involvement in drug trafficking. They come in various shapes and sizes and with their own skills and specializations; they operate in different geographical domains and different product markets; they use a variety of tactics and mechanisms for circumventing restrictions and avoiding law enforcement; and they vary considerably in the scope of their activities.

The UN Global Programme against Money Laundering being highly concerned with the after effects warned the member countries in an official paper:

"Wealthy Criminal Organization can wreak devastating social consequences on society. Laundered money provides fuel for drug dealers, arms merchants and other criminals to operate and expand their enterprises. Left unchecked, money laundering can erode the integrity of a nation's financial institutions by changing the demand for cash, making interest and exchange rates more volatile and by causing severe inflation in countries where criminal elements are doing business. The siphoning away of billions of dollars a year from normal economic growth poses a real danger at a time when the financial health of every country affects the stability of the global market."

Sometimes under an unwarranted indulgence of some of the most developed countries of the World in the name of countering turmoil brewing in a specific part of the globe, an ambitious outfit of a developing country grows unscrupulously under the strength of Narcotics trade which may boomerang back to its creator to engulf it as a Frankenstein. This happened with the Pakistan's ISI in which case the US Intelligence outfit CIA turned a blind eye to the ISI indulgence of Narcotics trade which was consciously promoted by General Zia, its President. Emboldened, the ISI fomented terrorists activities in Punjab and J&K. The aim has always been destabilization of India. The Punjab terrorists were trained in Pakistan and the Narco Gangs operated under some selected officers of the ISI. The Drug Lords were then enlisted by them to establish an unholy nexus with the terrorists, thus employing Narco-terrorism against India. The Drug barons of the Golden Crescent employed the terrorists to transfer drugs to India. From India the drugs were dispatched via the Western Seaboard or by air from Delhi or Bombay to Europe or the US, via the Gulf or Africa. A regular International chain was established by the second half of the eighties. Bombay, the financial headquarter of this unholy nexus, became the main source of finance of the Punjab terrorists. Punjab's terrorism was thus financed by drug money.

Narcotics trade has since become the base of organized crime. The reason is simple. This trade alone can generate the kind of money that can literally challenge the might of the state power. By adopting very convenient methods the smugglers try and bend the state machinery to their will. This involves all kinds of illegal activities from distribution of territory to pick-pockets to extortion, hired-killings, flesh trade to boot-legging and what not, including building up a back up supply of arms and ammunitions. Metropolises to megapolises around the globe are exposed to this phenomenon. Rightly thus today's underworld is an underworld of Narcotics.

"The Law and order machinery, the political parties and the bureaucracy are successfully infiltrated or subjugated by the awesome power of the sheer volume of the moneys involved. The industrialists often work as partners along with the bankers, as the money generated must find legitimate expression. Real estate, foreign exchange rackets, import export transactions, films, stock markets all forms of trading, where money involved is large, are the secondary operators of the Narco-terrorists. Money laundering is an essential part of Narcotics trade, which is often ignored by the enforcement agencies. In India the so-called NRI investment is 50% drug money.

"Money begets prestige, so the big fish in the drugs network have established themselves as respected citizens of the country. It is thus not surprising that all the political parties patronize these big fish. Apart from money it is the sheer impact of the most powerful and wealthy organizations of the underworld on the electoral future of the political parties that is making the political parties subservient to the Narco-trade either directly or indirectly." (Sudhir Sawant)

The Narco-traders have aptly interpreted the term globalization and taken advantage of it. Today their linkages and networks are worldwide. It should thus be anybody's guess how one Dawood Ibrahim can control his empire in India by simple proxy. The power of these gangs has no longer remained confined to the metro cities, or some selected states, but has spread its tentacles of operation and influence in hitherto untrodden areas and beyond the boundaries of nations.

The impact of Narcotics is also evident and has become a matter of concern on the fabric of society. It has catered to the needs of the teeming millions of frustrated unemployed youth and also those who want make a fast buck.

It provides a short cut to power and fame. Prior to 1991, to belong to the notorious "D" (Dawood) Company was considered a matter of prestige in Bombay.

When a state power backs the underworld network it has at its disposal resources and expertise which otherwise would be beyond the reach of the common criminals. The underworlds direct infiltration in the political system is already well known. Many MPs and MLAs are a part of the underworld controlled by narcotics. A politician is entirely dependent on external sources for his finance much more than his legitimate accountable sources. Drug money is playing a big role in financing the politicians who may even unwillingly fall into their trap but may not steer clear thereafter.

"Often the drug baron-industrialist nexus results in a political nexus. It is also a well-known fact that many so called industrialists are financed by the drug."

Our neighbour's formidable and potent outfit, backed and nurtured by drug money has infiltrated many organizations of the country. They have established contacts with every possible organization having regional variances, whether social, economic or political and infiltrated craftily into them. They sought active cooperation of the Peoples War Group, the LTTE and even ULFA and other insurgent groups and have launched various kinds of joint operations. They are reportedly penetrating the premier investigating agencies and the services and have even reached our island territories in the Indian Ocean. The underworld was utilized by these agencies for obvious mutual benefits. All sorts of differences on any issue in the North East, Tamil Nadu, Punjab, J&K and Naxalism have been blown up by the ISI to destabilize the country's integrity and reputation in the comity of Nations.

Considering the gravity of Drug-Crime nexus a concerted effort is called for by one and all of the international law enforcement agencies individually and whenever or wherever possible jointly to strike at the very roots of the Narco menace so as to arrest the onslaught of various other crimes which is frustrating all our efforts to establish peace and tranquility in the region.

The Asian Crime Prevention Foundation has been playing a major role at least in countering the formidable challenges in the sphere of crimes. They have been working out effective strategies for regional cooperation to combat illicit trafficking in drugs, firearms, humans, transnational organized crimes, money laundering, cyber crimes, environmental crime and violence against women and children. The role of non-governmental organizations has also been considered to be of utmost importance and as such there are recommendations to ensure active cooperation between the governments of the Asia-Pacific regions and the NGOs.

Another major issue, which needs to be addressed immediately, is the fight against hunger. While ideally or philosophically it will be in the fitness of things to effect a substantial check on the unbridled on growing population, but this war can be won only slowly and steadily, all the outfits of the state have to be geared up conscientiously. What, however, we should immediately embark upon is mitigating the problems of the suffering millions, especially those who are hungry. The latest World Bank prescription has also not considered this in its entirety.

The whole United Nations system, till recently, did not have a proper mechanism for inter-agency co-ordination to collect and collate data on hunger at the global level. It was only generally known that there are millions of men and women who starve and millions of children who suffer from stunted brain growth owing to certain deficiencies. The Food and Agricultural Organization took the initiative and came out last year with its report on 'State of Food Insecurity in the World". This has been done as follow up to the 1996 Food Summit held in Rome at their initiative, which was attended to by 186 countries. According to this report, India has the largest number of under-nourished at 204 millions, followed by China at 164 millions. South Asia accounts for 284 millions i.e. more than one third of the world population of the hungry at 824 millions. The data collected between 1987 and 1998 show that two out of five children in the developing world are stunted. one in three is under-weight and one in ten is wasted. The 1996 Summit had decided that by the year 2015 should reduce the number of the hungry by half, which was reckoned at 830 million in the developing world at that time. This called for a reduction of 20 millions in the number of the hungry every year, whereas the actual reduction has been of the order of 8 million only over a period of five years. Rightly the Father of the Nation had the insight to indicate that there was enough in the world for every body's need, though not for some people's greed. In the foreword to the F.A.O. report its Director General Jacques Diouf has not, however, dreamt when he recorded " it is my conviction that there is no reason not to have a hunger-free world sometime in the next century. The world already produces enough food to feed the people who inhabit it today and it could produce more. However, unless deliberate action is taken at all levels, chances are that hunger and malnutrition will continue in the foreseeable ·future."

With the present world production of food, if only 18% of humanity suffer from hunger, then there would definitely be a large number of people who eat more than they should. The publication "State of the World 2000" indicates the number of hungry as 1.2 billion, the number of over-fed at the same figure and another 2 billion people who have serious micronutrient deficiency in their diet. The three figures adding up to 4.4 billions are indicative of the number of hungry, malnourished and over-nourished. This figure is against the total world population of 6 billion.

Noble Laureate Amartya Sen has been rightly emphatic in his statement that hunger is seldom caused by the absence of food. The world was only too slow to accept his views so far. It is worth mentioning that nearly 80% of the mal-nourished children in the developing world live in countries, which are food-surplus.

It can, therefore, be concluded that hunger is a result of human decisions and can be eliminated if correct decisions are taken.

It is time after a prolonged slumber to wake up to these urgent Needs of the world and to take immediate steps to address the very basic problems of the human race in right earnest, utilizing all the resources available in the hands of the various international bodies so as to make this earth livable and survivable.

The world bodies should do well to develop an enlightened citizenship. An Indian king, poet and mystic Bhartrihari in his Niti-Sataka (Verse 64-) had expounded, about fifteen hundred years back, the four human types in a society, thus: ' There is one type of people called the sat-purusas, good people, who sacrifice their own self-interest and work for the welfare of other people; the next group consists of the samanyas, the majority, who also work for the welfare of other people, but without sacrificing their own self-interest; the third group are the manava-raksasas, demons among men, who destroy other people's welfare in order to gain their own selfish interest; but the fourth group on the contrary-alas, I do no know what to call them-destroy other people's welfare, even without gaining anything for themselves?'

Which type do we choose for ourselves? Let us decide.

Swami, Ranganathananda, the Revered President of the Ramakrishna Mission in his book "Enlightened Citizenship and Our Democracy" wants us to convert the nation into a mighty anthropological laboratory for total human development. Let us resolve in chorus what he urges:

Today, we have to build up a new democratic and humanistic **noosphere** (which is constituted of the mind-pulses and though currents of all the people of a society). Millions of democratic thoughts and democratic deeds build up a democratic noosphere that will create a healthy social environment which will buy up every struggling man and woman, constantly whispering into his and her heart: Brother man, Sister-woman, stand up and march onward on the long road of human development; we are all here to help you; god-speed to you! This is what we shall achieve by the wide cultivation of enlightened citizenship.

‹12›

Security in the New Millennium

The meaning and scope of security have become much broader. The number and types of security providers have grown enormously and the relationship between security providers has become more dense and complex. As well as armed terrorism, for example, states have to contend with eco-terrorism and cyber-terrorism (e.g. the 1 love you' bug). All three are cross-border phenomena of global scope and ramifications requiring active collaboration among the defence and constabulary forces, law-enforcement authorities and non-government groups and organisations.

1. Global Governance

The threshold of the new millennium is also the cusp of a new era in world affairs. The business of the world has changed almost beyond recognition over the course of the last one hundred years. There are many more actors today, and their patterns of interaction are far more complex. The focus of power and influence is shifting. The demands and expectations made on governments and international organisations by the people of the world can no longer be satisfied through isolated and self-contained efforts. The international policy making stage is increasingly congested as private and public non-state actors jostle alongside national governments in setting and implementing the agenda of the new century. The multitude of new actors adds depth and texture to the increasingly rich tapestry of international civil society.

* Vice Rector (Peace and Governance), United Nations University, Shibuya, Rector, Tokyo, Japan.

In today's seamless world, political frontiers have become less salient both for national governments whose responsibilities within borders can be held to international scrutiny, and for international organisations whose rights and duties can extend beyond borders. The gradual erosion of the once sacrosanct principle of national sovereignty is rooted today in the reality of global interdependence: no *country* is an island unto itself anymore. Ours is a world of major cities and agglomerations, with nodes of financial and economic power and their globally wired transport and communications networks. Cumulatively, they span an increasingly interconnected and interactive world characterised more by technology-driven exchange and communication than by territorial borders and political separation.

In this period of transition, the United Nations is the focus of the hopes and aspirations for a future where men and women live at peace with themselves and in harmony with nature. Over a billion people living in abject poverty will have had neither the spirit nor the means to cheer the arrival of the new millennium. The reality of human insecurity cannot simply be wished away. Yet the idea of a universal organisation dedicated to protecting peace and promoting welfare - of achieving a better life in a safer world, for all - survived the death, destruction and disillusionment of armed conflicts, genocide, persistent poverty, environmental degradation and the many assaults on human dignity of the 20th century.

The United Nations has the responsibility to protect international peace and promote human development. The UN Charter codifies best-practice state behaviour. Universities are the marketplace of ideas. Scientists have a duty to make their knowledge available for the betterment of humanity. The United Nations University has the mandate to link the two normally isolated worlds of scholarship and policy-making. It lies at the interface of ideas, international organisations and international public policy. In an information society and world, the comparative advantage of UNU lies in its identity as the custodian and manager of knowledge-based networks and coalitions that give it a global mandate and reach.

One recurring refrain in our projects in recent times has been the tension between the twin processes of globalisation and localisation; a second is the need for partnerships between different actors, including individuals, at all levels of social organisation; and a third is the comprehensive and interconnected nature of many of today's major problems that require urgent policy measures. Solutions must be individual-centred, within the framework of human security which puts people first; they must be integrated and coordinated; and they must be holistic, tackling the roots of the problems even while ameliorating the symptoms of stress and distress.

Globalisation refers both to process and outcome. National frontiers are becoming less relevant in determining the flow of ideas, information, goods, services, capital, labour and technology. The speed of modern communications makes borders increasingly permeable, while the volume of cross-border flows threatens to overwhelm the capacity of states to manage them. Globalisation releases many productive forces that, if properly harnessed, can help to uplift millions from poverty, deprivation and degradation. But it can also unleash destructive forces - 'uncivil society' - such as flow of arms, terrorism, disease, prostitution, drug and people smuggling, etc. that are neither controllable nor solvable by individual governments. At the same time, and indeed partly in reaction to globalisation, communities are beginning to re-identify with local levels of group identity.

Recommended solutions to the dilemma include decentralisation and subsidiarily, on the principle that the focus of action and solution should be where the problems are. There must be active participation of the local government, non-government organisations (NGOs), and the private actors in all phases of planning and implementation. Thus international democracy promotion should be directed at building local capacity - supporting, financially and technically, the various pillars of democratisation processes, the rule of law and the judicial system, and the legislatures, in addition to assisting the conducting of elections.

The combined effect of globalisation - both the process and the outcome – and localisation is to erode the legitimacy and effectiveness of national governments and inter-governmental organisations. There has been a corresponding decline in levels of resources and support for international organisations, including the United Nations. In the meantime, a host of new actors from civil society - NGOs, labour unions, churches - have become progressively more assertive in demanding a voice at all top decision-making tables. Sometimes developing countries attach their concerns to NGOs, while at other times NGOs attack the state of affairs in developing countries (slave labour, child labour, environmental laxness).

The solution to many of these challenges lies in global governance. The goal of global governance is not the creation of world government, but of an additional layer of international decision-making between governments and international organisations which is comprehensive and not merely piecemeal social engineering, multisectoral, democratically accountable, and inclusive of civil society actors in the shared management of the troubled and fragile world order.

Partnerships are called for between governments, international organisations, NGOs, other civil society organisations and individuals. Some countries are beginning to involve citizens more substantially in the political decisions-making process through well-designed public choice mechanisms like referenda. We are likely to witness increasing issue-specific networks and coalitions. The United Nations has the moral legitimacy, political credibility and administrative impartiality to mediate, moderate and reconcile the competing pulls and tensions associated with both the process and outcomes of globalisation. Human security can provide the conceptual umbrella that brings together the main themes of the Millennium summit - security, development, environment and governance - within one coherent framework. This would help to give practical content to the opening words of the UN Charter, 'We the people'.

2. Traditional Security Paradigm: Towards a World Free of Wars

War lies at the heart of traditional security paradigms, and military force is the sharp edge of the realist school of International Relations. The incidence of war is as pervasive as the wish for peace is universal. At any given time, most countries are at peace and long to keep it so. Yet most are also ready to go to war if necessary. Some of the most charismatic and influential personalities in human history - from Gautam Buddha and Jesus Christ to Mahatma Gandhi - have dwelt on the renunciation of force and the possibility of eliminating it from human relationships.

The 20th century captured the paradox only too well. On the one hand, we tried to emplace increasing normative, legislative and operational fetters on the right of states to go to war. Yet the century turned out to be the most murderous in human history, with over 250 wars, including two world wars and the Cold War, with more dead than in all previous wars of the past two thousand years. Another six million more have died since the Cold War ended.

Confronted with a world that cannot be changed, reasonable people adapt and accommodate. The turning points of history and progress in human civilisation have come from those who set out to change the world. This section is a story about a group of unreasonable people who met recently for the first Steering Committee of 'Global Action to Prevent War: An International Coalition to Abolish Armed Conflict and Genocide'.

The causes of war are many and complex. Our call to end it is single-minded and simple. Cynics insist that war is an inherent part of human society. To end war would indeed be to end history. Maybe. But so too have crime and poverty always been part of human history. Any political leader who admitted to giving up on the fight to end crime or poverty would quickly be returned to private life by voters. Paradoxically, in the case of war it is those who seek to abolish it who are considered to be soft in the head.

The deadly situation does not have to continue into the new century. We already have the resources and the knowledge that can drastically cut the level of armed violence in the world and make war increasingly rare. What has been missing is a programme for the worldwide, systematic and continuing application of these resources and knowledge. Global Action offers such a programme, and it is building a worldwide coalition of interested individuals, civil society organisations, and governments to carry it out.[1]

For internal conflicts, we propose a broad array of conflict prevention measures to be applied by the UN, regional security organisations and international courts. For conflicts between neighbouring states, we recommend force reductions, defensively-oriented changes in force structure, confidence-building measures and constraints on force activities tailored to each situation. The possibility of conflict among the major powers can be reduced by fostering their cooperation in preventing smaller wars and through step-by-step cuts in their conventional and nuclear forces, eliminating their capacity to attack each other with any chance of success.

Global Action's conflict prevention and conventional disarmament measures will promote nuclear disarmament. Nuclear cuts in turn will facilitate conflict prevention and conventional disarmament. Achievement of nuclear disarmament will very probably require both reduced levels of conflict worldwide and some effective and acceptable way to cut back the conventional forces of the major powers, especially their force projection capability with naval and air forces. Countries like China, Russia and India are not likely to relinquish their nuclear weapons if the main effect of doing so is to enhance the already large conventional superiority of the United States. Other governments are unlikely to be prepared to reduce their conventional armed forces drastically unless there is evidence that nuclear weapons are on the one-way road to elimination.

---

1. Global Action's website address is **www.globalactionpw.org**

Global Action's deliberate focus is on violent armed conflict. The world also faces fundamental crises of poverty, human rights violations, environmental degradation, and discrimination based on race, gender, ethnicity, and religion. All of these challenges must be met before human security and a just peace can be fully achieved. To meet these challenges, many efforts must be pursued; no single campaign can deal with all of them. But efforts to address these global problems can and should complement and support one another. The abolition of war will make it possible to focus all remaining energy and efforts on resolving the fundamental structural problems.

The analogy we like is with domestic violence. Faced with incidents of violence within the family, the first and most urgent order of business is to stop the violence. Only then can we look at probable causes and possible solutions, including if necessary separation and divorce.

3. From National Security to Human Security

The shift from the 'national security' to the 'human security' paradigm is of historic importance. The object of security changes from the state to the individual; the focus changes from security through armaments to security through human development; from territorial security to food, employment and environmental security. The fundamental components of human security - the security of people against threats to life, health, livelihood, personal safety and human dignity - can be put at risk by external aggression, but also by factors within a country including 'security' forces. Over the course of the 20th century, 30 million people were killed in international wars, 7 million in civil wars and an additional 170 million by their own governments.[2]

In his Millennium Report, Secretary-General Kofi Annan writes of the quest for freedom from fear, freedom from want and securing a sustainable future. A recurring theme in his report is the importance of making the transition from the

2. 'Freedom's Journey', survey in The Economist, 11 September 1999.

culture of reaction to the culture of prevention. This is even more fundamental for the attainment of human security than for national security, as even a cursory glance at threats to human security will show.

Mankind - including the rich countries - will not be able to live free of fear, will not be able to secure a sustainable future, so long as over a billion people live in servitude to want. That is, freedom from want is precondition of the other two elements in the trinity. The safest and most peaceful communities are composed of individuals who have their basic needs and aspirations met.

The multi-dimensional approach to security sacrifices precision for inclusiveness. In order to rescue it from being diluted into nothingness, we need to focus on security policy in relation to crisis. Short of that it is more accurate to assess welfare gains and losses rather than increased security and insecurity. Security policy can then be posited as crisis prevention and crisis management, both with regard to institutional capacity and material capability.

Even if we limit 'security' to anything which threatens the core integrity of our units of analysis (namely human lives), many non-traditional concerns merit the gravity of the security label and require exceptional policy measures in response: environmental threats of total inundation or desertification; political threats of the complete collapse of state structures; population flows so large as to destroy the basic identity of host societies and cultures; structural coercion so severe as to turn human beings into de facto chattels; and such like. The annual mortality correlates of Afro-Asiatic poverty (low levels of life expectancy, high levels of maternal and infant mortality) run into several million. Annual deaths-preventable killings-even on this scale cannot be accommodated within the analytical framework of 'national security'; they can in 'human security'.

The traditional, narrow concept of security leaves out the most elementary and legitimate concerns of ordinary people regarding security in their daily lives. It also diverts enormous amounts of national wealth and human resources into armaments and armed forces, while countries fail to protect their citizens from chronic insecurities of hunger, disease, inadequate shelter, crime, unemployment, social conflict and environmental hazards: 'Na roti, na kapara, na makan - par Bharat mera mahan'.[3]

When rape is used as an instrument of war and ethnic 'impurification,' when thousands are killed by floods resulting from a ravaged countryside and when citizens are killed by their own security forces, then the concept of national security is immaterial and of zero utility. By contrast, human security can embrace such diverse phenomena. To insist on national security at the expense of human security would be to trivialise the concept of security in many real-world circumstances to the point of sterility, bereft of any practical meaning.[4]

A recent report on health as a global security challenge concluded that health and security converge at three intersections.[5] First, faced with domestic economic crises and shrinking foreign assistance, many developing countries have had to make difficult budgetary choices to reduce the level of public services. But the failure of governments to provide the basic public health services, including garbage removal, water treatment and sewage disposal, has two further consequences. It erodes governmental legitimacy, and encourages the spirit of 'self-help' and 'beggar they neighbour' among citisens at the expense of the public interest. Often the competition degenerates into

---

3. The first part is a popular saying in India, the second is a patriotic boast. Two have been combined for ironic effect: Neither food nor clothing, nor shelter–but India is great?

4. For an attempt to apply the human security concept to the Asia-Pacific region, see William T. Tow, Ramesh Thakur and In-taek Hyun, eds, *Asia's Emerging Regional Order: Reconciling Traditional and Human Security* (Tokyo: United Nations University Press, 2000).

5. *Contagion and Conflict: Health as a Global Security Challenge. A Report of the Chemical and Biological Arms Control Institute and the CSIS International 'Security Programme* (Washington DC: Centre for Strategic and International Studies, January 2000).

violence. Thus the withdrawal of the state from the public health domain can be both a symptom and a cause of failing states. Second, there has been an increasing trend in recent internal armed conflicts to manipulate the supplies of food and medicine. Indeed the struggle to control food and medicine can define the war strategies of some of the conflict parties. And third, the use of biological weapons represents the deliberate spread of disease against an adversary.

The narrow definition of security also presents a falsified image of the policy process. The military is only one of several competing interest groups vying for a larger share of the collective goods being allocated authoritatively by the government. Environmental and social groups also compete for the allocation of scarce resources. There is, therefore, competition, tension and conflict among major value clusters. The concept of military security as a subset of the national interest serves to disguise the reality of inter-value competition. By contrast, the multi-dimensional concept of security highlights the need for integrative strategies that resolve or transcend value conflicts. If they are rational, policy-makers will allocate resources to security only so long as the marginal return is greater for security than for other uses of the resources.

Once security is defined as human security, security policy embraces the totality of state responsibilities for the welfare of citizens from the cradle to the grave. The mark of a civilisation is not the deference and respect paid to the glamorous and the powerful, but the care and attention devoted to the least privileged and the most vulnerable. Children in particular need and should have the most protection in any society. Regrettably, many hazards to children's survival, healthy growth and normal development, in rich as well as poor countries, constitute a pervasive threat to human security at present and in the foreseeable future.

UN calculations show that just in the last decade, 2 million children have been killed, I million orphaned, 6 million disabled or otherwise seriously injured, 12 million made homeless, and

10 million left with serious psychological scars. Large numbers of them, especially young women, are the targets of rape and other forms of sexual violence as deliberate instruments of war. The steps taken in defence of the rights of children remain small, hesitant and limited. The biggest danger is compassion fatigue: we will get so used to the statistics that they will cease to shock us, and we will learn to live with the unacceptable.

Being wedded still to 'national security' may be one reason why half the world's governments spend more to protect their citisens against undefined external military attack than to guard them against the omnipresent enemies of good health. Human dignity is at stake here. How can one experience the joys and the meaning attached to human life, how can one experience a life of human dignity, when survival from day to day is under threat?

4. From Arms Control to International Humanitarian Law

Human security gives us a template for international action. Canada and Japan are two countries that have taken the lead in attempting to incorporate human security in their foreign policies. A practical expression of this was the Ottawa Treaty proscribing the production, stockpiling, use, and export of anti-personnel landmines. The first to impose a ban on an entire class of weapons already in widespread use, the Convention was a triumph for an unusual coalition of governments, international organisations and NGOs. Such 'New Diplomacy' has been impelled by a growing intensity of public impatience with the slow pace of traditional diplomacy. Many people have grown tired of years of negotiations leading to a final product that may be accepted or rejected by countries.[6] They look instead for a sense of urgency and timely action that will prevent human insecurity, not always react to outbreaks of conflict.

---

6. Jessica Tuchman Matthews, 'Redefining Security', *Foreign Affairs* 68 (Spring 1989), p. 176 Matthews was writing in the context of environmental negotiations.

It would be as big a mistake to interpret the Ottawa Treaty from the analytic lens of national security instead of human security, as to judge it by criteria devised for the evaluation of arms control regimes. Instead, it falls into the stream of measures which make up international humanitarian law.[7] Such measures derive from motives different from those which prompt the negotiation of arms control regimes, are concerned with different subject matters, involve radically different compliance mechanisms and ultimately have different political functions. The basic purpose of international humanitarian law is not the exacting one of securing the absolute disappearance of particular forms of conduct, but rather the more realistic one of producing some amelioration of the circumstances which combatants and non-combatants will confront should war break out. While its rules are cast in the language of prohibition, it operates through the process *of anathematisation*.

Sceptical observers of the Ottawa process have focussed on such important non- signatories as the United States, Russia, China and India; the allegedly perilous simplicity of the treaty, which creates scope for disagreement as to its exact meaning; and the relative ease with which a perfidious state party could move to violate its provisions. These criticisms are for the most part misconceived, and arise from a misunderstanding of the functions which the Ottawa Treaty can appropriately be expected to perform. In principle, every country whose participation is vital to the credibility and integrity of *an arms control regime* must be party to the treaty. *A humanitarian treaty* seeks to make progress through stigmatisation and the construction of normative barriers to use and deployment. While major-power endorsements of the convention would have added significantly to its political weight, amending the treaty provisions to accommodate their preferences would have greatly diluted the

---

7. This section summarizes Ramesh Thakur and William Maley, 'The Ottawa Convention on Landmines: A Landmark Humanitarian Treaty in Arms Control?', *Global Governance* 5:3 (July September 1999), pp. 273-302.

humanitarian content of the regime. The integrity of the convention as a humanitarian treaty was held to be more important than the inclusion even of the United States. The humanitarian impulse proved stronger than the arms control caution. Even those key states which have not signed the treaty have voiced sympathy for its objectives. To that extent, it has changed the parameters of discussion of anti-personnel mines from a strictly military framework to one which is strongly shaped by humanitarian concerns.

5. Non-Government Organisations (NGOs)

In recent major diplomatic landmarks like the Ottawa Treaty banning anti-personnel landmines, the Rome Treaty establishing the International Criminal Court, and humanitarian interventions in Kosovo and East Timor, the impact of NGOs on international public policy has been very evident. The consequence of the rise of NGOs as significant policy-influencing actors is to tilt the balance away from hard to soft security.

There are four broad reasons for the rise of NGO influence. Political space for them opened up with the end of the Cold War. New issues like human rights, environmental degradation and gender equality came to the forefront of public consciousness. These are issues on which NGOs enjoy many comparative advantages over governments in terms of experience, expertise and often, let it be noted, public credibility. These are also issues on which it is more difficult to marginalise and exclude NGOs than was the case with the hard security issues during the Cold War.

Second, the global scope and multilayered complexity of the new issues increased the need for partnerships between the established state actors and proliferating NGOs. They are partners in policy formation, information dissemination, standard-setting advocacy, monitoring and implementation.

Third, the opportunities provided to NGOs have expanded enormously as a result of modern communications technology that enables people to forge real-time cyberspace communities on shared interests, values and goals. The Internet and the fax machine have expanded the range, volume and quality of networking activity. Globally networked NGOs can serve as focal points for mobilising interests shared by people living in different countries.

Fourth and finally, people with special skills and expertise have increasingly been drawn to work for and with NGOs, thereby muting some of their earlier amateurishness. The more effective and credible NGOs are increasingly professionalised in personnel and operations, including research, lobbying, fundraising, advocacy and networking.

The expanding worldwide networks of NGOs embrace virtually every level of organisation, from the village community to global summits; and almost every sector of public life, from the provision of microcredit and the delivery of paramedical assistance, to environmental and human rights activism. Much of the UN's work in the field involves intimate partnerships with dedicated NGOs. They can complement UN efforts in several ways:

- The presence of NGOs in the field can be a vital link in providing early warning for dealing with humanitarian crises;
- Their specialised knowledge and contacts can be important components of the post-crisis peace-building process;
- They can mediate between the peace and security functions of intergovernmental organisations and the needs and wants of local civilian populations;
- They can exert a positive influence on the restoration of a climate of confidence for rehabilitation and reconstruction to take place.

This is not to imply that states are being replaced by NGOs and international organisations – far from it. Nor does it mean that all NGOs are 'good' ones, always on the side of angels. Instead we must confront, address and redress the problem of unelected, unaccountable, unrepresentative and self-aggrandising NGOs. They can be just as undemocratic as the governments and organisations they criticise, and represent single-issue vested interests such as the gun lobby. By contrast, most industrialised-country governments are multipurpose organisations trying to represent the public interest by the choice of the voters. In many developing countries, societies are busy building sound national governments as the prerequisite to effective governance: good governance is not possible without effective government.

But it does imply that national governments and international organisations will have to learn to live with the rise of NGOs. Indeed those who learn to exploit the new opportunities for partnership between the different actors will be among the more effective New Age diplomats.

6. Human Rights

NGOs have been especially active, often intrusive and sometimes even obtrusive on human rights. Fifty years ago, conscious of the atrocities committed by the Nazis while the world looked silently away, the United Nations adopted the Universal Declaration of Human Rights. It is the embodiment and the proclamation of the human rights norm. Covenants in 1966 added force and specificity, affirming both civil-political and social-economic-cultural rights, without privileging either set. Together with the Declaration, they mapped out the international human rights agenda, established the benchmark for state conduct, inspired provisions in many national laws and international conventions, and provided a beacon of hope to many whose rights had been snuffed out by brutal regimes.

A right is a claim, an entitlement that may neither be conferred nor denied. A human right, owed to every person simply as a human being, is inherently universal. Held only by human beings, but equally by all, it does not flow from any office, rank or relationship.

The idea of universal rights is denied by some who insist that moral standards are always culture-specific. If value relativism were to be accepted literally, then no tyrant - Hitler, Stalin, Idi Amin, Pol Pot - could be criticised by outsiders for any action. Relativism is often the first refuge of repressive governments. The false dichotomy between development and human rights is often a smokescreen for corruption and cronyism. Relativism requires an acknowledgment that each culture has its own moral system. Government behaviour is still open to evaluation by the moral code of its own society. Internal moral standards can comply with international conventions; the two do not always have to diverge. Because moral precepts vary from culture to culture does not mean that different peoples do not hold some values in common.

Few if any moral systems proscribe the act of killing absolutely under all circumstances. At different times, in different societies, war, capital punishment or abortion may or may not be morally permissible. Yet for every society, murder is always wrong. All societies require retribution to be proportionate to the wrong done. All prize children, the link between succeeding generations of human civilisation; every culture abhors their abuse.

The doctrine of national security has been especially corrosive of human rights. It is used frequently by governments, charged with the responsibility to protect citisens, to assault them instead. Under military rule, the instrument of protection from without becomes the means of attack from within.

The United Nations - an organisation of, by and for member states - has been impartial and successful in a standard-setting role; selectively successful in monitoring abuses, and almost feeble in enforcement. Governments usually subordinate considerations of UN effectiveness to the principle of non-interference.

The modesty of UN achievement should not blind us to its reality. The Universal Declaration embodies the moral code, political consensus and legal synthesis of human rights. The world has grown vastly more complex in the 50 years since. But the simplicity of the Declaration's language belies the passion of conviction underpinning it. Its elegance has been the font of inspiration down the decades, its provisions comprise the vocabulary of complaint.

Activists and NGOs use the Declaration as the concrete point of reference against which to judge state conduct. The Covenants require the submission of periodic reports by signatory countries, and so entail the creation of long-term national infrastructures for the protection and promotion of human rights. UN efforts are greatly helped by nongovernmental organisations and other elements of civil society. NGOs work to protect victims and contribute to the development and promotion of social commitment and to the enactment of laws reflecting the more enlightened human rights culture.

Between them, the United Nations and NGOs have achieved many successes. National laws and international instruments have been improved, many political prisoners have been freed and some victims of abuse have been compensated. The most recent advances on international human rights are the progressive incorporation of wartime behaviour and policy within the prohibitionary provisions of humanitarian law, for example in the Ottawa Treaty which subordinated military calculations to humanitarian concerns about a weapon that cannot distinguish a soldier from a child. Last year the world community established the first International Criminal Court. The US absence from both shows the extent to which human rights have moved ahead of their strongest advocate in the past.

7. Humanitarian Intervention

The refusal to accept the discipline of universal norms of international humanitarian law is especially difficult to fathom in the case of a country that insists on the right to humanitarian intervention. We cannot accept the doctrine that any one state or coalition can decide when to intervene with force in the internal affairs of other countries, for down that path lies total chaos. Nevertheless, the doctrine of national sovereignty in its absolute and unqualified form, which gave the most brutal tyrant protection against attack from without while engaged in oppression within, has gone with the wind. On the other hand, war is itself a major humanitarian tragedy that can be justified only under the most compelling circumstances regarding the provocation, the likelihood of success - bearing in mind that goals are metamorphosed in the crucible of war once started - and the consequences that may reasonably be predicted. And the burden of proof rests on the proponents of force, not on dissenters.

If the Gulf War marked the birth of the new world order after the Cold War, Somalia was the slide into the new world disorder and Rwanda marked the loss of innocence after the end of the Cold War. Worse was to follow in the 'Safe Area' of Srebrenica in July 1995 in a tragedy that, in the words of the official UN report, 'will haunt our history forever'.[8]

While Rwanda stands as the symbol of inaction in the face of genocide, Kosovo raised many questions about the consequences of action when the international community is divided in the face of a humanitarian tragedy.[9] It confronted us with an abiding series of challenges regarding humanitarian intervention: Is it morally just, legally permissible, militarily feasible and politically doable? What happens when the different lessons of the twentieth century, encapsulated in such slogans as 'No More Wars' and 'No More Auschwitzes,' come into collision? Who decides, following what rules of procedure and evidence, that mass atrocities have been committed, by which party, and what the appropriate response should be?

To supporters, NATO cured Europe of the Milosevic-borne disease of ethnic cleansing. The spectre of racial genocide had come back to haunt Europe from the dark days of the Second World War. Military action outside the UN framework was not NATO's preferred option of choice. Rather, its resort to force was a critical comment on the institutional hurdles to effective and timely action by the United Nations. To critics, however, 'the NATO cure greatly worsened the Milosevic disease'.[10] The trickle of refugees before the war turned into a flood during it,

8. *Report of the Secretary-General Pursuant to General Assembly Resolution 53/35 (1998)* (NCT York: UN Secretariat, November 1999), para. 503.

9. See Albrecht Schnabel and Ramesh Thakur, eds, *Kosovo and the Challenge of Humanitarian Intervention: International Citizenship, Selective Indignation and Collective Action* (Tokyo: Unite Nations University Press, 2000).

10. Richard Falk, 'Reflections on the Kosovo War,' *Global Dialogue* 1:2 (Autumn 1999), p. 93.

and afterwards the Serbs were ethnically cleansed by vengeful Albanians.

The sense of moral outrage provoked by humanitarian atrocities must be tempered by an appreciation of the limits of power, a concern for international institution-building, and a sensitivity to the law of unintended consequences. In today's unstable world full of complex conflicts, we face the painful dilemma of being damned if we do and damned if we don't:

1. To respect sovereignty all the time is to be complicit in human-rights violations sometimes;

2. To argue that the UN Security Council must give its consent to humanitarian war is to risk policy paralysis by handing over the agenda to the most egregious and obstreperous;

3. To use force unilaterally is to violate international law and undermine world order.

The bottom-line question is this: Faced with another Holocaust or Rwanda-type genocide on the one hand and a Security Council veto on the other, what would we do? Because there is no clear answer to this poignant question within the existing consensus as embodied in the UN Charter, a new consensus on humanitarian intervention is urgently needed.

The UN Charter contains an inherent tension between the principles of state sovereignty, with the corollary of non-intervention, and the principles of human rights. In the first four decades, state sovereignty was privileged almost absolutely over human rights, with the one significant exception of apartheid in South Africa. The balance tilted a little in the 1990s and is more delicately poised between the two competing principles at the start of the new millennium. The indictment of President Slobodan Milosevic as a war criminal, as well as the arresting saga of former Chilean President Augusto Pinochet, shows the inexorable shift from the culture of impunity of yesteryears to a culture of accountability at the dawn of the 21st century.

The UN Security Council lies at the heart of the international law-enforcement system. The justification for bypassing it to launch an offensive war remains problematic, and the precedent that was set remains deeply troubling. By fighting and defeating Serbia, NATO became the tool for the KLA policy of inciting Serb reprisals through terrorist attacks in order to provoke NATO intervention. Communities bitterly divided for centuries cannot be forced by outsiders to live together peacefully. Another lesson that has been reinforced is that it is easier to bomb than to build. The willingness of the strong to find a campaign of destruction stands in marked contrast to the reluctance of the rich - who happen to be the almost the same group of countries - to find far less money for reconstruction. In turn this seriously, if retrospectively, undermines the humanitarian claims for having gone to war.

Many of today's wars are nasty, brutish, anything but short, and mainly internal. The world community cannot help all victims, but must step in where it can make a difference. However, unless the member states of the UN agree on some broad principles to guide interventions in similar circumstances, the Kosovo precedent will have dangerously undermined world order. Not being able to act everywhere can never be a reason for not acting where effective intervention is both possible and urgently needed. Selective indignation is inevitable, for we simply cannot intervene everywhere, every time. But community support for selective intervention will quickly dissipate if the only criterion of selection is friends (where the norm of non-intervention has primacy) versus adversaries (when the right to intervene is privileged).

In addition, we must still pursue policies of effective indignation. Humanitarian intervention must be collective, not unilateral. And it must be legitimate, not in violation of the agreed rules which comprise the foundations of world order. Being the indispensable power can tempt one into being indisposed to accept the constraints of multilateral diplomacy. But being indispensable does not confer the authority to dispense with the legitimacy of the UN as the only entity that can speak in the name of the international community. The reason for much disquiet around the world with the precedent of NATO action in Kosovo was not because their abhorrence of ethnic cleansing is any less. Rather, it was because of their dissent from a world order which permits or tolerates unilateral behaviour by the strong and their preference for an order in which principles and values are embedded in universally applicable norms and the rough edges of power are softened by institutionalised multilateralism.

8. United Nations

It used to be said during the Cold War that the purpose of NATO was to keep the Americans in, the Germans down and the Russians out. Does Kosovo mark a turning point, changing NATO into a tool for keeping the Americans in, the Russians down and the United Nations out?

International organisations are an essential means of conducting world affairs more satisfactorily than would be possible under conditions of international anarchy or total self-help. The United Nations lies at their legislative and normative centre. If it did not exist, we would surely have to invent it. Yet its founding vision of a world community equal in rights and united in action is still to be realised.

For the cynics, the United Nations can do nothing right and is the source of many ills. For the romantics, the UN can do no wrong and is the solution to all the world's problems. Its failures reflect the weakness of member states, prevented only by a lack of political will from fulfilling its destiny as the global commons, the custodian of the international interest and the conscience of all humanity.

The Charter of the United Nations was a triumph of hope and idealism over the experience of two world wars. The flame flickered in the chill winds of the Cold War, but has not yet died out. In the midst of the swirling tides of change, the UN must strive for a balance between the desirable and the possible. The global public goods of peace, prosperity, sustainable development and good governance cannot be achieved by any country acting on its own. The United Nations is still the symbol of our dreams for a better world, where weakness can be compensated by justice and fairness, and the law of the jungle replaced by the rule of law.

The innovation of peacekeeping notwithstanding, the United Nations has not fully lived up to expectations in securing a disarmed and peaceful world. As with sustainable development, which seeks to strike a balance between growth and conservation, the United Nations must be at the centre of efforts to achieve sustainable disarmament: the reduction of armaments to the lowest level where the security needs of any one country at a given time, or any one generation over time, are met without compromising the security and welfare needs of other countries or future generations.

The United Nations system can take justified pride in mapping the demographic details of the human family, as also the stupendous improvements to human welfare that have been achieved. The advances in health, life expectancy, satisfaction of basic needs and other desires were truly phenomenal over the course of the *20th* century. The symbolic six billionth child was born just recently.

At the same time, as the sun rises on the new century and illumines some of the darker legacies of the last one, we should engage in sober reflection and somber introspection. It is simply not acceptable that:

- At a time of unprecedented economic prosperity and stockmarket boom in some parts of the world, millions of people should continue to be condemned to a life of poverty, illiteracy and ill-health;
- The combined GDP of the 48 least developed countries should be less than the assets of the world's three richest people;
- The annual income of 2.5 billion - 47 percent - of the world's poorest people should be less than that of the richest 225.

The need for international assistance in many continents is an unhappy reminder of man's inhumanity against fellow-man and his rapaciousness against nature. Secretary-General Kofi Annan has noted that there were three times as many major natural disasters in the 1990s as in the 1960s. Moreover, most disaster victims live in developing countries. Poverty and the pressures of population force growing numbers of people to live in harm's way at the same time as unsound development and environmental practices place more of nature at risk. The rich reap the benefits, the poor pay the price.

Success that is sustained requires us all to make a greater commitment to the vision and values of the United Nations, and to make systematic use of the UN forum and modalities for managing and ending conflicts. People continue to look to the United Nations to guide them and protect them when the tasks are too big and complex for nations and regions to handle by themselves. The comparative advantages of the UN are its universal membership, political legitimacy, administrative impartiality, technical expertise, convening and mobilizing power, and the dedication of its staff. Its comparative disadvantages are excessive politicisation, ponderous pace of decision-making, impossible mandate, high cost structure, insufficient resources, bureaucratic rigidity, and institutional timidity. Many of the disadvantages are the product of demands and intrusions by 188 member states who own and control the organisation, but some key members disown responsibility for giving it the requisite support and resources. For the United Nations to succeed, the world community must match the demands made on the organisation by the means given to it.

The United Nations represents the idea that unbridled nationalism and the raw interplay of power must be mediated and moderated in an international framework. It is the centre for harmonising national interests and forging the international interest. Only the UN can legitimately authorise military action on behalf of the entire international community, instead of a select few. But the UN does not have its own military and police forces, and a multinational coalition of allies can offer a more credible and efficient military force when robust action is needed and warranted. What will be increasingly needed in future is partnerships of the able, the willing and the high-minded with the duly authorised. What we should most fear is partnerships of the able, the willing and the low-minded in violation of due process. What if the UN Security Council itself acts in violation of the Charter of the United Nations? Unlike domestic systems, there is no independent judicial check on the constitutionality of Security Council decisions. No liberal democracy would tolerate such a situation domestically; why should liberal democrats, who generally lead the charge for humanitarian intervention, find it acceptable internationally?

The United Nations has to strike a balance between realism and idealism. Its decisions must reflect current realities of military and economic power. It will be incapacitated if it alienates its most important members. But it will also lose credibility if it compromises core values. The United Nations is the repository of international idealism, and Utopia is fundamental to its identity. Even the sense of disenchantment and disillusionment on the part of some cannot be understood other than against this background.

The learning curve of human history shows that the UN ideal can neither be fully attained nor abandoned. Like most organisations, the UN too is condemned to an eternal credibility gap between aspiration and performance. The real challenge is to ensure that the gap does not widen, but stays within a narrow band. Sustained, coordinated efforts can turn killing fields into playing fields and rice fields. Success comes from having the courage to fail. If you have never failed, then you have not tried enough: you have not pushed yourself hard enough, not tested the limits of your potential.

‹13›

India and Regional Development Cooperation

*Yoginder K. Alagh**

India supports regional economic cooperation. It has initiated processes of tariff reform. It supports trade facilitation. It has taken unilateral initiatives including Pakistan. Its trade with SAARC is rapidly expanding. It has made serious efforts at investment and other cooperation on many fronts including power, transport and water resource projects. India is a dialogue partner of ASEAN and an important sponsor of the Association of Indian Ocean Rim Countries. Our country is building a road project in Myanmar in the North South direction and has cooperated in completing a rail link for its friends in Central Asia with the Arabian Sea. Kazakhstan, Kyrghizstan, Uzbekistan and Tadpkistan now have through Bandar Abbas a land and sea route to India. The Government is committed to strategies of economic cooperation beyond its borders and many more infrastructure projects are being discussed including some for water, electricity and transport. The first trans border energy projects involving gas flows in the Eastern Region are already being implemented.

With the countries of the SAARC, ASEAN, Central Asia and the Indian Ocean Rim, India's relationship has been long-lasting and the country remains ready to provide all possible

* Ex-Vice-Chairman, Sardar Patel Institute of Economics and Social Research, Ahmedabad, Gujarat; Ex-Vice-Chancellor, JNU, New Delhi and Chairman, Civil Services Examination Review Committee (UPSC), New Delhi, India.

assistance to projects engaged in the mutual task of nation building. We have every intention of accelerating existing projects on cooperation. We are willing to continue sharing with them, in the spirit of traditional partnership as well as of South-South Cooperation, our experiences and expertise in all areas including infrastructure development, water resources, transport, human resource development and also scientific and technological cooperation. Beyond economic opportunity, we also have a deeply felt commitment to participate in this historic process of furthering peace and development in this region.

There are proposals for energy supplies to India, which initially take gas from Tripura and the North-East and pipe it through Bangladesh to energy demand sectors in Eastern and Southern India. In the long run, there are also proposals to supply gas/hydel power both from Myanmar to India as also Central and West Asia to India; and LNG from the Middle East to India.

ASEAN industrialists who are already developing communications and energy infrastructure in countries like Malaysia and Laos and have some interests in India, have expressed an interest in the development of communications and energy projects in India.

The Confederation of India Industry (CII) has developed an interesting presentation where the North-Eastern States of India can link with wider markets in the region (these include Myanmar, Thailand, Laos, Cambodia and Vietnam) provided proper attention is placed on policy measures and communications linkages. They have argued for an integrated plan of river, air, road and telecommunications infrastructure. As is well known, apart from a small tract in Myanmar, the Asian highway is now ready and in some sense it is easier to go from our North-East to Thailand and Indo-China rather than to Mumbai. The Mekong is not that far away from our borders with China and Myanmar and in the new integrated development plans for the Mekong basin communication is given a major emphasis. (I was one of the three international expert invitees to the Integrated Mekong Basin Plan meetings of the Mekong River Commission held in April this year and details are available in that meeting).

Most serious analysts of the Special Category States Plans will agree that there is a need for these States to identify new sources of growth. I was in the Planning Commission in the mid-'70s as Adviser (Perspective Planning) and this was the period when the current strategy for these areas - of diversification of hill agriculture, improvement of communications and minimum needs planning - was set up, including projects on Jhum cultivation. M. Sivaraman had played a leading role in the establishment of the North-East Council as also a large number of para statal corporations for sustainable agro based and forest development. Most of these corporations have not succeeded. The high Central plan assistance in per capita terms given in the North-Eastern States has not led to sustained growth so far.

We need to give very serious thought to the concept of developing our North-East as a part of a larger regional entity. The history of development in this region and its cultural considerations have, needless to say, be given high priority and may dictate a degree of caution. We are a large, democratic, federal country with great reserves of resources and can bring considerable flexibility to bear on such problems which is an asset. I do not believe that non-democratic systems have greater capability than us in handling such socio-economic and socio-political development issues. We have in the long run everything to gain by taking a more comprehensive outgoing approach. This will also give a signal to the Indian people who are citizens of the border states that the country depends on them in its outward progress. I believe that a circumscribing mindset will only aggravate problems. A machinery should be set up for developing a strategic view on development and security concerns brought in to discuss the whole issue of regional cooperation in the North-Eastern parts of India.

Need for a Policy Framework

There are a number of studies which show that the resolution of long standing questions of sharing of resources require initiatives at the highest political level, technical and socio-economic system builders at the lowest level and at the implementation level. We now discuss the design of such a system and then some aspects of the present context and future possibilities in the SAARC region. We also try to show that in cross-country analysis a degree of caution is required in making sweeping generalisations and genuine understanding of concepts used in economic and socio-political discourse is an essential prerequisite for the development of projects and plans of regional cooperation.

An Example of the Mekong

I recently found an interesting example of integrated techno-economic planning in the Mekong Basin, which deserves description - also since it shows an appreciation of Indian technical work. In April 1996, the Mekong River Commission and the UNDF had organised an Expert Meeting to discuss the Long Term Basic Indicative Plan for the Mekong Basin to develop a Work Plan for it. River Valley Planners were invited from four countries with experience of innovative plans. These included an Australian to present the Murray Darling Plan, a Brazilian the Sao Paolo River Plan, and a Spaniard the Spanish National Water Plan. I was invited to present the Sardar Sarovar Narmada Plan, in view of the international acceptance of this Plan as an outstanding effort at water resources planning. I will note three aspects of this agreement. First, the Mekong River countries - Myanmar, Thailand, Laos, Vietnam, Cambodia and China - have reached an agreement on the use and development of the Mekong River in 1993. It may be recalled that there was a history of conflict on the Mekong and some of these countries had actually fought wars with each other in the not too distant past. The agreement contains rules of operation with respect to the development of water resources. The second is an interesting feature of the agreement - a detailed understanding of the water rights of the people of the Mekong. Three examples will illustrate this. The agreement has a clause on the minimum requirement of the reverse flow into the Tonle Sap Lake in the Mekong Flood Period. Now this is a very interesting proposition - an international recognition that the inhabitants of a lake have water rights in the filling up of a lake in the peak water flow season of a reverse flow in a drain. This kind of meticulous attention to detail was simply not considered in water resources planning, say two decades ago. There are examples of neglect of water rights, for example, in Gujarat, the very justified Sipu Water rights issue raised by Chunni Kaka Vaidya. The second example is the three-pronge approach in the Mekong Agreement to problem solution. At the highest level, the Commission consists of high-level political persons namely Vice Premiers of the participating countries. They resolve any political problem that may arise in implementing the Agreement and also give the Commission a vision of its work. At the second level there was a mechanism in the Commission to work out comprehensive plans and policies and sort out details of a programmatic nature. At the third level, there are groups of implementers who would implement the vision taken at the highest level as operationalized at the second expert level.

We, however, tie ourselves up in knots in these problems internally. Take the issue of hydrology. I remember when I was Chairman APC and later Chairman BICP, on technical issues, the Courts and others would never question the findings of autonomous technical Committees or Commissions. Nowadays, however, the cavalier manner in which the hydrological findings of the Central Water Commission are treated in public discourse, is amazing. Social workers, journalists and others who do not even have an understanding of the difference between maft and cusecs, give definitive pronouncements on the availability or otherwise of water and thousands of crores of rupees of investment can be blocked or the use of available water done in an extremely haphazard manner, we have responsibility in setting the technical standards of discussion of such questions.

A look at successful canal management projects shows how economic and agronomic data are used to design control and regulation systems. I had described this in modelling terms a long time ago and the Nitin Desai Committee had set it up as a planning standard. Yet these standards of use of software modelling aids are an exception. Very few groups even understand that soil, climate and the farmers' economic responses can be used to design delivery systems. Econometric work, which isolates the underlying regularity of India's peasant behaviour, can substitute for the on-demand schedules of the large farms of France in the hydrologically controlled Canal de Provence or the American California Aquaduct. It is interesting that outside India, there is now an appreciation of Indian technical work on integrating the Asiatic Peasant economy into modern irrigation systems design, originally developed in the West.

It is interesting that at the first meeting for the Basic Indicative Long Term Plan of the Mekong Basin, the concluding statement included the following references to the Narmada.

1. Dr. Alagh, in Session B, provided an excellent example of how agricultural econometric models are used in water resource planning to help design and manage large irrigation systems. Mr. Hart, in his presentation on the California water plan, indicated how urban econometric models can be used to help forecast urban water demands.

   Of course, all types of models require input data and calibration of sufficient accuracy to be useful. However, as pointed out by Dr. Loucks, simulation models can often be used to help define the type and accuracy of data required for water resource planning and is a surrogate measure of its capability to conduct comprehensive, integrated water resource planning.

   In short, computer models often help water planners and managers accomplish more with less water and at less cost."

2. Promotion of economic development through the construction of hydropower reservoirs, irrigation systems, and navigation facilities figured prominently in the early basin plans in the Murray-Darling, California, and Spanish Plans. In the more recent Narmada and Yangtze plans they are a central element."

It may be noted that after negotiations we have now resolved our problems with Bangladesh on the issue of sharing of the Ganga Waters and there is now an agreement that practical approaches will be taken to the sharing of other rivers with common benefits to both countries. There are also reports of joint energy and communication projects.

Structural Characteristics of the South Asian Region

We have tried to put together the essential features of the South Asian economies.

India and other countries in the region have a reasonable level of investment activity as compared to the better performing, developing market economies. The other countries have had much lower levels of investment centres. But investment levels had crossed 20 per cent of the GDP in the 1990s. In Pakistan it was lower while for Bangladesh it was 21 per cent. Apart from India, with a domestic savings rate of 21 per cent of GDS, all the other countries had rates lower than 10 per cent, with Bangladesh clocking 3 per cent. Also, half of their investmentis financed by International borrowing. In India, this percentage is around one-

TABLE 1

SELECTED ECONOMIC INDICATORS: SOUTH ASIAN COUNTRIES

Country	Growth Rate GDP/Pop (% Compound Annual)			Gross Investment % of GDP		Gross Domestic % of GDP		Per Capita GNP USS Savings	
	65-89	80-89	80-90	1988	1998	1988	1998	1988	1995
1	2	3	4	5	6	7	8	9	10
Bangladesh	2.8	3.7	2.3	12	21	3	15	170	204
India	4.2	5.7	2.1	24	25	21	23	330	439
Nepal	3.2	4.7	2.7	20	21	8	9	170	208
Pakistan	5.1	6.3	3.1	18	17	9	13	350	366
Sri Lanka	4.1	4.2	1.8	21	24	9	17	420	517

Source : For India, successive issues of C.S.O., Government of India, *National Accounts Statistics*, Annual. For Pakistan, Ministry of Finance, Economic Adviser's Wing, *Pakistan Economic Survey*, Annual. For these two countries growth rates have been worked out by semi-log regressions of GDP at factor cost against time. For the remaining countries, the estimates are derived from Asian Development Bank, *Asian Development Outlook*, 1990, p. 223. Column 7 is from the same source and Column 4 from p. 251, but for India it is taken from the 1991 Census.

TABLE 2

SELECTED SOCIAL INDICATORS FOR COUNTRIES OF SOUTH ASIA

Country	Female Life Expectancy at Birth (Year) 1988	Literacy Rate	% Income Accruing to Highest 20% Lowest 20%	Rural Poverty %
1	2	3	4	5
Bangladesh	51	22	4.2	51
India	58	38	5.1	37
Nepal	51	12	NA	43
Pakistan	55	19	5.9	31
Sri Lanka	73	83	11.7	36

Note: For India, the World Bank figure is 29, which is an underestimation. This figure is derived from the National Sample Survey, Government of India, *Key Results of Employment and Unemployment Survey*, Special Report No. 1, 1990, p.54. The estimate is for 1987.

Source: World Bank, **World Bank Report**, 1990, pp. 178, 236, 240

TABLE 3

STRUCTURAL RATIOS OF SOUTH ASIAN COUNTRIES: 1988/1995

Country	% GDP in Manufact- uring	Exports	Fertilizers Consump- tion Kgs/Hec		Energy Consump- tion Kgs/Hec.	Resource Balance1 % GDP
1	2	3	4 1988	1995	5	6
Bangladesh	14	7	77	136	50	-9(75)
India	30	6	52	82	211	-3(12)
Nepal	17	6	23	32	23	-20(50)
Pakistan	24	11	83	116	210	-5(36)
Sri Lanka	27	24	109	106	162	-10(49)

Note: 1.   Resources balance as percentage of gross investment is given in parentheses. Resource balance refers to the difference between export of goods and non-factor services and imports of goods and non-factor services and is a measure of foreign dependence in a two gap model.

   2.   Figures are for 1989 and the source is Asian Development Bank, **Asian Development Outlook**, p. 239. For 1995, FAO.

Source: World Bank, **World Development Report**, 1990, pp. 182.

eighth of gross investment and in some years it has been even lower (Tables 1 and 3).

The slow growth of national income has meant a relatively slow transformation of the national economy. The manufacturing share of output has risen marginally in most countries of South Asia with the exception of India and, to some extent, Sri Lanka and Pakistan. The position is far worse as regards to the structure of the labour force. The countries of the region have a high rate of labour force participation, both male and female. This is characteristic of Asian countries. Female rates of labour force participation in Pakistan are, however, extremely low. The structure of the labour force in terms of agricultural/non-agricultural shares has remained constant in the countries of the region as indicated by the Bangladeshi economist Syed Osmani. (Notes 2). In India, there was a gradual shift from agriculture in the decade of the 1970s, a trend that became more pronounced in the 1980s.

In the early 1980s, agricultural population as a percentage of the total was estimated at 82 per cent and 92 per cent for Bangladesh and Nepal respectively. In Pakistan and India, this proportion was 51 per cent and 60 per cent respectively. It was even lower for Sri Lanka (Table 4). Population pressure on arable land was highest in Bangladesh and Nepal and was also high in India and Pakistan (2.5 persons per hectare of arable land). Interestingly, the per head dietary energy supply was only marginally short of requirement in India, Pakistan and Nepal (96 per cent, 95 per cent and 93 per cent respectively, the FAO norm being 105 per cent), but was much lower in Bangladesh (84 per cent). Given the different levels of agricultural development, this reflects differential food purchasing power and agricultural diversification regimes (Table 4). A crude measure (Table 2) of inequality (income accruing to the highest 20 per cent of the population as a ratio to that accruing to the lowest 20 per cent) indicated that Bangladesh was the most equal (4.2), followed by India (5.1) and Pakistan (5.9). Strangely, Sri Lanka (11.7 per cent) rated low on this measure. Perhaps unequal income distribution can be compensated by public policy.

TABLE 4

STRUCTURAL AGRICULTURE AND FOOD SUPPLY IN SOUTH ASIA: 1983

Country	Agrl Population (% of Total)	Agrl Population/ ha of Arable Land	Agrl- GDP/ Agricultural Population USS 1986	Dietary Energy Supply/ Requirement per person (%)	Agric Growth % annual 1989/95
1	2	3	4	5	6
Bangladesh	82	8.7	84	84	1.7
India	60	2.7	114	96	3.0
Nepal	92	6.3	114	93	-1.4
Pakistan	51	2.5	190	95	3.9

Source: Gerry Rodgers, Population Growth and Poverty in South Asia and FAO.

Caution in Cross Cultural Studies of Social Indicators

The proportion of the population below the poverty line has been declining very gradually in India and Pakistan. Sri Lanka always had a more equal distribution of consumption. While reliable statistics are not available, poverty levels in Nepal and Bangladesh are generally higher. Gerry Rodgers has noted agricultural productivity to be about 90 per cent higher in India as compared to Bangladesh, and around 75 per cent higher in Pakistan as compared to India. But per head calorie supply as a percentage of requirements was reported to be around 94 per cent in both countries and was even lower in Bangladesh (Table 4).

In both India and Pakistan, poverty estimates are derived from household surveys of consumer expenditure. In Pakistan, these are conducted far less frequently than in India and the sample size is much smaller. Nevertheless the data obtained from household surveys is sufficient to permit analysis. Some of the earlier estimates, which were presented by the eminent Pakistani economist, S.M. Nasim, are as follows (Table 5).

TABLE 5

INCIDENCE OF POVERTY IN RURAL PAKISTAN (PERCENTAGE)

Country	Below Poverty Line 1 (95 % of minimum of 2100 Calories		Below Poverty Line II (92 % minimum of 2100 Calories		Below Poverty Line III (90% of minimum of 2100 Calories	
	Household	Popn	Household	Popn	Household	Popn
1963-64	79	72	62	54	54	45
1966-67	73	64	63	52	55	44
1968-69	74	64	63	53	56	46
1969-70	76	68	56	46	45	36
1970-71	79	71	58	47	48	38
1971-72	82	74	65	55	54	43

Source: S.M. Nasim, Rural Poverty and Landlessness in Pakistan, in ILO, Poverty and Landlessness in Rural Asia, 1977, pp. 41-66.

It is interesting that taking the cut-off point of poverty as 2,100 calories, Nasim estimated around 80 per cent of the population to be below the poverty line but he considered it appropriate to modify this line:

In 1963-64, the first of the years for which information is available on the distribution of consumption and calories, over 85 per cent of rural households in Pakistan (80 per cent of the population) were below this norm. Thus, it must be concluded that for Pakistan, the level of income that ensures adequate calorie consumption but almost certainly implies serious deficiencies in non-calorie nutrition requirements, is too high to be used as a realistic poverty line. Instead, Nagira suggested three different poverty levels respectively representing the amount of income with an intake of 95%, 92% and 90% of the minimum required calories (Table 5).

It would be clear to Indian economists that given the data, Nasim was bending over backwards to moderate the proportion of population below the poverty line and yet Pakistani critics followed the opposite path. Muzahid has presented the familiar argument on intra-class variation in calorie consumption within an expenditure class. (Note 3) Irfan and Amzad (Note 4) and

(Table 6) estimated lower percentages of the population below the poverty line (refer to Table 6).

TABLE 6
RURAL POVERTY IN PAKISTAN

| Year | % of Households | | % of Population | |
	Poor	Very Poor	Poor	Very Poor
1	2	3	4	5
1963-64	40.5	30.6	41.0	32.2
1966-67	46.3	35.0	50.7	38.8
1969-70	51.0	38.4	54.5	43.2
1979	39.8	26.5	41.2	29.3

It is interesting to note that even in contemporary discussion in Pakistan, the issue of poverty is relatively less emphasized. However, in a recent overview of employment, distribution and basic needs, the Pakistani economist Moin Bagai (Note 5) placed major emphasis on income distribution data, arguing that income distribution is more equal in Pakistan as compared to other countries of the region as revealed by the work of the Pakistani economist Jawaid Afzar. In fact Afzar's (Note 6) work has indicated that the level of the Gini Coefficient in Pakistan emerged since the distribution of rural income was more equal in East Pakistan (now Bangladesh) as compared to West Pakistan. Once the separation occurred, inequalities increased. Bagai has argued: "The explanation for a much heightened perception of inequalities and income distribution in the late 1960s against this mixed evidence of overall trend lies mainly in the changing pattern of relative inequalities in the rural/urban areas"(Note 7). Regarding poverty studies, Bagai has devoted only one and half pages to it as compared to 20 pages to the distributional aspects, and has endorsed the view that 'considerable restraint has to be exercised in interpreting their results'. (Note 8)

The facets of poverty and their interpretation is a rigorous question of empirical inquiry and it will not be discussed here, but it would be interesting to point out to a student of economics that faced with roughly similar factual data, economists interpreting countries with a similar tradition of analysis and training, react very differently. Pakistani economists obtaining higher estimates of poverty either reduced the norm and/or used different kinds of data until more acceptable "levels" were reached. In the case of India, the opposite view is taken. For instance, in the classical study by Dandekar and Rath, when two different rounds of the NSS indicated a reduction in inequality, Dandekar argued that this was contrary to the general observations of the Indian economy and attributed the difference between the CSO estimates of per capita expenditure and those emerging from NSS estimates to richer households to show that inequality had worsened. (Note 9)

Indian economists who have worked on poverty are doyens of the profession. At the Planning Commission, I had occasion to work with them as the Chairman of the Taskforce on Minimum Needs and Effective Demand (Note 10), which continues to be the base of poverty estimates in India. In the mid-term appraisal of the Seventh Plan, the author was instrumental in getting the Perspective Planning Division of the Planning Commission to revise upwards the estimates of poverty that it had prepared for the Seventh Plan, and also played a role in the formation of the Lakdawala Committee on the re-examination of the conceptual base for poverty estimates. The author has worked with Pakistani economists like Moin Bagai, Rashid Amzad and Bagai's successor Arshad Zaman, and these scholars command the highest respect.

The issues at hand however do not relate to the individuals involved. Approaches to the study of developmental and distributional issues are invariably intertwined with the perceptional problems emerging from the society in which the experts work. Moin Bagai, for example, while somewhat critical of poverty and formal distributional studies, has shown a heightened awareness of some of the cultural values of the societies in the region in the following words:

"The qualitative difference between the western-oriented lifestyle of the elite groups and the majority of the population who continued to pursue a cultural pattern which permitted pursuit of human advancement despite pervasive poverty by modern standards cannot be bridged by marginal attempts at improving income distribution. The lifestyle of 'Civil Lines', which originated as the enclaves of alien rulers and had tended to include newly emerging successful groups in the Third World societies are an invisible curtain segregating its more enterprising elements from the mainstream of society. (Note 11)

Even in the West, economists in the United Kingdom and the United States adopt very different approaches to studying economic growth. For example, American economists approach growth more optimistically as compared to their British counterparts. Thus, while Cambridge Massachusetts talked of technological progress and golden age equilibrium models of growth and only much later worked out the mathematics of switching theorems, Cambridge England was always worried about razor edges, destabilizing technical progress, uneven income distribution and demand deficiency and other difficulties. Perhaps, approaches to economic problems lie embedded in historical memories. Both India and Pakistan have a shared colonial past. In spite of South Koreans' high economic integration with Japan, it is driven by historical memories of colonization and wants to catch up. Every major enterprise remembers its occupation and experience and aims to surpass, if possible, but in any case to reach, the Japanese standards. It is rather difficult for India and Pakistan to get similarly involved with Britain but economists in both countries tend to see somewhat similar phenomena with very different coloured spectacles. Perhaps the size of the country makes a difference. Alternately, the problem may lie elsewhere in approaches to early forms of national experience. The issue obviously needs further study and debate.

In fact, many analysts make comparisons of poverty estimates of India with many other countries, which use very different concepts. For example, poverty estimates in Indonesia, following a method suggested by the World Bank, uses consumption of a minimum level of rice as a cut-off point (150 Kg/per caput/ annual). With this cut-off point, it is argued that poverty in Indonesia has gone down to a sixth from around two fifths of the population in the early'60s. In India on the other hand, poverty is said to have gone down only from around two fifths to a third. But if the Indonesian norm were taken into account, Indian poverty levels would be less than a sixth of the population.

Again, take social indicators on which economists like Dr. A. Sen and Dr. Mahabul Haq are very critical of Indian performance in a comparative Asian setting. The relevant policy issue in such a discussion is not just levels, but changes in indicators, so that the discussion of different policies can be intelligently carried on. Table 7 gives a picture from 1960/1990 of different countries of different social indicators. Since, as pointed out earlier, India's development performance has been relatively self-reliant in the sense that it has a low domestic savings - investment gap and therefore foreign aid has been a much smaller part of its experience as compared to other South and West Asian countries, its record of improvement in social indicators compares well with ASEAN countries and is much better than other South Asian countries. On account of a longer history of colonial exploitation, levels of social indicators in India were at the time of Independence much lower than the other countries, but have improved and the gap has narrowed considerably. Thus for example regarding improvement in life expectancy, adult literacy and population per physician, India's statistics out of seven countries is the third highest as compared to the Asian tigers and NIC.

Future Perspectives

Structural reform and more decentralized methods of policy-making are at the heart of raising the growth rate and evolving more sustainable development patterns in South Asia. As we have argued earlier, development strategies, which emphasize cooperation rather than conflict have enormous possibilities. In the late'80s, Benazir Bhutto former prime minister of Pakistan

TABLE 7 : HUMAN RESOURCE DEVELOPMENT: SELECTED COUNTRIES, 1960-1990

	LIFE EXPECTANCY AT BIRTH			INFANT MORTALITY RATE[a]			ADULT ILLITERACY RATE[b]			PRIMARY ENROLLMENT RATIO[c]			SECONDARY ENROLLMENT RATIO[d]			POPULATION PER PHYSICIAN		
	1960	1990	Chge 1960/90	1960	1990	Chge 1960/90	1960	1990	Chge 1960/90	1960	1989	Chge 1960/90	1960	1989	Chge 1960/89	1960	1984	Chge 1960/84
EAST ASIA & PACIFIC																		
Philippines	53	64	11	134	41	93	28	10	18	105	111	6	26	73	47	na	6570	na
Malaysia	54	70	16	105	16	89	42	22	20	96	96	0	19	59	40	7020	6090	1930
Thailand	52	66	14	149	27	122	32	7	25	83	86	3	13	28	15	7950	1660	6290
South Korea	54	71	17	120	17	103	29	4	25	94	108	14	27	86	59	3540	2380	1160
Indonesia	41	62	21	159	61	93	61	23	38	71	118	47	6	47	41	46780	33370	9410
SOUTH ASIA																		
India	43	59	16	165	92	73	72	52	20	61	98	37	20	43	23	4850	2330	2520
Sri Lanka	62	71	9	71	19	52	25	12	13	95	107	12	27	74	47	4490	5520	970
ALL DEVELOPING COUNTRIES	46	63	17	233	69	164	na	40	na	na	105	na	na	43	na	na	4980	na

a. Number of infants per thousand live births in a given year, who die before reaching one year of age.

b. Proportion of the population over the age of fifteen who cannot, with understanding, read and write a short, simple statement on their everyday life. Base period illiteracy rate is for 1960 except for Indonesia and India (1961); Malaysia (1970); and Sri Lanka (1963).

c. Gross enrolment of all ages at the primary level as a percentage of primary-school-age children.

d. Computed in the same manner as the primary enrolment ratio.

Source: World Development Report, various issues; The State of the World's Children, 1989.
Compiled by Munish Alagh.

had initiated thinking on a basic needs plan for the Sub Continent. I had as a participant in the first SAARC Planners meeting at Kathmandu supported this initiative from the Indian side. There is considerable work which shows that unless development vision changes there will be problems in each country. Many of the analysts have shown that a continuation of the past into the future would create problems. Guha and Alagh (Note 12) have indicated that if current savings trends continue and growth rates are forced high, unless productivity improves the inflation rate would increase to 10 per cent per annum in India. Jawaid Afzar, in a classic paper on basic needs in Pakistan, has noted a yearly population growth rate of 3 per cent, an annual savings rate of 12 per cent to be inconsistent with a 6 per cent growth rate and a basic needs strategy in Pakistan (Note 13). Similar patterns can be discussed for agricultural growth (Table 8 & 9); alternative strategy forecasts have indicated that rural poverty levels in India and Pakistan should be brought down to below 25 per cent, if the widespread processes of sustainable land and water development strategies are to become the accepted framework rather than exceptional cases. It is these experiences and related industrialization strategies which have to inform the process of regional cooperation.

TABLE 8
ALTERNATIVE GROWTH PATHS 1990-2000 (% ANNUM)

Year	GDP		Agriculture GDP	
	Low	High	Low	High
1	2	3	4	5
Bangladesh	3.6	6.0	1.1	3.9
India	4.0	6.0	2.1	3.9
Nepal	3.5	6.3	1.4	3.5
Pakistan	4.8	7.2	3.8	4.2
Sri Lanka	3.5	6.8	1.8	3.0

Source:- Different Projections done by expert groups; lower and higher estimates taken.

Jawaid Afzar has pointed out the alternatives for Pakistan: Should the investment rate of 18 per cent be sustained? With a population growth rate of 3 per cent per annum which will not substantially decline in the immediate future, Pakistan needs a GNP growth rate of about 6 per cent to make major headway in provision of basic needs. A marginal capital output ratio of 3 would require an investment rate of 18 per cent. Pakistan is implementing an investment programme, which contains some capital-intensive imports. Furthermore, arresting the spread of salinity and conserving land productivity calls for heavy investment in agriculture. Nevertheless, it is argued with some merit that the capital output ratio can be lowered by altering the investment mix, by substituting investment in agriculture and in small-scale industry for investment in physical infrastructure and heavy industries.

For India, Pranob Sen has highlighted the importance of overcoming the public resources gap and correctly matching domestic savings with local and foreign investment requirements. Manohar Rao has observed that only a trade-dominated strategy will work in the next phase. Closed economy resource intensive paradigms seem to have been exhausted as growth sources. In poorer countries the problems are even more severe. (Note 14)

TABLE   9

REGIONAL AGRICULTURAL OUTCOMES

	Variable	Regional Low	Indicator High
1	Foodgrain Growth 1990-2000	2.6	3.3
2	Non-foodgrain Growth	1.2	4.6
3	Irrigated Area (%)	30	42
4	Fertiliser kg/Harvested Area in 2000	40	168
5	Exports as % of Agricultural Output	20	35

Note: Lows are based on modified historical projections.

Source: FAO, *Regional Implications of Agriculture 2000.*

The main questions to be raised in defining the agenda for inter-regional cooperation in South Asia therefore are:

The nature of community-based land and water development experiments of a sustainable kind already underway – the issues of defining the rights of producers and workers in terms of land rights, for example, and the related questions of community participation. Such issues become important in reclamation of degraded lands, land development and water harvesting in arid and rainfed areas and also the proper functioning of decentralized irrigation systems in canal based irrigation. (Note 15)

At the regional level, this becomes the question of sharing experiences and expediting cooperative land and water resource development projects. (Note 16) Agriculture and rural development schemes on improved land and water development regions - diversification of cropping systems and diversification into non crop-based agricultural and rural development.

At the regional level, the sharing of experiences in integrating markets with such community-based experiences is important as also development of policies and projects or more efficient input supplies, delivery systems and agro-processing technologies. Projects for cooperation with third countries/ regions should be examined.

Small-scale industrialisation and links with national and global markets need to be examined.

The scope for core sector industrialisation and regional cooperation in the industrial area needs to be widened and accelerated, including tariff and other policies, in which India should take the lead.

It needs to be appreciated that problems of understanding of a socio-political nature are the primal issues as the technical discussion for example, between Pakistan and Indian economists clearly reveals and a more sympathetic consideration of different views and approaches needs to be given clearly high priority.

It is clear that the print has come to end the grouping phase of cooperation in South Asia and start thinking on the next phase.

References:

1. Y.K. Alagh, *Regionalized Scenarios for the Indian Subcontinent* (Fast, EEC, Brussels, 1992).

2. S.M. Nasim, *Rural Poverty and Landlessness in Pakistan*, in ILO *Poverty and Landlessness in Rural Asia*, Geneva: ILO, 1977, p. 46.

3. G.B.S. Muzahid, *A Note on Measurement of Poverty and Income Irregularities in Pakistan*, Pakistan Development Review, Autumn 1978.

4. M. Irfan and Rashid Amzad, *Poverty in Rural Pakistan*, In Haq and Bagai, no. 8, pp. 206-59.

5. Moin Bagai, *An Overview*, ibid, pp. I-XXXIV.

6. Jawaid Afzar, *Distribution of Income in Pakistan*, ibid, pp. 31-66.

7. Bagai, ibid, p. xiv.

8. Ibid, p. xxi.

9. V.N. Dandekar and N. Rath, *Poverty in India*, Bombay: Sameeksha, 1972.

10. Government of India, Planning Commission, Task Force on Projections of Minimum Needs and Effective Demand, Delhi: Manager of Publications, 1974.

11. Bagai, no. 8, p. xxxiii.

12. The papers by Sen, Rao, Guha and Alagh are strategy papers included in a volume on macro-economic policy in India. See Y.K. Alagh, R.J, Mody and R. Desai (Eds.) Stabilization and Structural Change: Essays in the Honour of D.T. Lakdawala, Delhi: Vikas, 1991.

13. Jawaid Afzar, *Identification and Quantification of Basic Needs in Pakistan*, in Haq and Bagai, no. 8, pp. 292-313.

14. A.R. Khan, *Basic Needs Targets: An Illustrative Exercise in Identification and Quantification with Reference to Bangladesh*, Bangkok: ILO/ARTEP, 1985.

15. In the Indian case Alagh has discussed the details of water

management issues in specific projects in Next Phase of Water Planning, in M.V. Nadkarni, A.S. Seetharamu and Abdul Aziz (Eds.) *India: The Emerging Challenges: Essays in Honour of Prof. V.K.R.V. Rao*, New Delhi: Sage Publications, 1991

16. See B.C. Verghese, *Ganga: The River of Hope*, London, 1991.

◀14▶

America and India in Asia-Pacific

Ashok Kapur*

Introduction: The Bilateral and International Setting: 2000

The 50-years-old relationship is a story of failed policies (e.g. the US insistence on Indo-Pakistani parity - 1947-1998) and missed opportunities. For 50 years, both sides lectured each other but they did not successfully engage each other even though the two societies are democracies, there are potentially multiple channels of discourse (academic, commercial, media, cultural, science and technological, immigration and inter-governmental) and there are tangible interests in the picture - with points of convergence as well as divergence. Unfortunately, during the Cold War and its aftermath, the Indo-US relationship has never been free of friction and mistrust. Can this pattern change in the contemporary context of an evolving strategic environment in Asia Pacific?

Following Indian nuclear and missile tests in 1998 and Indian declarations that Chinese and Pakistani policies and capabilities created threats for Indian security, and the following international controversy which Indian actions created, the US and the Indian governments engaged in a high level dialogue. The Talbott-Jaswant Singh talks went on for over 100 hours, the longest in the troubled and conflicted history of this bilateral relationship. Ironically, it took the Indian nuclear blasts and

---

*   Professor, Department of Political Science, University of Waterloo, Ontario, Canada.

missile tests to get the American attention and to get American practitioners to focus on Indian security concerns vis-à-vis China and Pakistan.

The Vajpayee government was making it known that India, like China, expects to seek international and regional influence by exercising economic, military and political power, and that now the strategic and economic agenda was more important than the Nehruvian ideological sacred cows like non-alignment, the Third World as a zone of peace, the North-South developmental dialogue and unilateral self-restraint in the nuclear and missile sphere (the Nehruvian baggage of nuclear disarmament is still there but this is a matter of rhetoric not conviction). The 1998 event was not only a sign of re-definition of Indian political and nuclear diplomacy, it also brought India into the international mainstream where power and security rested on fierce pillars: strong economic performance, a strong political organization that produced coherent and convincing policies which engaged friends and enemies alike, and a visible military strength which made enemies think about the cost of aggressive action.

India's action also signalled a challenge to the widespread international belief that the future of Asia depended only on China, Japan and the USA. China and Japan face serious economic and political difficulties at home and their future direction is uncertain. There are already two Chinas within the mainland: the first, the Maoist model, consists of the isolationist, peasant-based economy which does not challenge the communist authority in Beijing; in the second there are the rich and poor Chinese, the coastal traders have foreign links, they may or may not pay their taxes to Beijing and the tension between the two models has enormous potential to create internal economic, social and political turmoil. Japan is not under American control. The Japanese elite who sought international and regional influence by economics only has been discredited by economic failure and the new generation of Japanese leaders (or potential leaders) are thinking of Japan's destiny in terms of the three pillars of power noted above. Japan is in transition and it has the military infrastructure (large navy, strong defence budget, superior military technology, e.g. space) as well as a lively internal high level and societal debate that seeks a higher Japanese defence profile.

Under these circumstances, more not less friction should be expected within the major power nodes in Asia, and in their relationships with other major and minor powers. It is in this context that Australia and India recently mended their ties despite Canberra's fierce reaction to the Indian tests. India and Australia have several common interests: fear of an expansive China, concern with instability in South East Asia as in Indonesia and the need to avoid Indo-Australian naval competition when the Indian navy could be cooperative with the Australian navy (and the senior partner, the US navy) in the touchy sea lanes from the South China seas to the Indian Ocean. The Indian Navy's "area of interest" now extends from the Arabian Sea to the South China seas. The latter is India's naval frontier like Tibet. India will need more submarines, frigates and transporters to give military teeth to its "area of interest" and this will take a decade or so, i.e. before the Chinese Navy is in a position to extend its presence in the Indian Ocean area. At the moment, Chinese naval activity consists of reconnaissance by the odd submarine and fishing boats; they fly the Burmese flag but are staffed by Chinese military personnel and the boats are full of maps and communication gear but no fish!

The Talbott-Singh dialogue was built on two parameters: the American non-proliferation agenda and the Indian security agenda. This dialogue ran out of gas in 1998-99. Still, it has cosmetic value. However, I believe the fluid Asian strategic context places a burden on American and Indian practitioners and scholars to stay engaged on a variety of economic, strategic and political issues and not to let a single issue like the CTBT or the Kashmir hijack derail the dialogue. The articulation of honest differences of views is the essence of democracy, and now a sustained debate is needed, one that recognizes the different historical and cultural experiences, the different geographical imperatives, and different policy concerns that reflect the domestic as well as external imperatives in the Asia-Pacific region in the 2000-2010 time frame.

2. <u>Although the USA is presently the pre-eminent power in Asia, it cannot pursue its interests unaided: it must negotiate with major and minor powers including "rogue states" like North Korea. Nor can the USA avoid for long the obligation to participate in the development of a stable balance of power in Asia that manages friction among the Five Centres of Asian power, viz. USA, PRC, Japan, Russia and India, in the coming decade.</u>

Figure 1 is the framework to consider the following questions, which relate to the aforesaid statement.

FIGURE 1 : THE VARIABLES IN ASIA'S STRATEGIC FUTURE, 2000-2010

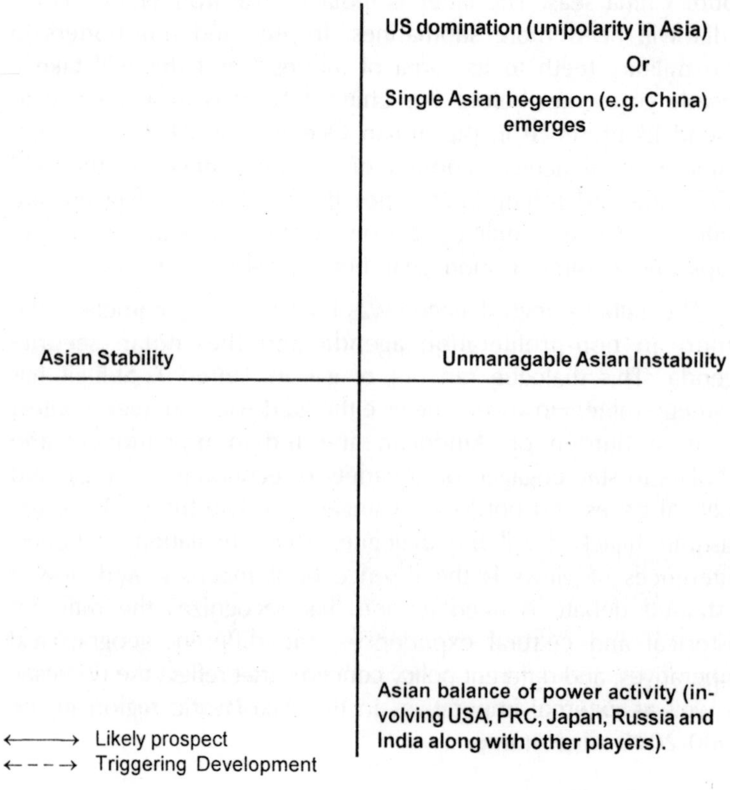

US domination (unipolarity in Asia)

Or

Single Asian hegemon (e.g. China) emerges

Asian Stability   Unmanagable Asian Instability

Asian balance of power activity (involving USA, PRC, Japan, Russia and India along with other players).

←——→ Likely prospect
←— —→ Triggering Development

FIGURE 1 : THE VARIABLES IN ASIA'S STRATEGIC FUTURE, 2000-2010

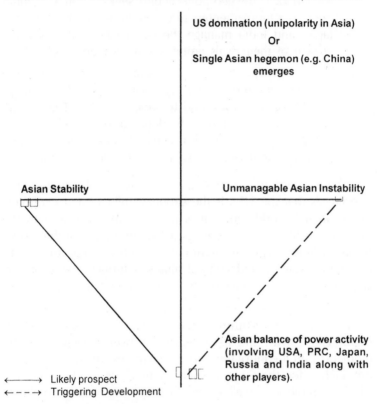

Is stability in Asia (Eurasia) to be achieved in the coming decade through America's continuing pre-eminent position in Asia, i.e. through unipolarity or will it be achieved by an Asian (Eurasian) balance of power which is still evolving, which at the moment is not self-sustaining and which requires US direction vis-à-vis the live centres of influence in different parts of Asia?

If the Asian (Eurasian) balance of power is not self-sustaining, can the USA reconcile the two logics of statecraft currently in play in Asian (Eurasian) affairs, i.e. the logic of the marketplace seek closer China relations but the second logic, the geo-political one, seeks to contain China? There is a supplementary question: how will China, Russia, Japan and India manage the two logics as they see the growth of their rivals ambitions and capabilities?

❑ Is instability in Asia (Eurasia) "good" if it is manageable, if it does not produce a single hegemon, and if it helps commerce, i.e. from food to weapons sales? That is, can insurgency and instability be deemed to be good business and good politics if leaders and institutions can manage it so that system breakdown is avoided in the future?

These questions are based on one fact and one premise. The fact is that the USA is the strongest military and economic power in the world today. It is powerful in space and in the oceans. It leads a set of alliances in different parts of the world. It has influence in international institutions that deal with economic, military and cultural affairs. Internally the economy is strong and the population feels good about itself.

The premise concerns the "but". Despite its enormous capabilities and influence, can America dominate Asian relationships with the asymmetrical power it enjoys at the moment? Can it control the impersonal forces which have carved out niches for themselves, such as religious fundamentalism, Chinese ambition as well as internal instability, Russian weakness and nationalist resurgence, Japanese re-thinking about its destiny in the military, economic and the diplomatic spheres, Indian re-thinking about its destiny in the same vein, and so on?

The "but" is important because the American foreign policy and military apparatus as it is constituted can deal effectively with sub-critical, high probability, moderate or low impact events but not so with high impact shocks like nuclear and missile tests by non-allied states or high profile terrorism against American targets. The American system fares poorly with public challenges to its authority and prestige in international institutions and in the eyes of the American public. Moreover, the capacity to deal with sub-critical situations rests on a condition of economic well being, and even this capacity may be degraded in a condition of economic stress.

The "but" implies that America needs all the help it can get from its strategic partners in Asia but to secure this, a paradigm shift in American linking and strategy is required.

3. The CTBT is a major hindrance in the further development of Indo-US political and strategic relations. The treaty has scientific and cultural consequences because it seeks to retain USA's scientific edge while diminishing the scientific edge of other powers. Both sides need to be honest about the cultural basis and scientific as well as cultural consequences of non-proliferation that fosters technical discrimination. As long as the USA maintains this fixation with superiority, military modernization among Asia's major and minor powers is inevitable in the foreseeable future. The USA should shed its fixation with non-proliferation and shift its attention to the development of a pentagonal Asian balance of power.

The CTBT issue should not become an ideological fixation or a litmus test of progress in Indo-American discussions. Non-proliferation is value-laden strategy and it expresses civilizational controversies and ambitions. It is unrealistic for the USA to call a halt to India's military modernization in atomic science, space and electronics given the absence of a political settlement between India and her rivals. In the circumstances, a call for Indian disarmament is a call to India to act like a defeated state, which it is not. Consider Japan's case. It was defeated in 1945, it acquired US nuclear and defence protection but the moment this is removed or if the level of protection loses its credibility in the view of the Japanese elite and public opinion, Japan will act differently. Japan has all the means to go nuclear. It has quietly built up its atomic, space, electronic and naval capabilities. It is capable of changing quickly, and the process of change appears to have started. India's military modernisation has been underway since 1962 and it continues to be necessary for India to consolidate and to increase its defence and deterrent capacities so as to be able to project its positions in its area of interest in the Indian Ocean and in the Himalayan zone, just as military modernisation by USA, China, Russia and Japan is justified by a concern with a problematic strategic environment.

The Indian case against the CTBT is compelling.

❑ It will create lifelong pressure against India by the US-led world community; it has harassment potential. In the Talbott-Singh talks, the US wanted to know the location of Indian fissile materials; it wanted transparency. With this knowledge and a fissile material cut-off ban, accounting by India will be required constantly. This will lead to terrible harassment like Richard Butler's in the case of Iraq. (The US also wants details about India's C 3 arrangements and this poses the danger of interference with the system in a crisis)

❑ Non-proliferation is not simply arms control; it is foreign policy and national culture. The US wants to keep its scientific edge vis-a-vis all its rivals and friends (including UK and France) and to stop new entrants in the nuclear and space business like India and others from developing high technology capacities that could challenge US primacy in military, scientific and commercial affairs. In addition, the USA is urging India to adopt consumerism as a national value. (The US approach is also Manmohan Singh's approach). Hence, non-proliferation that cuts off or even retards indigenous high technology development in the frontiers of science has military, cultural and political-diplomatic consequences. It means that in the judgment of the international regime builders some civilizations should be scientifically advanced, and some less so, and this is a strategy to manage the clash of civilisations (to borrow S. Huntington's idea). The US is actively pursuing this approach, recognising that others such as the Japanese are acquiring a scientific edge.

❑ Our view is that civilizational rivalries are important. They reflect and reinforce cultural diversities and values and form the basis of a multicultural world community where diversity is accommodated through multilateralism. Civilizational rivalries are necessary for industrial and scientific progress. For Indians the issue is not that civilizational rivalries between China and India or between USA and India should end; on the contrary they stimulate innovation in the scientific, industrial, military and the political organizational spheres so that new challenges can be met. Rather the issue is that they must not end in military conflict that brings civilizations to an end (i.e. nuclear holocaust or civil war that ends civil society is not desirable). For this we need a combination of organized (civilized) and public civilizational competition, scientific, industrial and military achievement (should military conflict become inevitable) and effective diplomacy (measured by negotiated results and not by the number of speeches made), which avoid unnecessary military conflicts that do not serve the public good.

❑ The issue for India is not that the scientific, industrial and military gap between USA and India is worrisome. The concern is about the nature of American policy rather than the asymmetry in the distribution of power between the two. The concern is that America, a democracy, is insisting on using its influence to create a gap between India, another democracy, in favour of China, a communist authoritarian regime and Pakistan, a military theocracy. Figure 2 outlines the scientific and military consequences of the gap between India on the one hand, and China-Pakistan on the other hand. Given that the rivalry between India and China is now in the open, the American position is counter-productive vis-à-vis a politically conscious country of India's size.

FIGURE 2 :

**THE PROBLEM WITH THE CTBT FREEZE:
HOW WILL THE GAP BE MANAGED?**

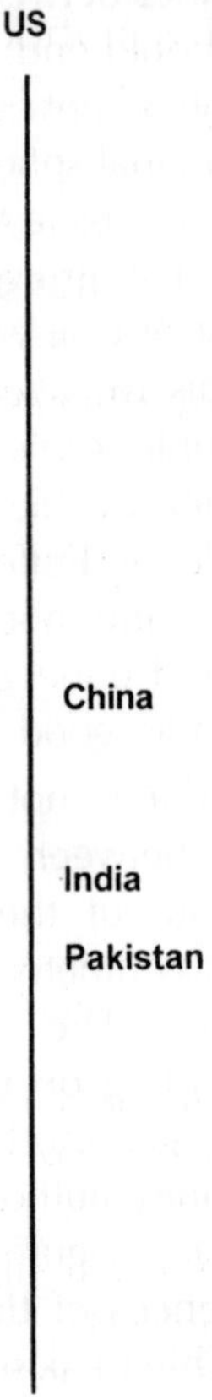

US

China

India

Pakistan

———— Alliance (Pakistan is to PRC as Israel is to USA)

— · — Military rivals who threaten each other but are not engaged in a serious effort towards conflict resolution. Where are the negotiators, the bridge builders?

FIGURE 2 :

THE PROBLEM WITH THE CTBT FREEZE:
HOW WILL THE GAP RE MANAGED?

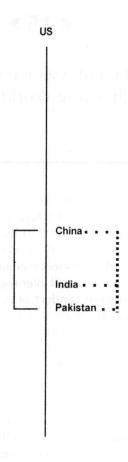

Alliance (Pakistan is to PRC as Israel is to USA)

Military rivals who threaten each other but are not engaged in a serious effort towards conflict resolution. Where are the negotiators, the bridge builders?

‹15›

India and Asia-Pacific in the Changing World Order

Hoshiar Singh *
R.S. Yadav **

The end of the Cold War represents a significant development in international relations, which had serious implications for both India and the Asia-Pacific. It led to the end of geo-political and geo-military relations of the Cold War era and geo-economic regionalism acquired prominence among the states of the Asia-Pacific.[1] New intra-regional and inter-regional alignments are being built to facilitate smooth conduct of economic transactions both at the bilateral and multilateral levels. Even the political issues and security concerns are being resolved through cooperative understanding. Hence, the changed order in the Asia-Pacific region is witnessing the trends of interdependence, engagement, economic development, cooperative multilateralism and comprehensive security.[2]

Simultaneously, this development has far-reaching implications for India and has led to the reorientation of India's foreign policy outlook. The major change adopted by India has been the beginning of economic reforms and adjustment with the emerging euphoria of globalisation and liberations. On the one hand, it resulted into the emergence of "Look East Policy"

---

* Pro-Vice-Chancellor, Kurukshetra University, Kurukshetra, Haryana; President, Indian Political Science Association, India.

** Reader, Department of Political Science, Kurukshetra University, Kurukshetra, Haryana, India.

and on the other hand, it facilitated the improvement and strengthening of ties with countries like China and the USA. The improvement of relations with the latter is in the form of a U-turn in policies that has culminated into "militing-to-military" cooperation in the Asia-Pacific. Therefore, the development of warm ties with the South East Asian Scales, along with the improvement of relations with China, Japan and USA led to a close cooperation between India and Asia-Pacific.

However, at the outset, it must be made explicit that India's interests in the Asia-Pacific centre around India-South East Asia relations because:

(i)   Politically, India is likely to interact more with the countries of South East Asia rather than other sub-regions of the Asia-Pacific;

(ii) Economically, India is neither part of the APEC at present nor it is going to be its member till 2007. Consequently, India's main economic role in this region will be through ASEAN, which is gaining prominence in the region; and

(iii) Strategically it is true that the issue of India's defence and security could not be well understood by limiting its concerns up to South Asia. Besides, through ARF and bilateral ties within the USA, India is well set to play this role in the Asia-Pacific through ASEAN.

Thus, the improvement of relations with other powers of Asia and the Pacific just provide a broader framework for their ties. Hence, a modest attempt is made here to study India's relations with South East Asian states to discern the broader India-Asia-Pacific ties. By limiting the scope of this paper to a sub region, i.e. South East Asia, will better serve the purpose of discerning major trends and tendencies of India's post-Cold War foreign policy towards Asia-Pacific.

I

The disintegration of erstwhile Soviet Union (1991) and developments in Eastern Europe (1989) affected the global structure significantly. It not only led to the end of the Cold War, but also carried serious implications for all countries of the world. India and the South East too would not remain unaffected by this phenomenon. The qualitative and structural changes brought about by the end of the Cold War led to new orientations in the foreign policies of India and countries of South East Asia. On the one hand, India starts moving towards South East Asia to build strong economic, strategic and political ties with them. On the other hand, South East Asia, by leaving all inhibitions of the past, came closer to India to develop warm and friendly relations with it. This convergence between them has been due to numerous politico-strategic and economic realizations brought about by the end of the Cold War in international relations. An in-depth examination of these developments will establish this point more convincingly.

i)   At the global level the bi-polar system has been replaced by one significant pole, i.e. USA. It has neither brought about an "end of history"[3] or era of "American Century"[4] as perceived by some American scholars, nor established a "New World Order", establishing US hegemony as perceived by George Bush.[5] But it certainly led to the emergence of a qualitatively new international order replacing the old one.[6] However, the "leadership role" and predominant position of the USA is not ruled out.

Certainly there are challenges to its superiority in terms of the economic situation in Japan and emerging economic integration in Europe. But its overall predominance has increased in the global decision making with the collapse of the socialist bloc. Now no other state is powerful enough to challenge its military might in the world. As far as the South East is concerned, till 1990 it enjoyed a favourable position in the US foreign policy outlook because, except for the Indo-China region, most of South East Asia was pro-West in orientation. But in the post-Cold War era, the US started withdrawing from this region as no serious threat now emanates from here as the ideological barrier between ASEAN and other states (particularly Vietnam) have diminished and are all under one economic group.

However, despite this withdrawal, American interests in the Asia-Pacific can't be discounted. Hence, the role of the US is not ruled out completely.

(ii) With the collapse of the bipolar conflictual world order, the trends point towards the growing importance of regionalism in global politics. The regional concerns are more associated with economic cooperation rather than political alignments. In this context, regional economic blocs in the form of European Union (EU), North Atlantic Free Trade Area (NAFTA), South Asia Free Trade Area (SAFTA), ASEAN, Indian Ocean Rim-Association for Regional Cooperation (IOR-ARC), and Asia Pacific Economic Cooperation (APEC) emerged or were strengthened. EU and NAFTA represent more of the American conceits and Europe's thrust of dominance or at least reduction of dependence on the USA in the changed global milieu. Groupings like SAFTA and IOR-ARC however are new initiatives in the changed milieu by nations to re-adjust their policies in the context of the changing global economic pattern. Within this framework ASEAN represents a very successful regional initiative that gives exemplary lessons to other states. In the post-Cold War era it has not only consolidated its economic strength but has succeeded in making it more comprehensive and integrated by enlarging itself from ASEAN-6 to ASEAN-10, thereby representing the whole of South East Asia. The formation of Asia Pacific Economic Cooperation (APEC) stands for the American resolve to tap ASEAN economies and trap Japan and China in the multilateral liberalized economic system and it represents ASEAN's linkage with the regional group (i.e. ASEAN) and its efforts to join APEC have received momentum. They have also joined hands over numerous other activities, like sub-regional cooperation, joining in trilateral relationships, forming of new regional groupings (i.e. IOR-ARC), development of inter-group relationships (ASEAN-SAARC) etc. Hence, India – South East economic ties not only began but also strengthened due to these contemporary changes.

(iii) Post-Cold War developments have not only ended the ideological barriers at the global level but have also facilitated the removal of some barriers of misperceptions in South East Asia. Two major developments, which are of an inter-related nature, have initiated closer India and South East Asian relations. At one level, the changes in South East Asia have blurred the distinctions of states that are pro-West and pro-Soviet in their foreign policy orientations. In the past, it probably has created a void between the Indo-Chinese region countries and the ASEAN states; the close Soviet-Vietnam linkages and the issue of Cambodia prevented the former from becoming part of the ASEAN regional system. But now with the end of Soviet-Vietnamese linkage and resolution of the Cambodian crisis the background for Vietnam to come closer with them has come into being. The earlier ideological misconception is removed and through the new economic reform programme, the Indo-China region has been able to establish links with the economics of other ASEAN states.

(iv) Finally, the developments in the post-Cold War era created a fluid situation for the world in general and South East Asia in particular, which brought forth numerous problems for both India and the states of South East Asia, which in turn helped in building up of relations. In South East Asia, though the political problem of Cambodia was resolved, the war-ravaged economy of the whole Indo-Chinese region had to be strengthened. Besides, the economic consolidation of the whole of South East Asia was a matter of priority for all these states. The ASEAN economic boom also needed to expand so that the new market could flourish. But the declining American interest created a strategic vacuum that had to be filled, so as to balance Chinese and Japanese interests, which had increased to a great extent in the contemporary geo-strategic scenario. The recent currency crisis added to the problems of South East Asia. Today they need the help of certain economies or areas, which can bail them out of the present chaos they are in.

Thus, the end of the Cold War provided ample opportunities for India and the states of South East Asia to come closer to one other. Economic exigency of the changed world system provided the ground for cooperation. The geo-strategic scenario not only helped in removing the basic irritants between them, but also provided scope for long-term strategic partnership. These changes can be observed in their foreign policy orientations, through the political changes that are suited to the requisite time. The emerging realization among the political elites, in the light of new bilateral, regional and global compulsions, have led to a fundamental shift in their political relations. The implications of such shifts are both negative and positive, and will provide the framework for further investigations. In the light of these findings, their future ties could be predicted and it could be possible to envisage the extent to which India's post-Cold War initiatives towards South East Asia have succeeded in fulfilling the larger goals of India's foreign policy.

II

Economic dimension has acquired a significant place in India's relations with these states. Compulsions of both of them have brought them closer to each other. India's keenness to develop smooth South East Asian economic ties are based on:

1) The economic strength of South East Asia, which has tremendously increased due to the rise in its intra-regional trade and therefore, it is in India's interest to take measures to boost its trade with this region,

2) India's "inward looking" trade makes it to a great extent quite dependent upon its ties with the countries of this region,

3) Nowadays, it is presumed that large investments in manufacturing activities in overseas countries decide the trade volumes. Hence investment in ASEAN countries would boost India's trade,[8]

4) India could make use of the investment opportunities in South East Asian states which are likely to shift the "flying geese" pattern of investment away from ASEAN countries towards neighbouring country like India

5) Indian technologies still appropriate for being transferred to the countries of South East Asia,

6) Even the joint research and development programme in agro-based and textiles industries between India and the South East are very sound,

7) The evolution of the proposed ASEAN Free Trade Asia (AFTA) in the next ten years would provide new business opportunities for India for locating its investments in the expanded ASEAN region.

The need for economic cooperation has been a two-sided affair, as the South East also rated India very high on its economic priorities due to following factors:

1) India, with its large and sound human resource base, could provide ample opportunities to ASEAN surplus capital to reap advantages by investing in India,

2) India's skill and entrepreneurship in establishing small and medium-scale industries could open up more employment in South East Asia, particularly in the Indo-China region,

3) India's track record of economic reforms and the liberalization process has certainly scored over some of its Asian competitors in attaching investments,

4) China's withering economic image in the eyes of ASEAN had ushered in a strong economic tilt towards India,

5) India with a democratic form of government (with economic and political stability) coupled with the availability of cheap labour and ample scientific and technical manpower is looked upon by many South East Asian countries as a better place for investment.

(a) Trade :

With the end of the Cold War, the trade scenario between India and South East Asia strengthened due to emerging complementariness between their economies. On the one hand, with the Soviet disintegration, India lost nearly 22 per cent of its earlier trade being conducted with the countries of the Socialist block hence an alternative for such trade becomes inevitable. Simultaneously, since July 1991 it started the process of economic reforms due to which there was a shift from an "inward looking economy" to that of an "outward oriented economy". On the other hand, the post-Cold War era witnessed the regionalization of world trade in the Anglo-American world by the formation of the "European Union" (EU) and North Atlantic Free Trade Area (NAFTA). This brought the ASEAN countries at a crossroad and compelled them to devise an appropriate strategy in response to the emerging consolidation of the regional trading blocks.[11] Some academics have rightly pointed out that with the formation of these blocs, loss suffered in terms of trade by Asia, including ASEAN, was nearly 4 per cent.[12] Thus, if India was busy diversifying its trade in other areas due to the collapse of Eastern Europe and the Soviet Union in the new changed scenario of globalization, then ASEAN was also fighting the problem of "Fortress Europe" and "Fortress America" by new strategies of cultivating countries like India, building relations with SAARC and devising new institutions in the form of ASEAN Free Trade Area (AFTA). In this context, trade relations between India and ASEAN converged.

Besides this, the conclusion of GATT into WTO provided new opportunities both for india and South East Asia individually and jointly to tap the emerging opportunities for export in selected countries and areas where they are better placed. It is particularly true about India and Southeast Asia's potentialities in agro-horticultural products, services (particularly software and financial services), and selected manufacturing items.

This resulted in the strengthening of trade ties between India and South East Asia, which is clear from the increase in India's exports to this area. ASEAN accounted for 3.6 per cent of India's exports to the world in 1980, which by 1992 increased to 6 per cent.[13] In value terms as well India's exports to ASEAN

TABLE 1: INDIA-SOUTHEAST ASIA TRADE, 1993-94 TO 1996-97
(IN MILLION US $)

Sl. No.	Country	1993-94		1994-95		1995-96		1996-97	
		Imports	Exports	Imports	Exports	Imports	Exports	Imports	Exports
1.	Brunei	0.00	0.33	0.11	2.15	0.03	6.93	0.06	6.26
2.	Cambodia	N.A.	N.A.	N.A.	N.A.	N.A.	N.A.	N.A.	N.A.
3.	Indonesia	107.53	210.54	289.07	249.11	440.71	633.07	608.98	592.90
4.	Malaysia	223.53	221.62	439.65	257.01	862.75	375.75	1030.91	531.99
5.	Myanmar	108.46	19.30	113.72	20.32	155.16	28.84	168.65	28.84
6.	Philippines	5.33	52.19	10.56	89.19	20.52	137.85	16.76	185.55
7.	Singapore	561.77	673.90	807.12	691.03	1064.17	861.70	1080.94	977.51
8.	Laos	N.A.	0.21	0.53	0.11	N.A.	0.30	N.A.	0.41
9.	Thailand	51.27	319.46	153.95	364.75	162.18	451.97	199.42	450.60
10.	Vietnam	39.20	25.11	39.62	52.54	14.81	118.86	1.75	117.57
		1096.79	1522.71	1854.33	1726.16	2320.33	2615.27	2107.47	2491.63

Source: Govt. of India, Ministry of External Affairs, India and ASEAN: Dialogue Partnership (New Delhi, 1997), pp. 6-13

1993-94 = + 425.92   1994-95 = + 128.17
1995-96 = + 294.94   1996-97 = + 384.16

had more than quadrupled to reach the $1.3 million level in 1992.[14] This also marked India's trade with these countries from deficit to surplus since 1992. In the later period India's trade in terms of both imports and exports to this area grew significantly as is obvious from Table –1.

This increase in bilateral trade shows how these countries are economically coming closer to each other. Though it is also evident from this table that some countries of South East Asia are over-represented while others are under-represented in terms of India's two-way trading relationship but that could be rectified by the bilateral efforts of the countries concerned. Also it would get a further boost with the emerging economic progress of those countries. However, it is to be admitted that India's acquisition of "sectoral dialogue partnership" in 1992 and "full dialogue partnership" in 1995 have significantly boosted this progress. With ASEAN-6 turning into ASEAN-10 by incorporating all the countries of South East Asia, the already strong trade ties between India and South East Asia will be further strengthened.

Due to the increased trade share in each other region trade has significantly improved. If taken country wise, this difference could be visualized by some bilateral trade percentage in 1988 and 1994-95: Indonesia (4.9 to 15.7 per cent); Malaysia (8.7 to 20.5 per cent), Philippines (4.4 to 3.0 per cent), Singapore (43.7 to 42.8 per cent); and Vietnam (1.2 to 2.7 per cent).[16] Despite these ups and downs the overall trades between India and with ASEAN reached a $ 1075.9 million in 1995 with a noticeable increase of 4.3 per cent to 6.92 per cent from 1989 to 1994-95. According to the 1997 assessment, it touched the US $ 6 billion, which accounts for around 8 per cent of India's total trade and is marked by the high growth rate and exports propensity. Thus despite some minor ups and downs, bilateral trade with some ASEAN countries has grown significantly. India is targeting a US $15 billion trade turnover with ASEAN by the year 2000-2001.[17]

In terms of commodities there exists great diversity and multiplicity in terms of India's exports to this region. India's major exports to ASEAN countries include oil meals, edible nuts, cotton yarn, fabrics, drugs, pharmaceuticals and fine chemicals: inorganic, organic and agro-chemicals, primary and semi-finished iron and steel, machinery and transport equipment; processed minerals, iron and steel bars, textile machinery, etc. Sugar and rice have also begun to be exported to some of the ASEAN countries at competitive prices. Sugar processing machinery, electrical equipment and machinery, railway rolling stock, telecom equipment, gems and jewellery, boat manufacturing and design, automotive parts, etc. Above all information technology including software development, consultancy and training in both hardware and software, provide tremendous opportunities for enhancing India's exports. Similarly, there is tremendous scope for Indian companies to participate in construction activities, and the health and education sector. Indian processed fruits and vegetables have great potential in the ASEAN markets.[18]

However, the recent fiscal crisis has ended the "golden age" of the South East Asian economy that began with the 1995 New York Plaza Accord.[19] This had a wide-ranging impact on this region's economy, society and polity. It may be expected that trade will be the first casualty under this phenomenon. It has been observed in this context that due to this, leaders of these countries "may adopt a more nationalistic stance in economics and politics unless the vulnerability of their economics to global pressure is addressed".[20] Consequently, ASEAN may again follow an inward-looking approach and stress on a more intra-region oriented outlook. But it seems a little too early, rather the process of their opening to the outside world is likely to continue unless this crisis turns into a global crisis for the capitalist system. Thus, as soon as this region recovers from the present economic chaos, prospects for inter-South East Asian trade are very bright.

(b) **INVESTMENTS** - (i) Since 1991, India's liberalization programme is paying great attention to attract foreign direct investment from all the countries of the world. Consequently, the number of changes in its finance and fiscal policy are introduced to attract FDI. These changes have done away with the licensing system for imports; reduction in import duties; liberalization of the exchange rate regime; making rupee convertible; incentives to NRIs; removal of restriction on repatriation of capital invested, repatriation of dividend, royalty, technical fee, etc. Besides, some other factors, which make FDI more attractive, are also available which influences the investor's decision. These are the size of the market and its growth potential; political and economic stability; linkages and proximity with other important markets, availability of trained manpower and wage structure; and industrial and institutional infrastructure.

Simultaneously, some countries of South East Asia are facing domestic economic compulsions to deploy their surplus funds abroad in Asia in the post-Cold War era. In this context, China and India provide major attractive destinations for locating such investment. The flying geese pattern of FDI (especially from Asian sources including Japan, Taiwan and South Korea), which benefited the ASEAN economies in the 1970s and 1980s, has now shifted from ASEAN countries. Second, the real effective exchange rate is not as competitive in some of the ASEAN countries when compared to other destination countries of Asia-Pacific including of late, India. Third, the new markets in India and China are further opening up and competing for attracting FDI. Fourth, investors of ASEAN countries are investing and relocating their units elsewhere outside South Asia. Thus due to the above factors, South East Asia looked towards India as a new destination for its FDI, which is evident from the flow of FDI from different South East Asian countries to India from 1991 to 1997 as given in Table-2.

(ii) In the post-Cold War era, there has been a tremendous increase in the two-way joint venture between them. During 1991-1996, South East Asian countries had 5,400 such projects in the pipeline involving US $1,740 million, as is evident from Table-3. Similarly, up to 1996 India established 152 joint ventures in this region, which involve nearly US $89 million. This is clearly evident from Table-4.

Thus the Indian liberalization programme has made it possible for Indian companies, both in the government and private sectors, to conduct business in South East Asian countries. The numbers of such companies are increasing day by day. From the

TABLE 2: SOUTHEAST ASIA'S FOREIGN DIRECT INVESTMENTS IN INDIA, 1991-947 (UP TO 30 SEP. 97)

(Rs. in million)

S.N.	COUNTRY	1991	1992	1993	1994	1995	1996	1997	TOTAL
1.	MALAYSIA	1.80	744.30	84.80	252.80	138860.90	423.31	19616.45	34983.76
2.	THAILAND	-	25.20	3684.20	99.80	19680.90	765.22	238.94	24494.26
3.	SINGAPORE	13.70	602.10	667.40	2655.00	9910.40	3197.72	6619.42	23665.73
4.	PHILIPPINES	-	50.00	132.42	41.00	729.50	2836.84	49.00	3838.76
5.	INDONESIA	-	19.00	3.80	-	3133.00	375.00	105.00	3635.80
6.	VIETNAM	-	-	-	-	-	0.33	-	0.33
7.	BRUNEI	·	-	-	-	-	-	-	-
8.	LAOS	-	-	-	-	-	-	-	-
9.	CAMBODIA	-	-	-	-	-	-	-	-
10.	MYANMAR	-	-	-	-	-	-	-	-
11.	Total from all Countries of SE-Asia								
12.	Total from all countries of the World	5341.10	38875.40	88593.30	320717.20	320717.20	433264.78	433264.78	1390131.73
13.	Percentage of the World	-	-	-	-	-	-	-	-

Source: SIA News letter, Vol. VI, No. 6, October 1997, pp. 6-8.

TABLE 3: SOUTHEAST ASIA'S INVESTMENTS AND PROJECTS
IN PIPELINE IN INDIA, 1991-97

(Rs. in million US $)

S.No.	Country	Total Approvals	Projects in Pipe line	Major Areas of Investments
1.	Singapore	418.77	750	Roads and highway, mass
2.	Thailand	693.01	200	rapid transit system,
3.	Malaysia	439.07	4000	Seaports, Airports, Air port
4.	Philippines	108.05	50	related services, Power,
5.	Indonesia	100.88	400	Tele-communication,
6.	Brunei	000.00	N.A.	Petroleum, Tourism, Tourist related services,
7.	Laos	N.A.	N.A.	Industrial estate,
8.	Cambodia	N.A.	N.A.	Technological parks,
9.	Vietnam	000.01	N.A.	information technologies
10.	Myanmar	N.A.	N.A.	etc.
	TOTAL	**1760.01**	**5400**	

Source : Govt. of India, Ministry of External Affairs, India and Asean:
Dialogue Partnership (New Delhi, 1997), p.17.

TABLE 4: INDIAN INVESTMENTS IN SOUTHEAST ASIA
(as on 31st December 1996)

S.No.	Country	Total Joint Venture	Total Amount in US $ million	Major Areas of Investments
1.	Singapore	58	20.307	Software Developments,
2.	Thailand	27	16.510	Gems and Jewellery,
3.	Malaysia	45	29.350	Manufacturing, Textile,
4.	Philippines	01	0.380	Trading, Chemicals,
5.	Indonesia	20	20.258	Minerals and Metal Ores,
6.	Brunei	00	0.00	Construction, Shipping,
7.	Laos	01	1.620	Sugar, Telecom sector
8.	Cambodia	N.A.	N.A.	etc.
9.	Vietnam	N.A.	N.A.	
10.	Myanmar	N.A.	N.A.	
	TOTAL	**152**	**88.425**	

Source : Govt. of India, Ministry of External Affairs, India and Asean:
Dialogue Partnership (New Delhi, 1997), p.17.

government side, State Trading Corporation, MMTC and Shipping Corporation of India are located in Singapore. In the private sector, companies like ITC, Peerless group, Kirloskar, Greaves, Ispat alloys, Vedika investment services, Mastek, Sumeet, Ranbaxy, Godrej, JG Glasses, Birla Group, Hindustan Safety Glass, etc. have succeeded in their ventures in these countries.[22]

But the situation is very fluid regard joint ventures between India and South East Asia. This is aside from the fact that some bilateral problems and some common difficulties between them need serious consideration. First the total FDI flows from the South East Asian countries are very meagre. It was about 4.09 per cent of the total FDI India received during 1991 to 1994. This situation has become all the more difficult in the wake of the recent crisis in this region since July 1997. Second, even among the total FDI India received from this region there is grave imbalance among the countries that have contributed towards it. Trends during 1991 to 1994 indicated that 85 per cent of it was received only from two countries (Singapore and Thailand) and the contribution of another three countries (Philippines, Indonesia and Brunei) has been negligible and the contribution of another country (Malaysia) is also meagre. Finally, even on the Indian side, the lack of hard currency or export capital is a serious impediment in large-scale cooperation.

Thus, post-Cold War developments, along with the complementarities between India and South East Asia have provided ample scope for the growth of economic ties between them. India has taken number of initiatives under its "look East" policy to suit the conditions of such economic cooperation. This gesture of India was reciprocated by the initiatives of South East Asia under its "look West" policies. Emerging cooperation between them could be discerned from the analysis at twin levels. At one level, this is evident from the growth of their cooperation in trade, investment, services and the finance sector. At another level, this cooperation materialized with the support of well-augmented institution. The main institutional infrastructure has been extended by ASEAN, which recently converted itself into a true representative of the whole of South East Asia. Cooperation through ASEAN has not only consolidated economic ties between India and Southeast Asia, rather both may use this mechanism for playing a greater role in Asia-Pacific in the future.

III

India's thrust towards South East Asia has been due to a changed strategic milieu in the region, which is evident from numerous trends:

(i) First and foremost, the impact of the end of the Cold War has been the change in South East Asian perceptions towards India's naval expansion. In the 1980s, the Indian Navy become a subject of considerable debate among the Indian Ocean littorals, probably not so much because of the relatively faster expansion of its navy but because of ambiguity and lack of transparency regarding its doctrines, strategic concerns and objectives.[22] Though India never perceived any threat from the South East Asian states, South East Asia felt some concern about India's naval expansion. The basis for this apprehension, initially, was the Indo-Soviet treaty and the Soviet bases at Da Nang and Cam Ranh Bay in Vietnam. It was feared that India might play a supportive role to any Soviet or Vietnamese aggressive move in the region. [24] Another concern during the superpower's emerging detente was the perceived threat from Japan, China and India to compete with each other to fill the ensuing power vacuum. Whatever might be the cause of South East Asia's worry from India's naval presence, the end of the Cold War removed misconceptions, as the end of the Cold War radically transformed the security scenario in South East Asia, which ruled out any possibilities of India's collaboration with the Russians or Vietnamese in this region. This positive development opened up new vistas for the development of India-South East Asian relations.

(ii) In the post-Cold War era, security cannot be compartmentalized when the global reach of weapons and the scope for rapid deployment of forces has increased to the point where the threat of armoured intervention and conflict can never be ruled out, on any part of the world, and where the struggle for sovereignty over territory and resources is getting more and more acute. In this context, India emerged as the net gainer. First, being caught in vortex of its immediate security concern in and around South Asia in particular and the cold war politics in general, India has managed to wriggle out from that successfully. Second, the overall improvement in the region and global security atmosphere has enabled India to pursue its foreign policy goals more vigorously.[25] Consequently, India now started looking towards the Asia-Pacific in general and South East Asia in particular, with more seriousness of intent.

(iii) One major shift in India's foreign policy during the post-Cold War era has been its "look east" policy. Consequently, on the one hand, India starts building fences with the USA in the Asia-Pacific region. India's efforts under Kickleighter proposals for military-to-military cooperation with the US are a manifestation of this thrust. On the other hand, India is managing its relations well - both with China and Japan. With China, the improvement in relations is going in the right direction, where as with Japan considerable closeness in bilateral ties have been established. In this context, South East Asia comes into Indian calculations very significantly. A three-pronged approach towards this region has been adopted by India. First, political contacts are being renewed through exchange of visits by political leaders so as to make India relevant to the balance of the power system. Second, economic linkages are being established with the countries of this region, especially ASEAN, to strengthen its economic capabilities in the post-Cold War era. Third, the thrust is on developing strategic partnerships through various confidence-building measures and bilateral defence cooperation to work towards common security needs.[26] Thus, a new orientation was developed to strengthen all-round relations with South East Asia.

(iv) India's self reliance and growth in the defence sector also gave it confidence to play an important role in South East Asia. During the 1980s (1980 to 1987) India managed to build up its military capability, leaving it in a fairly good position.[27] Besides, its naval and air force modernization, with its new initiatives have made it capable of having a strong domestic arms industry in high technology weapons.[28] Development of light combat aircraft (LCA), the revised advanced light helicopter (ALH) and five missiles under the integrated guided missiles development programme are manifestations of such proof. The chances of export of LCA to developing countries in the future are very bright as it is estimated that Asian and African countries will need to replace as many as 8,000 fighters in the next twenty years. Modernization of numerous Soviet-built weapons, particularly the MIG fighter will further boost India's interests as two-thirds of the world's fighters are badly in need of refurbishing.[29] The enhanced military capabilities, along with South East Asia's arms acquisition programme in the post-Cold War era, brought India closer to them. Though India's attitude on CTBT and later Pokhran-II in May 1998 have developed some suspicions among the South East Asian states, its relations continue to remain warm despite some divergences on the nuclear issue between India and South East Asia. This can be clearly discerned from the recent Manila meeting of ASEAN.[30] ASEAN's refusal to condemn India by name is well appreciated by New Delhi and it augurs well for India-ASEAN relations. As a token of appreciation, India has come out with a number of measures (counter trade, liberal trade credits etc.) to help alleviate the current economic hardship faced by a number of ASEAN nations.[31]

After the end of the Cold War, numerous confidence-building measures by India and greater appreciation of India's role among the South East Asian states brought them together on strategic issues. But at that time no independent institutional arrangements regarding security matters existed in South East Asia. Hence

India-South East Asia cooperation started with collaboration in economic forms through the joining of ASEAN by India as sectoral dialogue and later on as a full dialogue partner. But during this process, various mechanisms for South East Asian security were suggested. Gareth Evans proposed a Conference on Security and cooperation in Europe (CSCE) version m Asia.[32] Some consideration for developing a system based on Asia-Pacific Economic Cooperation (APEC) was also suggested. Concert for power approach for this region was also considered. But all these approaches were rejected by ASEAN as they had a common weakness of overlooking the peculiarities of the region and failed to trace into account of the "ASEAN Way" of doing things.[35]

However, in the changed global and regional scenario through some of the "reactive" and "proactive" policies, ASEAN took some initiative for regional security in South East Asia. Its reactive moves were based on the basic convictions that:

(i)   any initiative to address Southeast Asian security should enumerate from within the region rather than without;

(ii)   the external involvement should be kept to the minimum; and,

(iii)   foreign military presence, however stabilizing an effect it might have, should be temporary.[36]

Proactive elements in its approach can be discerned from its policies:

(i)   member states should not allow bilateral disputes to flare up into open conflicts;

(ii)   the region be neutralized through the declaration of zone of peace, freedom and neutrality (ZOPFAN) as adopted in 1971;

(iii)   to conclude the Treaty of Amity and Cooperation (TAC) among ASEAN states as suggested in 1976; and,

(iv)   to utilize post-ministerial Conference (PMC) to discuss security issues, along with economic, with dialogue partners.[37] Since India has been significantly associated with the ASEAN, hence its approach to the security issue would also be considered sympathetically.

Finally, ASEAN comes out with a separate institution for defence and security matters in 1993. The ASEAN Regional Forum (ARF) was established as a multilateral forum to consider the issues of defence and security in Asia-Pacific. However, it is not like a military pact and it is not directed against any particular system. Regarding its functioning, a "concept paper" was introduced in 1995, which recommended an evolutionary approach to tackle security issues: (a) Promotion of confidence-building measures; (b) development of preventive diplomacy; and, (c) development of conflict resolution mechanism. [38] Since 1996, India has also joint this forum and is contributing to the security of this region.[39]

India and South East Asia have similar security concerns for this region in the post-Cold War era. Proximity of the two provides an ample scope for their military cooperation, particularly in the naval field. Joining hands with India, might also serve South East Asia's interest of balancing of China and Japan in the changed regional milieu. This is why it has been 'rightly observed that "a more connected India will better - and perhaps more productively - balance the influence of China and Japan in Asia".[40] On the other hand, India will be equally benefited because its maritime cooperation and peacekeeping experiences will boost its scope for further cooperation with the Asia-Pacific states. Besides, it will get the opportunity to explain that India has no intention to compete with other powers to fill the perceived power vacuum. Finally, it will provide a good chance to present its views on its nuclear capabilities, which has created a lot of misconceptions among the people of this region.

Though the new institutional set-up in the form of ARF could be beneficial to both India and South East Asia. If India can improve its image in the region, the latter could also benefit from India's defence capabilities to enhance its security environment. If India's nuclear policies are well perceived then South East Asia's efforts towards ZOPFAN and South East Asia nuclear weapons-free zone (ZWFZ) can be considered by India.

Thus, ARF will provide a new boost to stability, peace and economic progress for South East Asia and will open up new vistas for strategic and economic partnership of these states with India.

Thus, the post-Cold War scenario in South East Asia is very conducive for the growth and development of strategic cooperation with India. It is because the end of the Cold War has paradoxically brought about a phenomenon of an arms race among the ASEAN. Recent joint naval exercises done by India with these states has not only removed the misconception regarding India's naval hegemony prevalent among the states in the 1980s, but at the same time developed confidence among them. India's various confidence-building measures brought it more closer to them. India's indigenous defence capabilities provide assurance of its suitability to these states. Consequently in this era, India is carrying on joint naval exercises with them. India is also assisting in upgradation of their existing military equipments. At the same time, it is looking at this region as an emerging new centre for India's defence exports. In this process, it is following a twin approach with these states, associated in institutions looking for the security in this region, as well as bilateral defence deals with the states of South East Asia.

IV

India's economic and strategic relations with South East Asia did not develop in a vacuum. Rather political understanding between India and countries of South East Asia are the key to such developments. That is why Mohammad Ayoob was right when he once observed that, "New Delhi has come to the conclusion that if it is to have some clout in South East Asia and carry some weight in terms of the foreign policy calculations of South East Asian states, it would have to demonstrate its relevance to the region in political ... terms".[41] Consequently, India has to develop a deeper political understanding among the political elites of South East Asia. This understanding will lead to a change in the perceptions about India among the policy-makers, which ultimately will clear the way for all-round development of cooperation between India and South East Asia. Simultaneously, India, through its participation in different organizations of this region, has to learn the "ASEAN ways" of functioning and mould its policies accordingly. Through its "track-two" (non-governmental institutions) or even "track-three" (people-to-people) diplomacy with them, India has to learn new ways and means to develop close friendships with this region. The changed political alignment in the post-Cold War era has done away with the past misconceptions regarding India-Vietnam-Soviet Union linkages and its likely fallouts on Cambodian issue. Simultaneously India's engagements with the USA and ASEAN have cleared the doubts in the minds of pro-western states in this region. But while chalking out the future agenda, India has to change itself according to the political needs of these states. Besides, it has to play an important role in the emerging quadrilateral linkages between ASEAN-USA-China-Japan. Hence, if on the one hand, the need for India is to minimize its bilateral and regional political differences with South East Asia, then on the other hand, it has to place itself as a part pf South East Asian politics in particular and Asia-Pacific developments in general.

To meet the above challenges, India followed a two-pronged political approach towards South East Asia. At one level, serious efforts to develop an understanding with political elites, both at personal and institutional levels, were made. On the other hand, for the overall improvement of goodwill between India and these states, the former has been busy in building multilateral contracts with them. Thus, post-Cold War policy initiatives by India endeavour to bring India closer to them to serve both its short-term and long-term foreign policy objectives.

(i) During the post-Cold War era, the main plank of political diplomacy for India in South East Asia has been to come closer to the political elites of this region. That is why India has gathered all forces of dynamism - domestic and regional - and has been directly focusing on establishing synergies with a fast consolidating and progressive neighbourhood to its east in the Asian continent. In this context, South East Asia figures very prominently, as this region has been geographically inseparable, culturally conjoined and now, more than ever before, economically and strategically interdependent and complementary. Now the question arises as to how to tap this region in terms of India's foreign policy interests? This has been the key element for the practical aspects of India "Look east" policy. In this context, I.K. Gujral, the then Indian external affairs minister, was right when he observed on 24 July 1996 in the first PMC meeting of ASEAN after India got full dialogue partnership. He viewed that:

> "India will seek to promote high-level formal and informal political contacts and visits, official level consultations in bilateral, ASEAN-related and multilateral for a vigorous business-to-business interaction and match-making, focused and frequent interchange between one, dynamics and antis of learning, and an excellence and familiarization drive to establish direct connectivities between our respective media, cultural and artistic communities.[42]

To develop close contacts at both official and un-official levels has been the thrust of India's policy since 1991. The visits of a large number of high-level dignitaries from both sides show the inclinations on both sides to develop a closer understanding between the decision-makers in India and South East Asia. From the Indian side, the president visited Vietnam and Philippines and the prime minister paid visits to Indonesia, Thailand, Vietnam, Singapore and Malaysia since 1991. From the South East Asian states, thirteen visits by presidents/prime ministers/princes have been made from different South East Asian states. This fact is clearly evident from Table-5.

Apart from this dual-track diplomacy, people-to-people contacts have also been encouraged to cement the ties between India and South East Asia. Promotion to tourism, trade, cultural activities, academic exchanges, etc. have been enhanced to develop friendly contacts between the common men of two regions. Thus, this three-tier approach to diplomacy (official, unofficial and people-to-people) has been made instrumental in bringing about closer ties between India and South East Asia in the post-Cold War era. At the second level, political understanding between India and South East Asia has been encouraged through

TABLE 5: EXCHANGE OF VISITS OF PRESIDENTS/PRIME MINISTER OF INDIA AND SOUTHEAST ASIA, 1991-98

A.	VISITS OF INDIAN DIGNITARIES TO SOUTHEAST ASIA		
1.	President of India	Vietnam	24-27 April, 1991
2.	President of India	Philippines	28 April- 1 May, 1991
3.	Prime Minister of India	Indonesia	31 Aug- 5 Sept. 1992 (To attend meeting of NAM)
4.	Prime Minister of India	Thailand	7-9 April 1993
5.	Prime Minister of India	Vietnam	5-7 Sept. 1994
6.	Prime Minister of India	Singapore	7-9 Sept. 1994
7.	Prime Minister of India	Malaysia	2-5 Aug. 1995

B.	VISITS OF SOUTHEAST ASIAN DIGNITARIES TO INDIA	
1.	Prime Minister of Cambodia	3 Oct. 1991
2.	Prince of Thailand	7-21 April, 1992
3.	Prime Minister of Malaysia	31 March, 1993
4.	President of Singapore	21-30 Nov. 1993 (Private visit)
5.	Prime Minister of Singapore	23-31 Jan. 1994
6.	President of Indonesia	27-30 March 1994 (To attend meeting of G- 15)
7.	Prime Minister of Malaysia	27-30 March 1994
8.	Prince of Thailand	4-7 June 1994
9.	First Prime Minister of Cambodia	18-19 Jan. 1996
10.	Prince of Cambodia	16 Dec. 1996
11.	Prime Minister of Malaysia	19-22 Dec. 1996
12.	President of Philippines	2-5 March 1997
13.	Prime Minister of Vietnam	7-9 March 1997

the development of multilateral contracts with individual countries of this region. A profile of these contacts in divergent areas of mutual interests has boosted the ties between India and these states. Contacts between them ranges from agro-products to those of defence cooperation, depending upon their mutual requirements, infrastructure and the level of development in different states. A state-wise analysis of this cooperation would reveal the nature of such an understanding between them.

Thus, during this period, India has been enhancing political understanding with this region by way of moulding the perceptions of political leaders and through the development of bilateral multi-level contacts. To a great extent, India has been successful in this process before the emergence of the economic crisis in South East Asia in 1997. This crisis has given a temporary setback to the ties between India and this region. However, it is not going to be a permanent roadblock in their relationship. It is because this crisis might soon be over. In addition, India has also been making efforts to help these countries to come out of this economic trap. In its own moderate way, India has offered aid to the states of South East Asia in terms of:

(a) Long-term credit on the supply of materials that South East Asian countries would be importing from India. These materials could be engineering goods, machinery, automotives and steel.

(b) Prepared to indulge encounter trade with the South East Asian countries, which means instead of wasting precious foreign exchange, these countries may barter their products with those from India.

(c) India has shown its willing to provide them EXIM Bank credits and offer training to augment their human resources and development.

Moreover, India has been ready to help these countries under the enhancement of greater South-South cooperation. Hence, the chances of India and South East Asia coming together, with more sound political understanding, has been more than it used to be during the earlier era.

V

From the above analysis, it can be concluded that the changed international scenario, along with the growing realization among Indian elites' perceptions about the future importance of Asia-Pacific, led to the new phase of "re-discovery and a renaissance" in its relationships with this region. However, this has been possible by the reciprocal positive response shown by the South East Asian states towards India. The scope of numerous economic activities between India and Asia Pacific are immense as both are presently following the globalization/liberalization process through their various official and non-official policies. But it is too early to project this area to develop itself as Asia-Pacific Free Trade Area (AFTA) in the near future. Consequently, India's interactions are likely to remain limited to major ASEAN states. In strategic terms, though India has became part of the security system of this region by joining ARF and bilateral ties with the USA, yet complete consensus on security matters among major actors in this region is still to evolve. Besides, India, despite its greater naval presence and bilateral defence ties with South East Asian states, is not in a position to play a serious role in this region. The post-Cold War era witnessed greater political understanding among the policy makers in India and different states of South-East Asia and other major powers like the USA, China, Japan, etc. This, however, does not guarantee a major political initiative-taking position to India. Its role is conditioned by the limitations of both a bilateral and multilateral nature. Thus, it is certain that in the changing global order, India is looking towards the Asia-Pacific region with greater concerns and hopes. But India's economic, strategic and political role will be projected through the core sub-region of Asia-Pacific, i.e. South East Asia. Here also the future of India's ties with them will be dependent upon the change in their domestic and external milieu in terms of their political stability and economic strength on the one hand, and the role of the outside power and developments of their inter and intra-linkages in this region, on the other hand.

References

1. Asia-Pacific is a very complex and vast region without a clear geographical definition. However, in the broader sense it refers to Asian countries and regions along with the Pacific Ocean including China, Japan, Korea, Taiwan, Hong Kong, South East Asian region and the Far East region in Russia. However, in security terms, the USA and South Asia could not be excluded from it.

2. G.V.C. Naidu, *"Future of Institutionalism in Asia Pacific: The ARF and its implications for Asia"*, Strategic Analysis. 23(11), February 2000, p. 1958.

3. Francies Fukuyama, *"The End of History"*, National Interest. Summer 1989, pp. 3-18. *The End of History and the Last Man* (London. 1989)

4. Charles Krauthmmer, *"The Unipolar Movement"*, Foreign Affairs. Summer 1991.

5. For details see D. Banerjee, *"International Strategic Situations"*, Strategic Analysis, Vol. 17, no. 1, April 1994, pp. 25-26.

6. For details see Ted Galen Carpenter, *"The New World Disorder"*. Foreign Policy, no. 84, Fall 1991.

7. For details on the prevalent trends and scholars explanation about this emerging new world order see, Gurmeet Kanwal, *"The New World Order: An Appraisal - I & II"*, Strategic Analysis, Vol. 23, nos. 3 & 4, pp. 345-370 & 531 &562 respectively.

8. For details see, T.K. Bhaumik, *"Indo-ASEAN Cooperation in Investment"* in Shri Prakash et al, eds., *India and ASEAN: Economic Partnership in the 1990s and Future Prospects* (New Delhi, 1977), pp. 61-87.

9. Charan D. Wadhva and Sanjay Ambatkar, *"India's Sectoral Dialogue Partnership with ASEAN"*, in Shri Prakash et al, eds., *India and ASEAN: Economic Partnership in the 1990s and Future Prospects* (New Delhi, 1977), p.32.

10. Shri Prakash et.al, eds., *India and ASEAN: Economic Partnership in the 1990s and Future Prospects* (New Delhi, 1977), pp. 14 & 15

11. Charan D. Wadhwa, *"ASEAN and its Economic Relations with*

a *Restructured Europe"*, in Kanta Ahuja, et al., eds., *Regime Transformations and Global Realignments* (New Delhi, 1994).

12. Economists. 24 October 1992.

13. Charan D. Wadhva, *"India Southeast Asia Economic Partnership in the 1990s: Role of Government Policies"*, Ghosal, no. 24, p. 67.

14. Ibid.

15. S. Viswam, *"India's Look East Policy"* World Focus, Vol. 18, no. 6, June 1997, p.6.

16. Ibid.

17. Govt of India, Ministry of External Affairs, India and ASEAN: Dialogue Partnership (New Delhi, 1997), p. 15.

18. Ibid.,p.l7.

19. For details see, *"Southeast Asia: The policies of economic disarray"*, IISS Strategic Comments, vol. 3, no. 7, September 1997, pp. 1-2.

20. Ibid. p. 2.

21. Charan D. Wadhva, *"India Southeast Asia Economic Partnership in the 1990s: Role of Government Policies"*, pp. 59-60

22. B. Bhattacharya, *"Indo-ASEAN Investment Relations"* in Shri Prakash et.al, eds., *India and ASEAN: Economic Partnership in the 1990s and Future Prospects* (New Delhi, 1977), p. 59.

23. For details see G.V.C. Naidu, *"The Indian Navy and Southeast Asia"*, Contemporary South East Asia. Vol. 13, no. l, June 1991, pp. 72-85. For Pakistan's point of view on this issue see, Pervaiz Iqbal Cheema, *"Indian Naval Build up and Southeast Asian Security: A Pakistani View"*, Contemporary Southeast Asia, vol. 13, no. 1, June 1991, pp. 86-102

24. G.V.C. Naidu, *"India's Strategic Relations with Southeast Asia"*, in Ghosal, ed., *India and Southeast Asia: Challenges and Opportunities* (New Delhi, 1996) pp. 311-341.

25. G.V.C. Naidu, *India and ASEAN*, Strategic Analysis, vol. 19, No. 1, April 1996, p. 67.

26. Ibid., pp. 69-72.

27. Deepa M. Ollapally, *"India and the New 'Asian' Balance of*

Power", Strategic Analysis, vol. 22, no. 4, July 1998, pp. 520-21

28. Amit Gupta, *"Determining India's Force Structure and Military Doctrine"*, Asian Survey, vol. 35, no. 5, May 1995, pp. 448-541.

29. Sandy Gordon, *"South Asia after the Cold War"*, Asian Survey, vol. 35, no. 10, October 1995, p. 882.

30. For details see, G.V.C. Naidu, *"The Manila ASEAN Meeting and India"*:, Strategic Analysis, vol. 22, no. 8 November 1998, pp. 1163-1177.

31. Ibid, p. 1176

32. Gareth Evans, *"What Asia Needs is an Europe Style CSCA"*, International Herald Tribune. 27 July 1996.

33. David Dewitt and Paul Evans, eds. *The Agenda for Cooperative Security in the North Pacific: Conference Report* (Ontario, 1993), p. 18.

34. Amitav Acharya, *"An Asia-Pacific Concert of Powers"*, Trends, no. 63, 25-26 November 1995, p. 1.

35. For details see G.V.C. Naidu, *"The Manila ASEAN Meeting and India"*, 36. Strategic Analysis, vol. 22, no. 8 November 1998, pp. 1164-68.

37. Ibid.,p.ll69.

38. Ibid., pp. 1169-70.

39. The Asian Regional Forum: A Concept Paper (1995).

40. For details see Udai Bhanu Singh *"Indian and ASEAN Regional Forum"*, Strategic Analysis, vol. 19, no. 4, July 1996, pp. 577-87; G.V.C. Naidu, *"India-ASEAN and ARF"*, Strategic Analysis, vol. 19, no.6, September 1996, pp. 851-52; *"The Manila ASEAN Meeting and India"*, Strategic Analysis, vol. 22, no. 8, November 1996, pp. 1163-77; Udai Bhanu Singh, *"Indian and the ARF: The Post Pokhran II Phase"*, Strategic Analysis, vol. 22, no. 10, January 1999, pp. 159171606.

41. Editorial, *"Look East"*, Asia week 9 August, 1997, p. 13. 41. Mohammed Ayoob, *India and Southeast Asia: Indian Perceptions and Policies* (London, 1990), p. 86.

42. Asian Recorder, 26,. August- 1 September 1996, p. 258-60

43. Asian Recorder, 11-17 June, 1998, p, 273-47.

‹16›

Some Pitfalls and Challenges for Asia-Pacific under Globalisation

J. George Waardenburg*

1. Introduction

This contribution attempts to turn against the pitfalls of a mechanistic view of world developments. More specifically it argues against the view that the worldwide process of globalization, which we equate by and large with global economic integration or economic openness of its constituent countries, automatically benefits the development of these countries and the welfare of their populations. Similarly it argues against the view that the global penetration of Information and Communication Technology (ICT), one of the forces for globalization, provides unconditionally and automatically a blessing for all of the same countries and populations. In both cases, it is argued, there are still degrees of freedom for national policies to attempt actively to nevertheless bring about such benefits and blessings.

This contribution does not rest on specific research but on publications which summarize the research of others; the publications are not always referred to specifically but are recommended for further reading[1].

*   Centre for Development Planning, Erasmus University, Rotterdam, Netherlands.
[1]   The present author acknowledges gladly his insight derived from conversations with Dr. R.O. Naastepad and Dr. Servaas

2. Openness and Development

In the '50s, '60s and early '70s, an import substitution strategy directed at industrialization (ISI) was the dominant conventional policy wisdom and advice for developing countries. However, from the latter '70s onwards economic openness towards the outside world became the key word and key advice for development[2] reinforced by it being made by the IMF and World Bank a precondition for assistance with balance of payments problems as part of a structural adjustment policy. The four "Asian tigers" were brought to the fore as an illustration of the idea that (increased) openness leads to (increased) growth. A careful scrutiny and empirical tests of this idea showed that its theoretical underpinning was weak and its empirical validity was causally ambiguous, one-sided, and not well founded. The "Asian crisis" has invigorated these doubts.

This is not to deny that openness is important for long-run economic growth: indeed increased exports[3] allow for imports of essential capital and intermediate goods for growth and for

---

Storm (Rotterdam) and from discussions in the UN CSTD in preparation of the report on Knowledge Societies. The publications specifically recommended for further reading are: Mansell, Robin and Uta Wehn (eds.), *Knowledge Societies*: "Information Technology for Sustainable Development, for the United Nations Commission on Science and Technology for Development", Oxford University Press, Oxford, 1998.

Rodrik, Dani, *The New Global Economy and Developing Countries: Making Openness Work*, Overseas Development Council, Washington, John Hopkins University Press, Baltimore, 1999.

Storm, Servaas T.H., *Openheid en Economische Groei* (Openness and Economic Growth), ESB (Economic Statistical Information), 85, 4239, 21-1-2000, pp. 52-54, Rotterdam.

[2]   Together with internal liberalization, though recently a more balanced relationship between market and government forces are advocated for development.

[3]   A general export pessimism may also be one-sided.

exploiting economies of scale[4], indeed access to foreign capital is important provided one avoids its dangers, especially those of short-term borrowing, indeed importing ideas and institutions may be important provided one keeps control of such processes. But for long-term growth effects it should be combined with a strategy for physical and human investment, which is key to growth, and with nurturing institutions of conflict management, including participatory ones improving income distributions and poverty situations, in order to protect the country against the effects of external disturbances.

3. ICT and Development

Few global developments in the past few decades have been more impressive and incisive than the rise and spread of ICT. Its impact has not been limited to providing some interesting new tools for data handling and communication, but it has meant the transformation of considerable areas of work and living. Moreover this is going on at an incredibly high pace. But it has done so, as happens with so many things, much more in developed countries than in developing countries, in which large parts of the population have not even been touched by the "ICT-revolution", let alone reaped benefits from it.

The pitfall here is to think that this will change automatically. Therefore the United Commission on Science and Technology for Development (UNCSTD) established a Working Group to study the issue of access to and use of CT by developing countries and suggest recommendations for the UNCSTD to UN bodies and individual countries' governments how to deal with ICT in order to make it beneficial to development in a broad sense of the word.[5] In addition to its ca. 24 pages report, an extensive handbook type publication of ca. 300 pages on the same

---

[4]   The degree to which this is possible depends also on the size of the GDP.

[5]   A summary of the "Report of the Working Group on Information and Communication Technologies for Development" with its brief analysis and commendations is available as Annexure 3 in Mansell and Wehn (eds.) (1998). The report of 1997 itself is available from the UN CSTD's secretariat at UNCTAD, Geneva.

subject was prepared under the supervision of the same Working Group by Mansell and Wehn (eds.) (1998).

This publication intended to provide the full background and justification of the report, but could also be used on its own.[6]

Two principal conclusions of the report, adopted by the UNCSTD, the ECOSOC and finally the General Assembly of the United Nations, are as follows.

- "Although the costs of using ICTs to build national information infrastructures which can contribute to innovative 'knowledge societies' are high, the costs of not doing so are likely to be much higher.

- Developing countries are at very different starting positions in the task of building innovative and distinctive 'knowledge societies' and in using their national information infrastructures to support their development objectives."

Against the background of these conclusions the report recommends to the national governments and US bodies as follows:

❑ Each developing country and country in transition establishes a national ICT strategy. Where such strategies already exist, they should be reviewed to ensure that they take note of the guidelines proposed by the UNCSTD Working Group;

❑ Immediate action be taken by national governments to establish a task force or commission or to ensure that another entity is charged with establishing the guidelines for national ICT strategies. Reviews should be undertaken over a six-month period and a report should be prepared

---

6   A shortened and popular version of this publication was prepared by the International Institute for Communication and Development (IICD), Juffrouw Idastraat II, 2513 BE, The Hague, in the form of four booklets, which can be obtained from the IICD.

by each government outlining the priorities of its national ICT strategy, the mechanisms for continuous updating, and the procedures for implementation of the components of the strategy. Progress on the implementation of this recommendation should be reported to the next session of the Commission in 1999;

❑ Each agency of the United Nations system review the financing, production, and use of ICTs for social and economic development in their area of responsibility. This review should monitor the effectiveness of new forms of partnerships in the ICT area, and address the capability of each agency to provide technical assistance in that area. This needs to happen so that the United Nations system can be in the forefront in helping developing countries and countries in transition to implement their national ICT strategies.

For implementing these recommendations the report adds a great number of "suggested guidelines" which can serve as an agenda for the proposed task forces or commissions. Though this report and its recommendations were adopted some three years ago, they appear not to have become irrelevant for countries in the Asia-Pacific region notwithstanding the rapid developments in ICT and the impact of the "Asian crisis". Pondering them might therefore be useful in the context of considering Asia-Pacific and The Global Order.

The Role of India in a Changing Asia-Pacific Region

Son Ngoc Bui*

India is a big country with the world's second largest population, nearly one billion (less only to China's population). In terms of GDP India is ranked the fifth largest in Asia, being US$381,566 mil. in 1997, smaller than one of Japan (US$4,190,233mil), China (US$ 901,981mil.), South Korea (US$442,543mil.) and Australia (US$393,519mil.) in the same year (FEER, YearBook, 2000). India is one of the nuclear powers in the world.

India's support for Vietnam during the Cold War was highly meaningful in so far as contributing to the security and peace of Southeast Asia. The world is changing and the role and position of a country in international security and peace depends considerably on its military power and also on its economic development, and the extent to which its economy integrates into the world economy. With the economic achievements in the past decade, India will certainly have a significant role in contributing to the security and peace of the Asia-Pacific region.

A Changing World and a Changing Asia-Pacific Region

During the Cold War, economic aspects in international life were not outstanding; in contrast, the political ones overwhelmed them. The conflict between the former Socialist system and the

*   Researcher, Institute of World Economy. Hanoi, Vietnam.

capitalist one influenced almost all economic, political and social activities of the world. Military power was considered to have a major role in determining the position of a country in the world, and no socio-economic development models in the world were proved truly right. Moreover, economic competition among countries or systems heavily bore political colour.

The collapse of the former socialist system by the end of 1980s and early 1990s ended the Cold War. Since then the world has been observing significant changes in most of the fields of international life. Politically, the systemic and ideological conflict came to an end. A new international life is emerging and characterized by some points:

First, though the ideological and militarily conflict between two systems has ended, the racial, religious, and locally political conflicts tend to increase.

Second, bipolarity between the U.S. and former Soviet Union has been gradually replaced by the multipolarity among many different centres.

Third, models of market-oriented and/or liberalized economy seem to be proved right and effective for economic development, which increasingly became a major trend in the world. There seems to be no doubt, and no more discussion about whether market-type economy is effective or not. It seems that the only remaining question around the world is how to undertake such reforms effectively. The economic competition among countries in some sense is nothing but the competition in undertaking such liberalization and market-oriented economic reforms. The governments in many countries seem to compete with each other in reducing the government intervention in the economy, relaxing restrictions on socio-economic activities, and even encouraging market elements in their socio-economic development strategies.

Fourth, globalization and regionanlization are emerging as a common trend in many fields. It is hardly imagined that any country can resist and/or stay out of such trends.

The Asia-Pacific region is also observing tremendous political and economic changes over the last decade. Conflicts among countries in the regions have been replaced by dialogue and peace talks. Liberalization of the economies and market-oriented reforms has been undertaken in most of the countries in the region. The fact that Vietnam, Laos, Cambodia joint the ASEAN and new development of AFTA in recent years shows a regionalization trend in this region. Though there remain some racial and religious conflicts in The Philippines and Indonesia, generally speaking, the common trend in the region is dialogue, peace and co-operation.

During the cold war, military power, especially nuclear power, played a major role in determining the position of a country in international life. In the context of a changing world, having military and nuclear power may not be enough for a country to have a substantial role for peace and security of a region in particular, and of the world, in general. In order to be able to have a certain role to play for peace and security of a region and/or of the world, it is important for a country to have undertaken adequate economic reforms. These reforms are required to lead to considerable growth of the economy, to open the economy to the world, and to integrate the economy into the world economy and/or region.

Reforms and the Role of India in a Changing Asia-Pacific Region

In line with the common trend of economic liberalization around the world, India has been undertaking economic reforms. According to such economic reforms, the restrictions on the economic activities are being gradually lifted. The Nation (1/3/2000), for example, suggested that India relaxed its control over capital movements in and out for foreign investors. The IMF (survey 3/4/2000) suggested that during the decade of 1990s India can be seen as the most dynamic in Asia in attracting FDI with a 6 fold per year increase on the average reaching US$2.7 billion during the 1995-1998 period (especially as high as US$ 3.6 bill. In 1997), compared with US$ 470 mil. during the 1991-1994 period. **The share of FDI inflows into India in total FDI into Asia rose by three times, from 1.1% to 3.3% for the same period. In the meantime, the share of FDI into the region in total FDI in the world decreases from 20% to 18%. The measures such as dismantling the state monopoly in insurance, opening banks and encouraging competition in banking system, promptly privatizing sate-owned enterprises, allowing a larger share of foreign ownership in many fields (even allowing 100% foreign-owned** capital in movies and mining) are the main reasons for rapid FDI inflows into India. Other measures attracting FDI and promise by the government to further reform the economy have encouraged the foreign investors to pour more money into India.

The results of such reforms are observable. During the 1990-1999 period, the Indian economy grew by a respectable 6% per year (Asia Yearbook, FEER, 2000). And the Indian economy is estimated by some analysis to grow at 7.5% per year over the next five years, becoming another miracle of Asia (FEER 20/1/2000).

The exports of India to Asia account for 52 percent of exports to developing countries and 24 percent of total exports in 1997. The imports from Asia accounts for nearly 45 percent of imports from developing countries and 22 percent of total import in the same year. Thus, Indian economy has a close relation with the Asia region.

However, the scale of international trade of India is modest, ranked 13th against Japan, Hong Kong, China and other countries. Besides, the foreign investment remains trivial let alone the investment into Asia. Despite this, with adequate economic reforms being undertaken by the Indian government, it is believed that economic development will help India integrate into Asian region, and with traditional relations with the Asians, there is no doubt that India will have an important role to play in the peace and security of the Asia-Pacific region.

Conclusion:

Thus, being a big country with strong military and nuclear power, India made a great contribution to the peace of Asia in the past. Now that the world is changing, the respectable economic reforms in India will certainly result in substantial economic achievements. Such achievements in turn will help India further integrate into the Asia region. Then, with strong military power, economic achievements, and further integration into the region, India is truly believed to have an important role to play in the security and peace of the Asia-Pacific region.

‹18›

Demographic Situation of Vietnam in the Asian Context

R.S. Dube*

Demographic Setting

Table 2 presents estimated population of the different regions in mid-2000. Vietnam supports some 80 millions of people who are distributed over an area of 128 thousand square miles. This has given a crude population density of 615 persons per square miles. The country ranks 8th among the Asian countries in respect of the size of population and 12th in respect of the density (615/square miles) of population. As compared with other Asian countries it is more densely populated than Pakistan (490/square mile) or the North Korean region (466/square mile). The density of population is about two times more than that of China or Thailand (Table 3).

Population of Vietnam is largely rural in character. The share of urban population is 24 percent. Level of urbanization in this country is so small that it is lower than that in Thailand (31%), Myanmar (26%) and Pakistan (33%). The country ranks at 25th position among the Asian countries in respect of the percentage of their urban population (Table 4).

The level of gross national product (GNP) is much lower than most of the Asian countries. The country in fact lies in the lowest slab of the grouping prepared for mapping regional situation of

* Professor, Department of General & Applied Geography, Dr. H.S. Gour University, Sagar (M.P.), India.

GNP in the Asian region (MAP-2). The available data suggests that practically all Asian countries other than Laos ($ 320), Cambodia ($260) and Nepal ($210) have registered higher GNP as compared to Vietnam. Here the level of GNP is barely 4 percent of that in South Korea ($8600), 15 percent of that in Thailand ($2160) and 50 percent of that in China ($750). An observation of the patterns, which may be seen in MAP -2, indicates that in this respect Vietnam's situation is similar to the other continental countries of Asia. This aspect would require to be taken care of if quality of life is to be improved (Table 5).

The age composition exhibits the impact of recent changes in vital rates. One third of its total population is classed under 15 years of ages. This situation is again similar to the conditions prevailing in many developing countries of the world. The share of population in the advanced ages in Vietnam is above 65 years, which is higher by 6 percent in comparison to many of the South Central and South East Asian countries, suggesting a progressive age structure of population.

The rate of population growth suggests slackening up trend. An observation of the data summarized in Table 6 and MAP-1 shows that if current rates are taken into account, the population of Vietnam would double in 48 years. Though this span of time is much shorter than that in China (79 years) South Korea (82 years) and Kazakistan (161 years) the available symptoms do suggest that the country is making determined efforts enhance the length of doubling time on the lines of success achieved in Japan, Korea and China.

The Vital Rates

Available data on vital rates suggest that Vietnam has achieved remarkable success in respect of birth and death controls. The country ranks 20th and 23rd among the Asian countries in respect of birth and death rates respectively. In fact birth rate (20) in this country is about half of that in Bhutan (40), Laos (41) and Cambodia (38) and the death rate (6) is about 2.5 times lower than that in Cambodia (12) and Pakistan (11). The demographic performance in Vietnam in respect of the reduction of vital rates is superior to even that of Indonesia, India and Malaysia (Table 7, MAP 3 and Table 9, MAP 5).

The regional exposition of birth rate level in the Asian region is quite interesting. The zone stretching from Afghanistan to the Indo-Chinese peninsula has registered birth rate higher than the average for the Asian region. Whereas whole of the remaining areas are classed in the categories of lower birth rates. Significantly Vietnam lies at the eastern fringe of this high birth rate zone and marks a transition between the high and low birth rate areas of Asia. It is in this respect that experiences of Vietnam in the field of birth control programme may prove helpful for other neighbouring countries.

The situations of total fertility rates as summarized in Table 8 and depicted on MAP 4 also gives similar patterns. In Vietnam TFR is 2.5, which ranks 22nd among the Asian countries. If compared with the highest TFR (6.1) in Afghanistan the countries success in this case is commendable.

In case of the death rate Vietnam's position is comparable with that of the birth rate levels. Here death rate is 6, which is one third of that in Afghanistan where these rates are highest (18) in Asian region. The data summarized in Table 9 and mapped in MAP 5 show that in this respect the country is classed in the lower side of classes determined for this purpose and the country stands at the outskirts of the relatively high death rate belt that encompasses the whole zone from Afghanistan to Indo-China. Similar patterns are seen in case of the infant mortality rates and the level of expectation of life (Maps 6, Tables 10 and II). It may be noted that in respect of the IMR (37) and expectation of life (66 years) the position of Vietnam is 12th and 19th respectively among the Asian nations. This suggests that its performance in respect of the control of IMR has not yet succeeded to the level it has succeeded in case of general mortality.

As a consequence the natural increase of population is 1.4 making a rank of 23rd among the Asian countries and the regional exposition of the trend resembles with those of the vital rates (MAP 7 and Table 12).

These facts on the vital rates registered in Vietnam suggest that the country has achieved remarkable success in the implementation of the family‚limitation programmes. An observation of Table 13 shows that in Vietnam 75 percent of married women use contraceptions. This performance is matched only by China and South Korea, where 83 percent and 77 percent of such women use these methods. These efforts have operated in bringing down the birth rate in this country.

Quality of Life

To ascertain the comparative level of quality among the life of Asian countries, a composite index has been worked out based on four Socio-Economic-Demographic factors (Infant Mortality Rate, Total Fertility Rate, Percentage of Urban Population and GNP per capita). The Index of level of quality of life of Vietnam is found as 37 and that of India as 32 as can be seen from Table 14. All the Asian countries are grouped into five categories namely "Very Good", "Good", "Average", "Poor" and "Very Poor" depending up on their relative level of Index among the countries taken for this purpose.

Three countries namely Singapore, Japan and China Hong Kong, belong to the "very good" category having level of Index more than 80. Seven countries belong to "good" category having level of Index 50-79. Twelve countries belong to "average" category having level of Index 30-49. "Poor" category comprised of seven countries having level of Index 15-29. Three countries namely Laos, East Timor and Afghanistan belong to "very poor" category having the level of Index less than 15 as can be observed from Table 15.

It may be seen that Vietnam's performance for attainment of good quality of life as suggested by these score is yet to rise above the average standards among the Asian country. It may, however, be pointed out that countries like India, Pakistan and Cambodia are placed in the lower composite scores.

An observation of the data given in Table 16 shows that Vietnam's attainment is superior to India in case of demographic characteristics. The socio-economic level is however inferior as requested by the level of per capita GNP and proportion of urban population. It is intriguing that even though density of population in Vietnam is much lower than that in India, the socio-economic performance is poorer as compared with India. The available data included for present study also show that socio-economic factors are not necessary conditions for demographic control.

TABLE 1: THE ASIAN REGION (WEST ASIA EXCLUDED) SOCIO-ECONOMIC AND DEMOGRAPHIC CHARACTERISTICS

Countries	Popn. mid 2000 (million)	Births per 1000 pop.	Death per 1000 pop.	Natural Inc (annual) %	Doubling time in yrs.	Projected Population (millions) 2025	Projected Population (millions) 2050	Infant Mortality Rate	Total Fertility Rate	% of Popn. of age <15	% of Popn. of age 65+	Life Expectancy Total	Life Expectancy Male	Life Expectancy Female	% Urban Population	% of Adult Population 15–49 with HIV/Aids	% married women using contraception — All methods	% married women using contraception — Modern methods	GNP per Capita 1998 (US$)
Afghanistan	26.7	43	18	2.5	28	48.0	76.2	150	6.1	43	3	46	46	45	20	N	–	–	350
Bangladesh	128.1	27	8	1.8	38	177.3	210.8	82	3.3	43	3	59	59	58	20	N	49	42	470
Bhutan	0.9	40	9	3.1	22	1.4	2	71	5.6	42	4	66	–	–	15	–	–	–	440
India	1002.1	27	9	1.8	39	1363	1628	72	3.3	36	4	60	60	61	28	0.8	48	43	440
Iran	67.4	21	6	1.4	48	90.8	102.9	31	2.9	39	5	69	68	71	63	N	73	56	1650
Kazakhstan	14.9	14	10	0.4	161	14.6	13	21	2.0	29	7	65	59	70	56	N	66	54	1340
Kyrgyzstan	4.9	22	7	1.5	47	5.8	6.1	26	2.8	37	6	67	63	71	34	N	60	49	380
Maldives	0.3	35	6	2.9	23	0.5	0.7	27	5.4	45	3	71	71	72	25	–	–	–	1130
Nepal	23.9	36	11	2.5	28	38	49.3	79	4.6	41	3	57	58	57	11	0.1	29	26	210
Pakistan	150.6	39	11	2.8	25	227	285	91	5.6	43	4	58	58	57	33	0.1	18	13	470
Sri Lanka	19.2	18	6	1.2	60	23.9	25.9	17	2.1	26	7	72	70	74	22	0.1	66	44	810
Tajikistan	6.4	21	5	1.6	43	8.4	9.5	28	2.7	43	4	68	66	71	27	–	21	–	370
Turkmenistan	5.2	21	6	1.6	48	6.8	7.5	33	2.8	40	4	66	62	69	44	N	20	–	–
Uzbekistan	24.8	23	6	1.7	40	31.5	33.8	24	3.4	40	4	69	66	72	38	N	56	51	950
Brunei	0.3	25	3	2.2	32	0.5	0.7	8	2.5	34	3	71	70	73	67	N	–	–	–
Cambodia	12.1	38	12	2.6	27	21.2	29	80	5.3	43	3	56	54	58	16	2.4	–	16	260
East Timor	0.8	34	16	1.8	39	1.2	1.4	143	4.6	42	2	46	45	47	8	0.2	–	–	–
Indonesia	212.2	24	8	1.6	44	273.4	311.9	46	2.8	34	4	65	62	66	39	0.1	57	55	640
Laos	5.2	41	15	2.6	26	8.4	11.8	93	5.6	44	4	51	50	52	17	0.1	–	–	320
Malaysia	23.3	25	5	2.1	34	37	48.2	8	3.2	34	4	72	70	75	57	0.6	57	25	3670
Myanmar	48.9	30	10	2.3	35	68.1	87.8	83	3.8	37	4	54	53	56	26	1.8	17	14	–
Philippines	80.3	29	7	2.3	31	117.3	139.6	35	3.7	38	4	70	66	69	47	0.1	49	32	1050
Singapore	4	13	5	0.8	84	8	10.4	3	1.5	22	7	78	76	80	100	0.2	65	–	30170
Thailand	62	16	7	1	70	72.1	71.9	22	1.9	24	7	70	70	75	31	2.2	72	70	2160
Vietnam	78.7	20	6	1.4	48	109.9	123.7	37	2.5	34	5	66	63	69	24	0.2	75	56	350
China	1264.5	15	6	0.9	79	1431	1369	31	1.8	25	7	71	69	73	31	0.1	83	81	750
China, Hong Kong SAR	7.0	7	5	0.3	256	8.6	7.6	3.2	1	17	11	80	77	82	95	0.1	–	–	23660
Japan	126.9	9	8	0.2	462	120.9	100.5	3.5	1.3	15	17	81	77	84	78	N	64	57	32350
Korea, North	21.7	21	7	1.5	48	25.7	26.4	26	2.3	28	7	70	67	73	59	N	–	–	–
Korea, South	47.3	14	5	0.9	82	53.3	51.1	11	1.5	22	7	74	71	78	79	N	77	66	8600
Mongolia	2.5	20	7	1.4	50	3.4	4.1	34	2.7	25	4	63	60	66	52	N	57	41	380
Taiwan	22.3	13	6	0.7	97	25.3	25.2	6.6	1.5	21	8	75	72	78	77	–	–	–	–

TABLE 2 : THE ASIAN REGION (WESTERN ASIA) ESTIMATED POPULATION (MILLIONS): MID- 2000

S.NO.	COUNTRIES	NO. OF PERSONS
1	China	1264.5
2	India	1002.1
3	Indonesia	212.2
4	Pakistan	150.6
5	Bangladesh	128.1
6	Japan	126.9
7	Phillipines	80.3
8	Vietnam	78.7
9	Iran	67.4
10	Thailand	62.0
11	Myanmar	48.9
12	Korea South	47.3
13	Afghanistan	26.7
14	Uzbekistan	24.8
15	Nepal	23.9
16	Malaysia	23.3
17	Taiwan	22.3
18	Korea North	21.7
19	Sri Lanka	19.2
20	Kazakistan	14.9
21	Cambodia	12.1
22	China Hong Kong SAR	7.0
23	Kazakistan	6.4
24	Turkmenistan	5.2
25	Laos	5.2
26	Bhutan	4.9
27	Kyrgyzstan	4.9
28	Singapore	4.0
29	Mangolia	2.5
30	East Timore	0.8
31	China Macao SAR	0.4
32	Maldives	0.3
33	Brunei	0.3

Source: The Population Reference Bureau, 2000 World Population Datasheet, was height DC

TABLE 3 : THE ASIAN REGION (WESTERN ASIA)
POPULATION DENSITY

S.NO.	COUNTRIES	DENSITY (PER SQ. KM.)
1	China, Hong Kong SAR	16949
2	Singapore	16714
3	Maldives	2469
4	Bangladesh	2305
5	Taiwan	1593
6	Korea S.	1234
7	Japan	870
8	India	789
9	Sri Lanka	757
10	Phillipines	693
11	Vietnam	615
12	Pakistan	490
13	Korea North	466
14	Nepal	421
15	China	343
16	Thailand	313
17	Indonesia	289
18	Myanmar	187
19	Malaysia	183
20	Cambodia	173
21	Brunei	149
22	Uzbekistan	144
23	East Timor	137
24	Tajakistan	115
25	Iran	107
26	Afghanistan	106
27	Kyrgyzstan	64
28	Laos	57
29	Bhutan	48
30	Turkmenistan	18
31	Kazakhstan	14
32	Mongolia	4

**TABLE 4 : THE ASIAN REGION (WEST ASIA EXCLUDED)
PERCENT SHARE OF URBAN POPULATION 2000**

S.NO.	COUNTRIES	% URBAN POPULATION
1	Singapore	100
2	China Hong Kong SAR	95
3	Korea South	79
4	Japan	78
5	Taiwan	77
6	Brunei	67
7	Iran	63
8	Korea North	59
9	Malaysia	57
10	Kazakistan	56
11	Mongolia	52
12	Phillipines	47
13	Turkmenistan	44
14	Indonesia	39
15	Uzbekistan	38
16	Kyrgyzstan	34
17	Pakistan	33
18	Thailand	31
19	China	31
20	India	28
21	Tajikistan	27
22	Myanmar	26
23	Maldives	25
24	Vietnam	24
25	Sri Lanka	22
26	Bangladesh	20
27	Afghanistan	20
28	Laos	17
29	Cambodia	16
30	Bhutan	15
31	Nepal	11
32	East Timor	NA

**TABLE 5 : THE ASIAN REGION (WEST ASIA EXCLUDED)
PER CAPITA GNP, 1998 (US $)**

S.NO.	COUNTRIES	GNP
1	Japan	32350
2	Singapore	30170
3	Korea South	8600
4	Malaysia	3670
5	Thailand	2160
6	Iran	1650
7	Kazakistan	1340
8	Maldives	1130
9	Phillipines	1050
10	Uzbekistan	950
11	Sri Lanka	810
12	China	750
13	Indonesia	640
14	Pakistan	470
15	Bhutan	470
16	India	440
17	Kyrgyzstan	380
18	Mongolia	380
19	Tajikistan	370
20	Bangladesh	350
21	Vietnam	350
22	Laos	320
23	Cambodia	260
24	Nepal	210

Note: Data for other countries not available

**TABLE 6 : THE ASIAN REGION (WEST ASIA EXCLUDED)
POPULATION DOUBLING TIME (In years at Current Rates)**

S.NO.	COUNTRIES	DOUBLING TIME (YRS.)
1	Japan	462
2	China, Hong Kong SAR	256
3	Kazakistan	161
4	Taiwan	97
5	Singapore	84
6	Korea South	82
7	China	79
8	Thailand	70
9	Sri Lanka	60
10	Mongolia	50
11	Korea North	48
12	Vietnam	48
13	Turkmenistan	48
14	Iran	48
15	Kyrgyzstan	47
16	Indonesia	44
17	Tajikistan	43
18	Uzbekistan	40
19	East Timor	39
20	India	39
21	Bangladesh	38
22	Myanmar	35
23	Malaysia	34
24	Brunei	32
25	Phillipines	31
26	Nepal	28
27	Afghanistan	28
28	Cambodia	27
29	Laos	26
30	Pakistan	25
31	Maldives	23
32	Bhutan	22

TABLE 7 : THE ASIAN REGION (WEST ASIA EXCLUDED) BIRTH RATES (Birth/1000 Persons) 2000

S.NO.	COUNTRIES	BIRTH RATES
1	Afghanistan	43
2	Laos	41
3	Bhutan	40
4	Pakistan	39
5	Combodia	38
6	Nepal	36
7	Maldives	35
8	East Timor	34
9	Myanmar	30
10	Phillipines	29
11	Bangladesh	27
12	India	27
13	Brunei	25
14	Malaysia	25
15	Indonesia	24
16	Uzbekistan	23
17	Kyrgyzstan	22
18	Iran	21
19	Tajikistan	21
20	Turkmenistan	21
21	Korea North	21
22	Vietnam	20
23	Mongolia	20
24	Sri Lanka	18
25	Thailand	16
26	China	15
27	Kazakistan	14
28	Korea South	14
29	Singapore	13
30	Taiwan	13
31	Japan	09
32	China, Hong Kong SAR	07

**TABLE 8 : THE ASIAN REGION (WEST ASIA EXCLUDED)
TOTAL FERTILITY RATES, 2000**

S.NO.	COUNTRIES	TFR
1	Afghanistan	6.1
2	Bhutan	5.6
3	Pakistan	5.6
4	Laos	5.6
5	Maldives	5.4
6	Cambodia	5.3
7	Nepal	4.6
8	East Timor	4.6
9	Myanmar	3.8
10	Philippines	3.7
11	Brunei	3.4
12	India	3.3
13	Bangladesh	3.3
14	Malaysia	3.2
15	Iran	2.9
16	Uzbekistan	2.8
17	Kyrgyzstan	2.8
18	Indonesia	2.8
19	Tajikistan	2.7
20	Turkmenistan	2.5
21	Mongolia	2.5
22	Vietnam	2.5
23	Korea North	2.3
24	Sri Lanka	2.1
25	Thailand	1.9
26	China	1.8
27	Kazakistan	1.7
28	Taiwan	1.5
29	Korea South	1.5
30	Singapore	1.5
31	Japan	1.3
32	China, Hong Kong SAR	1.0

TABLE 9 : THE ASIAN REGION (WEST AND NORTH ASIA EXCLUDED)
DEATH RATES (No. of deaths per 1000 persons)

S.NO.	COUNTRIES	DEATH RATES
1.	Afghanistan	18
2.	East Timor	16
3.	Laos	15
4.	Cambodia	12
5.	Pakistan	11
6.	Nepal	11
7.	Kazakistan	10
8.	Myanmar	10
9.	India	09
10.	Bhutan	09
11.	Japan	08
12.	Bangladesh	08
13.	Indonesia	08
14.	Phillipines	07
15.	Kyrgyzstan	07
16.	Thailand	07
17.	Korea North	07
18.	Mongolia	07
19.	Urbekistan	06
20.	Turkmenistan	06
21.	Iran	06
22.	Sri Lanka	06
23.	Vietnam	06
24.	China	06
25.	Taiwan	06
26.	Maldives	05
27.	Tajakistan	05
28.	Malaysia	05
29.	Singapore	05
30.	Korea South	05
31.	China, Hong Kong SAR	05
32.	Brunei	03

TABLE 10 : THE ASIAN REGION (WEST AND NORTH ASIA
Infant Mortality Rates 2000

S.NO.	COUNTRIES	IMR
1.	Afghanistan	150
2.	East Timor	143
3.	Laos	104
4.	Pakistan	91
5.	Myanmar	83
6.	Bangladesh	82
7.	Cambodia	80
8.	Nepal	79
9.	India	72
10.	Bhutan	71
11.	Indonesia	46
12.	Vietnam	37
13.	Phillipines	35
14.	Mongolia	34
15.	Turkmenistan	33
16.	China	31
17.	Iran	31
18.	Tajikistan	28
19.	Maldives	27
20.	Korea North	26
21.	Kyrgyzstan	26
22.	Brunei	24
23.	Thailand	22
24.	Uzbekistan	22
25.	Kazakistan	21
26.	Sri Lanka	17
27.	Korea South	11
28.	Malaysia	0.8
29.	Taiwan	6.6
30.	Japan	3.5
31.	China Hong Kong SAR	3.2
32.	Singapore	3.1

TABLE 11 : THE ASIAN REGION (WEST ASIA EXCLUDED)
Life Expectancy, 2000

S.NO.	COUNTRIES	EXPECTATION OF LIFE (yrs.)
1.	Japan	81
2.	China Hong Kong SAR	80
3.	Singapore	78
4.	Taiwan	75
5.	Korea South	74
6.	Thailand	72
7.	Malaysia	72
8.	Sri Lanka	72
9.	Maldives	71
10.	Brunei	71
11.	China	71
12.	Korea North	70
13.	Uzbekistan	69
14.	Iran	69
15.	Tajikistan	68
16.	Phillipines	67
17.	Kyrgyzstan	67
18.	Vietnam	66
19.	Turkmenistan	66
20.	Bhutan	66
21.	Kazakistan	65
22.	Indonesia	64
23.	Mongolia	63
24.	India	61
25.	Pakistan	58
26.	Nepal	57
27.	Bangladesh	56
28.	Cambodia	56
29.	Myanmar	54
30.	Laos	51
31.	Afghanistan	46
32.	East Timor	46

TABLE 12 : THE ASIAN REGION (WEST ASIA EXCLUDED)
Natural Increase, 2000

S.NO.	COUNTRIES	NATURAL INCREASE
1.	Bhutan	3.1
2.	Maldives	3.0
3.	Pakistan	2.8
4.	Cambodia	2.6
5.	Laos	2.6
6.	Afghanistan	2.5
7.	Nepal	2.5
8.	Phillipines	2.3
9.	Brunei	2.2
10.	Malaysia	2.1
11.	Myanmar	2.0
12.	East Timor	1.8
13.	Bangladesh	1.8
14.	India	1.8
15.	Uzbekistan	1.7
16.	Tajikistan	1.6
17.	India	1.6
18.	Kyrgyzstan	1.5
19.	Turkdmenistan	1.5
20.	Korea North	1.5
21.	Iran	1.4
22.	Mongolia	1.4
23.	Vietnam	1.4
24.	Sri Lanka	1.2
25.	Thailand	1.0
26.	China	0.9
27.	Korea South	0.9
28.	Singapore	0.8
29.	Taiwan	0.7
30.	Kazakistan	0.4
31.	China, Hong Kong SAR	0.3
32.	Japan	0.2

TABLE 13 : THE ASIAN REGION (WEST ASIA EXCLUDED)
Percent of Married Women using Contraception

S.NO.	COUNTRIES	PERCENT MARRIED FEMALE CONTRACEPTION USERS
1.	China	83
2.	Korea South	77
3.	Vietnam	75
4.	Iran	73
5.	Thailand	72
6.	Sri Lanka	66
7.	Kazakistan	65
8.	Singapore	65
9.	Japan	64
10.	Kyrgyzstan	60
11.	Mongolia	57
12.	Indonesia	57
13.	Uzbekistan	56
14.	Philippines	49
15.	Bangladesh	49
16.	India	48
17.	Nepal	29
18.	Cambodia	22
19.	Tajikistan	21
20.	Turkmenistan	20
21.	Maldives	18
22.	Pakistan	18
23.	Myanmar	17
24.	Bhutan	08

Note: Data not available for other countries of the region.

TABLE 14 : THE ASIAN REGION (WEST ASIA EXCLUDED)
Index of Quality of Life

| COUNTRIES | CONVERTED SCORE | | | GNP PER CAPITA | INDEX OF QUALITY OF LIFE |
	IMR	TFR	% URBAN		
Singapore	100.0	90.2	100.1	93.2	95.8
Japan	99.8	94.1	75.2	100.0	92.2
China Hong Kong SAR	68.0	100.0	94.4	73.0	83.8
Taiwan	97.7	90.2	74.1	26.1	72.0
Korea South	94.7	90.2	76.4	26.1	71.8
Korea North	84.5	74.6	53.9	24.2	59.3
Kazakistan	87.9	86.3	50.6	3.5	57.1
Malaysia	96.7	56.9	51.7	10.8	54.0
Iran	81.1	62.7	58.4	4.5	51.7
Brunei	85.8	52.9	62.9	4.5	51.5
Mangolia	79.0	66.7	46.1	0.5	48.1
Turkmenistan	79.7	70.6	37.1	2.3	47.4
Thailand	78.0	82.4	22.5	6.1	47.2
Uzbekistan	87.2	64.7	30.3	2.3	46.1
Sri Lanka	90.6	78.4	12.3	1.9	45.8
China	69.0	84.3	22.5	1.7	44.4
Kyrgyzstan	84.5	64.7	25.8	0.5	43.9
Tajikistan	83.1	66.7	18.0	0.5	42.1
Indonesia	70.8	64.7	31.5	1.3	42.1
Philippines	78.3	47.1	40.4	2.6	42.1
Vietnam	63.0	70.6	14.6	0.4	37.1
India	53.1	54.9	19.1	0.7	31.9
Maldives	83.8	13.7	15.7	2.9	29.0
Bangladesh	46.3	54.9	10.1	0.4	27.9
Myanmar	45.6	45.1	16.8	0.2	26.9
Nepal	48.4	29.4	0.0	0.0	19.4
Pakistan	40.2	9.8	24.7	0.8	18.9
Cambodia	47.7	15.7	5.6	0.2	17.3
Bhutan	53.8	9.8	4.5	0.8	17.2
Laos	31.9	9.8	6.7	0.3	12.2
East Timor	4.8	29.4	6.7	0.3	10.3
Afghanistan	0.0	0.0	10.1	0.3	2.6

TABLE 15 : DISTRIBUTION OF ASIAN COUNTRIES ACCORDING TO THEIR LEVEL OF QUALITY OF LIFE

QUALITY OF LIFE	INDEX	NO. OF COUNTRIES	COUNTRIES
Very Good	≥ 80	03	Singapore Japan China, Hong Kong
Good	50 - 79	07	Taiwan Korea South Malaysia Kazakistan Iran Brunei
Average	30 - 49	12	Mongolia Turkmenistan Thailand Uzbekistan Sri Lanka China Kyrgyzstan Tajikistan Indonesia Philippines Vietnam India
Poor	15 - 29	07	Maldives Bangladesh Myanmar Nepal Pakistan Cambodia Bhutan
Very Poor	<15	03	Laos East Timor Afghanistan

TABLE 16 : COMPARATIVE POSITION: INDIA VS. VIETNAM

PARAMETERS	INDIA	VIETNAM
Birth Rate	27	20
Death Rate	09	06
Natural Increase	1.8	1.4
Doubling Time in Years at Current Rates	39	48
IMR	72	37
TFR	3.3	2.5
Percent Population		
<15	36	34
>65	04	06
Life Expectance		
Total	61	66
Male	60	63
Female	61	69
Percent Urban	28	24
Percent Married Women using Contraception	48	75
GNP (Per capita, 1998 US $)	440	350
Population per square mile	789	615

‹19›

Emerging Strategic Scenario in the Asia-Pacific
With special reference to the South-East Asian Nations Quest for Peace

*Pramod Mishra**

In the post-colonial phase of South-East Asia, out of a number of external powers like the US, China and the Soviet Union, the first has played a more predominant role. When with the sole objective of containing communism, the US formed a military alliance in South East Asia known as SEATO in September 1954, two states of the region — Philippines and Thailand joined as members. No doubt SEATO remained a very fragile and undependable arrangement. The US has also maintained a number of bilateral defence arrangements with a number of ASEAN countries like Singapore, Philippines and Thailand. China as another intrusive power in South-East Asia has always remained controversial in the region, although initially it was responsible for spearheading the communist movement in the Indo-China region (Vietnam, Laos and Cambodia), it has more often proved its nuisance value rather than playing any role to generate peace and stability in South-East Asia.

For the erstwhile Soviet Union, South-East has remained a low priority area in the post war period. Its main strategy in the region was the containment of US power, its global adversary.

* Fellow, Developing Countries Research Centre, University of Delhi, India.

Besides with the beginning of the Sino-Soviet rift, it also wanted to neutralize Chinese influence in the region. Besides, the growing pacific fleet of the Soviet Union wanted an opening to the Indian Ocean and the Persian Gulf through South-East Asia. But as we have emphasized earlier, the US remained the predominant power in South-East Asia and it continues its close linkage with the ASEAN at present.

ASEAN and ZOPFAN

In August 1967, five countries-Indonesia, Malaysia, Philippines, Singapore and Thailand launched the Association of Southeast Asian Nations in Bangkok to accelerate economic progress and increase the stability of the region. Its membership rose with the inclusion of Brunei (1984) and Vietnam (1995). By the close of the century, with the joining of Cambodia, Laos and Myanmar, it has completed a circle by taking in its fold all the ten South-East Asian States.

The Foreign Ministers of Indonesia Malaysia, Philippines, Singapore and the Special Envoy of the National Executive Council of Thailand in their meeting at Kuala Lumpur expressed a desire to bring about relaxation of international tension and achieving lasting peace in South East Asia. They recognized the right of every state large or small to lead its national existence free from outside interference in their internal affairs and took cognizance of the significant trend towards establishing nuclear-free zones in Latin America and Africa with the sole purpose to promote world peace and security by reducing the area of international conflicts and tensions. They agreed to secure the recognition of and respect for South East Asia as a Zone of Peace Freedom and Neutrality (ZOPFAN) free from any form of interference by outside powers. They also agreed to broaden the areas of cooperation which would contribute to their strength and close relationship. Thus by all means ZOPFAN provided a congenial backdrop to the quest of ASEAN states for a durable peace in the region free from any outside interference.

Treaty of Amity and Co-operation in South-East Asia

In the second ASEAN summit at Bali on February 1976, the five top leaders of the founding nations of ASEAN signed the Treaty of Amity and Cooperation in South-East Asia. It can be analyzed under four broad heads. First the basic purpose of the Treaty is to promote peace, and everlasting amity among their peoples on the basis of mutual respect for independence, sovereignty, equality, territorial identity of all nations, non-interference in the internal affairs of one another, settlement of disputes by peaceful means and renunciation of the threat or use of force.

The second part focuses on "Amity", thereby desiring " to develop and strengthen the traditionally cultural and historical ties of friendship, good neighbourliness and cooperation, which bind them together" and to "encourage and facilitate contact and intercourse among their peoples".

Third, they have given a special emphasis on "co-operation" amongst themselves in economic, cultural, technical, scientific and administrative fields" with the sole objective of linking development with security. Their purpose is to strengthen mutual co-operation on a bilateral basis and in the international scene on a multilateral basis. They are also very keen for "national resilience in all areas free from external interference on the one hand and "to achieve regional resilience, based on the principles of self-confidence, self-reliance, mutual respect, co-operation and solidarity" on the other.

Finally, they have resolved that all mutual disputes, which could disturb regional peace, should be settled by friendly negotiations, rather than taking resort to war. At the *Bali summit*, the Declaration of **ASEAN Concord** is also another significant step towards durable peace in the region.

APEC Paves the Way

With the active co-operation of the ASEAN states, Asia-Pacific Economic Co-operation (APEC) was launched in 1989 at

Canberra and it in turn paved the way for a regional security dialogue. One must take note of the fact that the so-called 'growth triangles' (China-Taiwan-Hongkong and Malaysia-Indonesia-Singapore) are forging particularly strong economic interdependencies.

APEC is seen by some observers as a framework in which security might ultimately be considered. In May 1993, the US Assistant Secretary of State, Winston Lord clearly admitted, that APEC helps anchor the USA in Asia, the implication being that this may have a spillover effect in the security field.

The signatories, while reaffirming the importance of NPT in preventing the proliferation of nuclear weapons, have recognized the right of any group of states to include regional treaties in order to assure the total absence of nuclear weapons in their respective territories. They are also determined to protect the region from environmental pollution and the hazards posed by radioactive wastes and other radioactive materials.

The SEANWFZ Treaty has twenty-two articles with an Annexe and a Protocol. Its major characteristics are as follows[5] : It bans the manufacture, acquiring, possession, transportation test or use of nuclear weapons within the territories (land, waters, seabed & airspace) of the ten states of South-East Asia, their respective continental shelves and Exclusive Economic Zones (EEZ). However, nothing in this Treaty shall prejudice the rights by any states under the provisions of the UN Convention on the Law of the Sea (1982) with regard to freedom of the high seas, rights of innocent passage of ships and air crafts within the territory of South-East Asia. Nothing in this Treaty shall prejudice the right of these of states to use nuclear energy by the signatory states must be under complete IAEA safeguards, to be signed by each party not later than eighteen months after the entry into force.

The administration of the Treaty provisions will be undertaken by establishing a Commission for SEANWFZ, where the Foreign Minister of each state-party will participate. Decisions of the Commission shall be taken by consensus, failing which, by a two-third majority of members present and voting. As a subsidiary organ of the Commission there will be an Executive Committee to ensure the proper administration of the Treaty and to ensure the control system.

As a sort of safety value some remedial measures to prevent any violation of the Treaty by any Party can be undertaken by the Commission after proper verification and reporting by the executive committee. It can also decide on any appropriate measure, including submission of the matter to IAEA and, where the situation might endanger international peace and security, to the Security Council and the General Assembly of the UN.

In case of any disputes arising from the interpretation of the Treaty, if within one month, the parties to the dispute are unable to achieve a peaceful settlement of the dispute by negotiation, mediation or conciliation, they can refer it to arbitration or to the International Court of Justice.

ARF - The Anchor of SEA Security

The ASEAN REGIONAL FORUM (ARF) was formally launched in Bangkok on 25th July, 1994, as a "forum for dialogue" in which members could exchange ideas about the Asia-Pacific region in particular and international politics and defence affairs in particular. It is an initiative mainly undertaken by the ASEAN to shape the security architecture not only of the Southeast Asian region, but also of the entire Asia-Pacific in the post-cold war period. This assured the ASEAN a crucial role in the decisions concerning the Pacific Rim, which is progressively emerging as the focus of development. Due to the substantial economic clout of the ASEAN region, it is natural that there would be growing military co-operation among the members' states of ARF, which would ultimately ensure that the 21st century is the Asia-Pacific century of ASEAN'S dreams.

When the ARF was launched under the chairmanship of Mr. Prasong Sonsire; the Foreign Minister of Thailand, the invitees included the Foreign Ministers of 18 countries. These were the six ASEAN states-Brunei, Indonesia, Malaysia, Singapore, Thailand and the Philippines; ASEAN's seven dialogue partners (Australia, New Zealand, Canada, South Korea, Japan, the United States and the European Union; the three observers (Papua New Ġuinea, Laos and Vietnam) and two consultative partners (China & Russia).

When the second ARF was held in Bandar Seri Begawan, Brunei on 1st August 1995 with Prince Mohammed Bolkiah, Brunei Foreign Minister as chairman, Vietnam had already joined as the seventh ASEAN member. Cambodia admitted as an observer in ASEAN also joined as a member of ARF on 28th July 1995. By this time, the focus of ARF had widened in the sense that from a simple forum for dialogue", it went for some inter-session activities through three sub-groups on confidence-building (jointly chaired by Indonesia and Japan); peace-keeping operations (jointly chaired by Malaysia and Canada) and maritime search and rescue operations (jointly chaired by Singapore and US). However, ARF still continued to go slow at a "measured peace". A "concept Paper" circulated by ASEAN in 1995 recommended on evolutionary approach to the problem of tackling security issues. It suggested three stages in which it could be tackled: promotion of confidence building measures, the development of preventive diplomacy mechanisms and development of conflict resolution mechanism. The third ARF in 1996 saw India and Myanmar joining as the two new members. The ASEAN members are very cautious not to expand the scope of the Asia-Pacific region beyond the Myanmar-India border and they would like their central security concerns confined to the South China Sea and the Korean Peninsula. If ARF expands further, it will become really difficult for ASEAN to retain the position of leadership in it.

There are many more countries interested to join the ARF as a dialogue partner. These include Mongolia, North-Korea, Pakistan, Kazakistan, and Kyrgyzstan and even European countries like France and U.K. But the ASEAN would like to go slow and take a measured stand on admitting new members.

Second Track Diplomacy

The quest for peace and security in South-East Asia is also attempted in other ASEAN related forums like to ASEAN Ministerial Meeting (AMM), and Post Ministerial Conference (PMC) and Council for Security and Co-operation in Asia-Pacific (CSCAP). For instance in AMM Joint Communiqué, the prominent Ministers of the ASEAN region also took cognizance of the increasing degree of comfort in the interactions among ARF participants. The ARF contacts are further supplemented by meetings at the PMC level. That forum of comfort in the interactions among ARF participants. The ARF contacts are further with a wider membership (beyond the ASEAN region) helps shape the security policy for the region.

The role of a non-governmental body like CSCAP also provides the ASEAN with innovative ideas regarding political and security co-operation in the region. The CSCAP was established in June 1993. It more or less functions as a parallel body to the ARF and supports the latter with useful insights. Many suggestions made here are finally adopted in the ARF. A link between Track One and Track Two activities is maintained through the Chairman of the ASEAN standing Committee. Thus the ARF continues with the advantages of the official, and the non-governmental with informal methods of functioning.

South-East-Asia Nuclear Weapon Free Zone Treaty: A Land mark for durable Peace.

The perusal of the ASEAN goal of ZOPFAN, was to fulfil its broad security objectives of speedily resolving the conflicts in the Korean Peninsula, the South China Sea and Cambodia and to prevent further proliferation of nuclear and chemical weapons. The ASEAN Heads of State or Government in their fifth summit meeting at Bangkok on 15th December, 1995, along with the seven ASEAN members, the representatives of three other South-East Asian States (Cambodia, Laos and Myanmar) signed the Treaty on the South-East Asia Nuclear Weapon Free Zone (SEANWFZ).

The Protocol to the Treaty shall be open for signature by China, France, Russia, UK & US. Each of these external nuclear powers after signing the Protocol shall undertake not to use or threaten to use nuclear weapons against any state-party to the Treaty. They will also undertake not to use nuclear weapons within the South-East Asia Nuclear Free Zone. Two external powers (China and US) have already raised some objections to the Treaty. China has reportedly objected to the Exclusive Economic Zones (EEZ) provisions, as it claims areas of the South China Sea regarded by ASEAN states as within their EEZ. Besides, both China and the US have reservations on the treaty provision regarding the entry of foreign ships and aircraft within the SEANWFZ area on the ground that it would potentially restrict their freedom to move nuclear-powered vessels or aircraft through the area.

‹20›

India in the Changing World in the Beginning of 21st Century

*Meyer Mikhail**

The irreversible trend towards globalization and liberalization of economy has opened new avenues for international interaction and dialogue on all levels, including the academic and scholarly efforts for cooperation in various fields of research. We view the future of the institution, I represent, as developing steadily in the direction of strengthening contacts with academic circles of various states in Asia and in the whole world and we estimate India as an important partner in this process. I am convinced, that organization of this conference in Delhi bears a symbolic significance: India, being one of the biggest democratic powers in Asia and in the world, is inevitably going to play an important role in the formation of the world order of the coming millennium.

Political developments in India always attracted close public attention in our country. In fact, Indo-Russian relationship proves that the close ties, which existed through years, have been preserved despite the calamities of history, and managed not only to survive, but also to strengthen, despite initial historical and geographical boundaries, and the impact of changing political situations, (including the crucial changes in geopolitical climate). We had a constant interest in India and its place in the changing

* Director, Institute of Asian and African Countries, Moscow State University, Moscow, Russia.

world with varying tendencies in political thinking. Despite obvious diversities in geography, history, political and social tradition, both states emerged through the changeover to democracy with a partition of a much larger state and has since then developed in the direction of creating multi-party competitive political systems.

India's political initiatives in the international sphere brought this country into the circle of the decision-making powers, whose political heritage and modern views are highly estimated and taken into consideration by the politicians and public opinion all over the world. The country with one million population' resource, with great economic potential and rich cultural and historical roots can't be neglected in the formation of new attitudes towards the models of political behavior of 21st century.

Indian civilization gave the world brilliant philosophers, whose invaluable contribution is a part of World High Philosophical Tradition and will remain the subject of scholarly studies for ages. It has cultural implications not only in the East, but also in the West. Indian civilization showed the world a certain mode of life based on humanity, charity, self-sacrifice, respect not only to human, but all living beings, on a certain state of soul, when an individual feels oneself as a part of nature, a part of the Universe. It is a constructive way of living and that is why it has a future. These ideas, inherent in Indian philosophy, are required in the actual socio-political sphere of today. They influence political and economic theories, bringing harmony into them and the feeling of unity of mankind; showing the relative merits of rival political theories and systems; measuring them in terms of upholding the moral and spiritual law; revealing their supremacy over disagreement and confrontation. Indian philosophers of the past reached a certain state of mind, which was purified from the feelings of antagonism and open to the universal feeling, that creates the proper basis for the relationship between peoples. Indian philosophical traditions are always associated with peace and wisdom and it is so important in our split societies.

.Philosophical traditions had a direct impact on Indian way of policy-making, which is of great value to politicians of nowadays. India gave bright examples of political thinking beginning from Kautilya and created a democratic political system, based on principles of common consent, unity and continuity of policy, demonstrating evolutionary type of development despite existing contradictions between political parties, leaders and social tensions, immanent to every multi-ethnic society.

India's history is a constant search for an optimal mode of political organization: from the maximum of centralization to the maximum of dispersion through various stages and forms between these two poles, demonstrating the flexibility of reformism and great potential of creating complex syncretic intermediate ideological systems.

India on the verge of the 21st century has changed greatly from the fifties - early seventies in the time of unlimited predominance of Congress party. The emerged system of alternative parties changing each other in power and the growing tendency for creating broad political coalitions, capable to fulfil ruling functions, makes the political experience of this country actual to Russia.

In India we face complicated coalitions of various types and levels: macro-coalitions and so-called "coalitions in coalitions". India underwent an evolution towards wide coalitions both on the central government level and on the regional by the verge of seventies - eighties and gained the experience of creating broad coalitions, uniting political parties of different ideological views - the experience that should be analyzed by Russian policy-makers. India has managed to pass through an inevitable strife for autonomy and separatism and kept its "unity in diversity". Experience in the field of maintaining relationship "center - states" is really a valuable one for multi-national federations like Russia.

India's role in the emerging order for regional peace and international security is growing steadily. The centrality of India's position in South Asia emerges from geographic, demographic and almost all other aspects of national power as defined in the modern world - resource base, population, size, GNP and so on. In the absence of a collective or even shared perspective on strategic and security issues, the only viable option for dealing with them, revolves around bilateral framework and approaches, except on issues global in nature, for example, nuclear issues and disarmament. All South-Asian countries, possessing the identical civilization basis, have a long continuum of cultural contacts and cooperative relationships, both in economics and politics, on one side, and a burden of contradictions, on the other. This duality in the political dialogue between neighbouring countries of the region, connected through centuries, created an ambivalent attitude toward India, a peculiar mixture of admiration and suspicion - the situation, reminding one of the experience of the relationship between Russia and the former republics of the Soviet Union, now transformed into independent states. The efforts of India in creating positive political climate in the region have become an important objective of analysis for Russian historians and politicians. Despite the difference in the construction and functioning of political regimes in South Asian states and the existing tensions between the countries of the region in economic and political fields, the tendency for unity in South Asia, surviving through the rivalry and represented by the activities of South Asian Association for Regional Cooperation (SAARC), may become a real force in strengthening the links between the political systems of the countries of the Indian Ocean area.

The 20th century was a period of intensive research on India both in East and West. Indian studies in Russia have a long history, beginning with Afanasy Nikitin, but real academic studies started in the late 19th - early 20th century, when the emphasis on ancient Indian studies in general and Sanskrit studies in particular, gradually shifted to the studies of contemporary Indian society as well. The tradition seems to have been started by Ivan Pavlovich Minaev, who is often called the founder of Russian indology. In any case, he was the first Russian professional indologist who traveled in India and left brilliant reminiscences of the then existing realities. He was an eminent scholar and his followers inherited his knowledge. The works of such prominent scholars as Scherbatsky, Rosenberg, Oldenburg, Vasilyev are well known all over the world. Indian philosophical traditions deeply influenced philosophers of Russia: references to them can be seen in the works of Solovyev, Rosanov, Berdyaev, Florensky. India inspired Russian poets and we can trace its motives in the poetry of the "Silver Age" in the verses of Gumilev, Brusov, Bunin, Balmont, Voloshin, Merezhkovsky, Blok, who at the same time became the poetical interpreters of Sanskrit and Pali texts and hymns and thus contributed to Indian s   t   u   d   i   e   s

The interests of the Russian Indological school were wide: the publication of the original texts in Sanskrit and Pali went together with the translations of canonical and uncanonical works by Russian scholars and their commentaries to them. The works of Russian scholars were far either from eurocentristic writings or from their alternative. They filled the gap between the Western and Eastern indological studies and revealed peculiar features of Indian culture, necessary for its adequate interpretation.

Soon followed the years when the traditions of Russian indology were, if not broken but blocked. Indological studies of the Soviet period passed through several stages in its development and they were in close connection with the changes in the socio-political climate in our country. Late fifties -early sixties opened new prospects to the scholars in social sciences and to the indologists as well.

Every epoch has its own specific interpretation of archives and other documents determined by the general look upon the historical events. Beginning of another important stage falls on the period we are now going through. This very stage has its distinguishing features and differs greatly from the previous one. Revaluation of the way our country has been developing for the last decades brought reestimation of the way in which our historiography interpreted the process of development of Asian civilizations, on a whole, and Indian, in particular. The most distinguishing feature of recent Russian historiography is its search for various methods of historical interpretation, its strife to overcome stereotypes, which were worked out by the established tradition of historiography, based on orthodox schemes. The discussion goes not only on the problems of 20th century India, there comes a revaluation of the whole process of the development of Indian civilization: the views that existed are becoming more flexible, more close to life.

An enormous amount of work is done in the field of Indological studies in our country. But such is the origin and the character of Indian culture that the last word in Indological studies will never be said. Every epoch, every new generation can reveal some particular features in it and every scholar can read and estimate it according to his own vision, his outlook.

We feel it our duty to contribute to these studies: the Department of South Asian History and the Department of Indian Philology in the Institute of Asian and African Studies have been functioning since the establishment of this institution in 1956; in 1991 the Centre of Indological and Buddhological Studies was formed on basis of the above mentioned Departments with the aims of coordinating scholarly efforts and research activities in the field of Indian civilization and Indo-Buddhist cultural tradition. CIBS has actively begun to cooperate with scholars from other departments of IAAS, as well as with scholars from other scientific bodies, such as Russian Academy of Sciences, Historical faculty of Moscow State University, the Russian University of Humanitarian Studies and others. The main objectives of CIBS are as follows: conducting research work in the field of Indo-Buddhist tradition, its history and origins, links and interactions with other religious, philosophical and cultural traditions inside India; incorporating the results of research work into educational process in the Institute of Asian and African studies; establishment of an indological library for scholars and students; establishing and maintaining links with similar educational, research and cultural institutions in Russia and abroad in form of conferences, exchange programs, joint publications, etc.

The coming millennium is going to be the era of international interaction and dialogue and we feel ourselves open to enlarge cooperation with the academic institutions and universities, interested in the problems of the development of Afro-Asian region and its role in the emerging global order. We recognize the benefits to be gained by all participating sides through the exchange programs aimed at promoting scholarly activities and international understanding.

‹21›

Globalisation & Importance of Investment in Human Capital and its Determinants

The essence of globalization are (a) spread of international trade in goods and commodities (b) free movement of labour across the countries (c) increase in monitization of exchange of goods (d) free flow of capital from one country to other. However the corner stone of new international economic order established by International Monetary Fund, World Bank and World Trade Organization comprises of (a) free flow of goods and (b) free flow of capital across the region of the globe (Chandra, 1999). These two dimensions of globalization have been derived from Factor Price Equalisation Theorem. This particular trend in the new international economic order, however ignores an essential component of globalization i.e. free flow of movement of labour across the countries. Hence the process of globalization has failed to recognize the benefit of free movement of skilled and unskilled labour.

The Human Development Report 1999 states that the benefit of globalization has not spread evenly among the nations and within the nation. It has in fact worsened the inequalities in income and employment. Therefore, there is a need to analyze the emerging trend in the labour market in India and to have the necessary prescription to overcome the challenges

---

* Senior Lecturer in Economics, Arunachal University, Itanagar, Arunachal Pradesh, India.

posed by the process of globalization. Here in this paper an attempt has been made (a) to analyze the linkage between liberalization and employment ; (b) to examine the importance and impact of human capital on employment in the globalization era; (c) to evaluate the determinants of investment in human capital taking micro level data from Rural Orissa.

Liberalization and Employment :

The relationship between liberalization and employment can be looked in two ways ;(a) whether existing labour market conditions strengthen liberalization; and (b) how liberalization affects employment and labour market (Dev, 2000 b). In the context of developing economy, we shall attempt the second approach to analyse the impact of liberalization on employment. Under the liberalization measures, structural adjustment aims at removal of rigidities and factor price distortions in the economy which would change the industry mix and factor mix in favour of labour (Bhagabati and Srinivasan, 1993; Joshi and Little, 1996). This structural adjustment measures theoretically aims at a shift towards the demand of labour intensive product in a labour abundant economy. This conclusion is mainly derived from Hecker-Ohlin and Stopler - Samuelson Theorem.

In India, organized sector employment constitutes only 8% and the unorganized sector accounts for 92% of the total employment. It was reported that during the period 1977-78 to 1993-94, employment elasticity in organized sector has been declining and that of unorganized sector increasing (Chakravarty 1999). In the study of Kundu (1997), it was reported that 'usual status' workforce participation has declined and current 'daily status' employment has increased during the period 1977-78 to 1993-94. These trends suggest that after economic liberalization which started in mid 80s, the employment generated are of 'casual' type.

In the context of liberalization the employment study of Chadha (1999) is more disaggregative, in terms of rural and urban. This study reported that in rural unorganized manufacturing sector, employment grew negatively during 1989-90 to 1994-95. Further desegregating the rural unorganized manufacturing sector it was found that during the same period employment fell about 3% in agro-based manufacturing, grew by less than 1% in non agro-based manufacturing, grew by less than 1% in non agro-based manufacturing and fell by 2% per annum in total manufacturing. In contrast urban unorganized manufacturing suffered a relatively lower degree of job loss.

The study of Dev (2000a) is important in terms of quality of employment generated in the post liberalization era. The conclusions that he derived are (a) there was no reduction in employment growth in total (b) there was no increase in unemployment rate (c) educated employment has been declining (d) the rate of growth in rural non-farm employment has declined (e) the quality of employment deteriorated due to casualization of labour.

The above studies give some trend in the emerging labour market in India. Casualities of labour and decline in rural non-farm sector employment during liberalization, are the two conclusions that can be derived from the above studies.

Future of Labour Employment:

IT Sector: With the spread of information technology in the era of globalization there is no need of movement of skilled labour across the region. India stands now one of the leading exporter of information technology and at present exporting nearly Rs. 1800 crore of IT product to the World market. Almost all the countries of the World are now experiencing a shift towards skilled work force in their employment structure (Dev, 2000b). Following table gives the detail account of shift that has taken place in the share of skilled worker in manufacturing workforce.

TABLE - 1: Share of Highskilled subsector in Manufacturing employment (%)

COUNTRY	1980	1995
India	30	34.6
HongKong	36.8	38.6
South Korea	33.5	52.3
Malayasia	36.2	51.2
Philippines	23.7	26.4
Singapore	62.8	77.6
Taiwan	39.1	49.6

Source : International Labour Organisation, as reproduced in Dev, 2000c

The table shows that the high skilled sector in the world economy is an emerging area where employment can be generated. The shift in workforce in favour of high skilled worker is not so high in India as compared to the East Asian Economies.

Agriculture :

The traditional agriculture and allied activities is still the dominant sector in the Indian economy. Being a signatory to World Trade Organization India has to liberalise its agriculture sector and open it to the world market. This would lead to a change in new cropping pattern and greater commercialization of agriculture. The rural agro-based activities are also likely to play a dominant role in the era of competition.

The research in this area shows that a reverse shift in employment from nonfarm activities to agricultural activities is taking place in the liberalization era (Chakravarty 1999). Sen (1999) argued that the non-farm activities which grew in the 80s was mainly due to heavy public expenditure in India. Now during the liberalization era the government is likely to retreat from private goods sector. Therefore an alternative mechanism has to be thought out such that the non-agriculture sector grows at a faster rate.

Human Capital and its Importance :

In the year 1960, Prof T.W. Schultz in his presidential address to the American Economic Association said *'Although it is obvious that people acquire useful skills and knowledge, it is not obvious that these skill and knowledge are a form of capital, that this capital is in substantial part of a product of deliberate investment, that it has grown in Western societies at a much faster rate than conventional (non-human) capital, and that its growth may well be the most distinctive feature of the economic system. It has been widely observed that increase in national output have been large compared with the increase of land, man-hours and physical capital probably the explanation for this difference'* (Schultz, 1961).

The above statement of Schultz reflects the importance of investment in human capital. During the last forty years theory of Economic growth has evolved to a stage, where the importance of investment in human capital has been recognized as the main engine behind the growth of many economies (Romer, 1986; Lucas, 1993). Lucas is trying to explain the miracle of East-Asian economies concluded that 'The main engine of growth is the accumulation of capital- of knowledge - and the source of difference of living standards among nations is the difference in human capital' (Lucas, ibid.). Considering the importance of human capital in economic growth the World Bank in a policy document on 'Reducing Poverty in India' comes to the conclusion that a one year increase in average education of the workforce can raise output by 13 percent and that the increased educational level can contribute around one-quarter of the increase in economic output. Farm based production function shows that in agriculture, education helps increase output by increasing the adoption of new technology and farming practices (World Bank, 1998).

In the context of growth of non-farm employment, the impact of education is quite high. In the study of six villages of Mehsana district of Gujarat , Unni (1996) examines the influence of individual, household and community characteristics on the likelihood that an individual, would be employed in the non-farm sector, as well as on the earning of such individual from such employment. Unnis' finding clearly suggests that education is the critical factor influencing both employment opportunities and earning from non-farm activities.

Education and its Contribution to Economic Growth

The contribution of education to economic growth has also been documented in many studies. World Bank (1993) documented the contribution of Primary education to East-Asian economies as follows:

TABLE 2

Country	Contribution of Primary Education to Economic Growth (%)
Thailand	87
Hongkong	86
Indonesia	79
Singapore	75
Malaysia	73
Taiwan, China	69
South Korea	58
Japan	58

Source: World Bank, 1993: as reproduced in Haq et el., 1998

The above table shows the tremendous contribution of Education to economic growth in South-Asian countries. In the case of India the contribution of education to economic growth was only 27% as computed by Loh (1995).

Education and Foreign Investment :

Multinational Enterprise posses advance knowledge which enables them to introduce new capital goods with a low cost technology. Some time the absorption of technology is limited by the quality of human capital. In a study of sixty-nine countries Borensztein, Gregorio and Lee (1998) found a positive association between level of secondary schooling and flow of Foreign Direct Investment. In India quality of human capital in terms of secondary schooling enrolment rate is 59% as compared to 93% of South Korea. This poor quality of human capital acts as an hindrance to FDI.

Determinants of Secondary Schooling:

It is clear that the quality of labour force has been cited in many analysis as one of the retarding force in the economic growth of India (Chadha, 1999; Ramaswamy, 1999). The secondary schooling which enhances the quality of labour force, plays an important role in economic growth of any country. In India secondary school enrolment rate is 59%. Here in this section an attempt has been made to find out the determinants of secondary schooling taking the data collected from two villages of Orissa.

The human capital approach to education emphasizes market determined value of education as the main determinant of individual demand for education (Schultz, 1988). However, some non-market forces play an important role in demand for education especially for children and adolescent and these non-market forces are manifested through household characteristics, which affect the time and opportunity cost of schooling (Handa 1996).

Taking a lead from Handa the demand for children's education can be derived from Backer-Lewis model of household decision making. Here the problem of the household is to maximise.

$$U\ (X_i,\ Z_i) \dotfill (1)$$

$$\text{Subject to } P_{xi}\ X_i\ +\ WL\ =\ WT\ +\ Y \dotfill (2)$$

$$\text{And } Z_i\ =\ Z_i\ (X.t.\ \Omega) \dotfill (3)$$

Here, the household is consuming two goods X and Z. U is the utility function of the household. X is the market and Z is the non-market goods. Equation (2) represents the income constraint of the household where P_{xi} = Price of Market goods X_i, w = Wage rate, L = Leisure , T = Time available and Y is the unearned income of the household, such as income derived from property, asset, dividends, etc.

The problem lies with the Z goods which is the non-market goods like children's education and health, etc. Non market goods are produced by the household and the production function is represented by equation (3). The inputs to these non-market goods are market-purchased intermediate goods and time input of the family and the efficiency parameter of the household represented by Ω. This Z function is a twice differentiable function represented by

$$Z_i = Z_i (X,t,\Omega) \text{ and } Z_i^1(X,t,\Omega) > 0, Z^{11}_i (X,t,\Omega) < 0 \dots\dots\dots (4)$$

where, I = 1.........n and n the number of non-market goods produced and consumed by the household.

By solving the above equations, the demand for Z_i can be obtained which will give the optimal level of consumption of Z goods. Here children's schooling (which is a Z-goods) demand function can be derived, which will be an increasing function of its cost. Household characteristics that increases the cost (or decrease the benefits) of educating a child will lower the household demand for education (Handa, 1996). Here the paper will use this approach and see how the household characteristics determine the demand for schooling.

Data :

Data for this analysis was collected from two randomly selected villages in Sambalpur District of Orissa. A questionnaire was used for the preliminary survey regarding the primary schooling attainment of the village. This preliminary survey was done for the PhD work of the investigator in January 1998. The households were contacted personally by the investigator randomly. The information regarding parents' education, child's age and schooling, caste, sex of the child, family size, land holding of the household, major source of income etc. were collected.

Determinants: Here from the data collected from the households, we exclude the children in the age group 0-13. The data that are used here is for the children in the age group 14-18, who are the potential entrants to the workforce. The analysis has found that only 197 children out of 283 have ever been enrolled in the school and 97 were never enrolled in school. Therefore the dependent variable is a binary variable which takes the value '1' if the child is ever enrolled in school and '0' if he is never enrolled. The explanatory variables are (1) Age of the child (AGE); (2) Adult more than 60 years of age (ADLT60); (3) Caste (CAST which takes value '1' in case of ST/SC and '0' otherwise; (4) Children less than 5 years of age (CHIL5); (5) Family size (FAMSIZE); (6) Father education (FATHEDN); (7) Fathers' age (FAITHAGE); (8) Female headed household (FHH), which takes value '1' if the household head is a female and '0' otherwise; (9) Land operated (LANDOPER); (10) Livestock owned by the household (LISTOCK); (11) Ln of Per capita income (LNPCI); (12) Mother's age (MAGE), (13)Mothers education (MOTHEDN); (14) Non farm income as a percentage of total income (NOFINPER) ; (15) Sex of the child (SEX), takes value '1' in case of male and '0' in case of male.

LOGIT analysis : The dependent variable is a binary variable takes value '0' and '1'. Therefore LOGIT analysis has been used to find out the determinants of enrolment in secondary school. The estimated education is given in table '3'.

TABLE-3

Dependent = 1, if the child is ever enrolled in school
Dependent = 0, if the child is not ever enrolled in school

Explanatory Variable	Coefficient	'T' value	
CONSTANT	-1.648	-11.368	* * *
AGE	-0.055	-11.59	* * *
ADLT 60	.054	4.34	* * *
CAST	0.278	11.21	* * *
CHIL5	0.09	6.32	* * *
FAMSIZE	-0.09	6.31	* * *
FATHEDN	0.063	10.096	* * *
FATHAGE	-0.002	-1.602	*
FHH	0.197	9.53	* * *
LANDOPER	0.005	1.418	
LISTOCK	0.018	9.458	* * *
LNPCI	0.037	2.384	* *
MOTHAGE	0.003	2.037	* *
MOTHEDN	-0.11	-10.488	* * *
NOFINPER	0.0018	4.61	* * *
SEX	0.06	4.45	* * *

Chi-square = 32885.997***, DF = 264

*** 99% level of significance

** 95% level of significance

* 90% level of significance

The above equation is a good fit of our model since the chi-square value is highly significant. The probability if a child's enrolment in the secondary school is positively linked with caste, number of children less then five years of age, father' education, female headed household, livestock, per capita income, mothers' education, non-farm income as a percentage of income and gender of the child. The positive sign of the variables CAST, FHH, and SEX shows that there is discrimination against ST/SC, discrimination against the child coming from female headed household and gender discrimination against the girl child in enrolment in secondary school. The important variables that affect the probability of secondary school enrolment are LANDOPER (not significant), LISTOCK, LNIPCI, NOFINPER. Therefore it may be concluded that diversified income in the household in favour of non-farm income increases the chances of children's enrolment in secondary school.

Conclusion :

The above analysis shows that investment in human capital in the form of schooling plays an important role in the era of globalization. The countries which are better of in schooling have performed well in economic growth. Schooling is the prerequisite condition to reap the benefit of globalization. The East-Asian miracle shows that growth generated through investment in human capital is higher than the growth generated through investment in non-human capital. Therefore, the micro determinants of schooling is very important in the formulation of human capital policy of any country in the days of globalization.

Considering the need and diversity of a country like India, the state cannot afford to provide a good where the Social Rate of Return (SRR) is less than the Private Rate of Return (SRR) is less than the Private Rate of Return (PRR). It is a established fact that secondary and tertiary education have a lesser SRR and a higher PRR than primary education. The provision of Education as a public goods in India is highly skewed in favour of secondary and tertiary education. In the days of globalization of government is likely to withdraw from secondary and tertiary education in favour of primary education. Therefore the demand side of secondary schooling needs more analysis and attention in the era of globalization.

References :

1. Bagchi, A.K., (1999): "Globalization, Liberalization and Vulnerability" *Economic and Political Weekly*, Vol. 34, No. 45, PP. 3219-3230.

2. Becker, G. (1981). 'A Treatise on the Family' Cambridge: MA Harvard University Press.

3. Bhagbati, J. and T.N. Srinivasan, (1993): India's Economic Reforms, *Ministry of Finance*, Government of India, New Delhi.

4. Borensztein, Gregorid and Lee, (1998): "How does Foreign Direct Investment

   Affect Economic Growth", *Journal of Development Economics*, Vol. 45, No. 1.

5. Chadha, G.K., (1999): "Trade Technology and Employment : Some missing Links in India's Rural Economy" *Indian Journal of Labour Economics*, Vol. 42, No. 4, pp. 881-908.

6. Chakravarty, Deepita., (1999): "Labour Market Under Trade Liberalization in India : Some issues concerning Reallocation" *Economic and Political Weekly*, Vol.34, No.48, PP. M.163-168.

7. Chandra, N.K., (1999): "Economic Growth and Sustainable Development in China" *Economic and Political Weekly*, Vol. 34, No. 45, PP. 3195-3212.

8. Dev, S. Mahendra.,(2000a):, "Economic Liberalization and Employment in South Asia - I" *Economic and Political Weekly*, Vol. 35, No. 1&2, pp. 40-51.

9. —————————————(2000b): "Economic Liberalization and Employment in South Asia-II" *Economic and Political weekly*, Vol. 35, No. 3, pp. 135-46.

10. —————————————(2000): "Economic Reforms, Poverty, Income Distribution, and Employment", *Economic and Political Weekly*, March-4, pp. 823-835.

11. Handa, Sudhansu (1996) "The Determinants of Teenage Schooling in Jamaica : Rich Vs. Poor, Female Vs. Male', *The Journal of Development Studies*, Vol. 32, No. 4, pp. 554-580.

12. Haq, M.Q. and K.Haq,(1998): Human Development in South Asia, Oxford University Press, Karachi.

13. Joshi, Vijay and I.M.D. Little, (1996): India's Economic Reforms: 1991-2000, Oxford University Press, Delhi.

14. Kundu, Amitabh.,(1997): "Trend and Structure of Employment in the 1990s, *Economic and Political Weekly*, Vol. 32, No. 24, PP. 1399-05.

15. Lucas, R.E., (1993): "Making A Miracle", *Econometrica*, Vol. 61, No. 2, PP. 251-272.

16. Majumdar, Tapas., (1997-98): " Economics of Indian Education for the next Century", *The Indian Economic Journal*, Vol. 45, No. 4, PP. 39-48.

17. Ramaswamy, K.V., (1999): "Exporting in a Globalized Economy" in K.S. Parikh ed.,India Development Report 1999-2000, Oxford University Press, New Delhi, pp. 191-200.

18. Romer,P.M.(1994): "The Origin of Endogenous Growth", *Journal of Economic Perspective*, Vol. 8, No. 1, pp. 3-22.

19. Schultz, T.W., (1961): "Investment in Human Capital", *The American Economic Review*, Vol. L1, No.1, PP. 1-17.

20. Schultz, T.P. (1988). *'Education Investments and Returns'* in H. Chenery and T.N. Srinivasan (ed) handbook of Development Economics, Vol. 1, Amsterdam, North Holland.

21. Unni, Jemmol., (1996): " Diversification of Economic Activities and Non-Agricultural Employment in Rural Gujarat" *Economic and Political Weekly*, Vol. 31, No. 33, pp. 2241-2251.

22. World Bank, (1998): "Reducing Poverty In India: Options for more effective Public Services", World Bank, Washington DC.

‹22›

Globalisation, Ethnicity and Ethnic Entrepreneurship in Asian Countries

*Govinda Chandra Rath**

The present paper traces a link between the widely said globalization and the concurrent trend of emerging ethnicity in Asian countries in its socio-economic paradigms. It further discerns how the innate power of various social communities makes them functional with maintaining their distinctiveness in one situation and face change in their life pattern in another situation in the course of their interaction with the larger economic processes of the world. In this context, the ethnic involvement in both the traditional and modern trades will be analysed from the larger perspective of globalization.

Prime Trend of Globalization

Globalization has been presented as that complex process of Europeanization that exerts uniform influence in the world's production process and at the same time induces a change in the world society too. The conventional definition of globalization ushered in a new phase in 1980s when it was replaced with new terms like 'internationalization' and 'Trans-nationalization' emphasizing on the operation of production on a cross-border basis and increasing interweaving of national economies through international trade. The later studies cast doubt on the complete integration, interdependence and openness of national

* Senior Lecturer, G.B. Pant Social Science Institute, Allahabad, Uttar Pradesh, India.

economies as the consequences of globalization. These studies conclude that the leading OECD economies concerns for international business are still largely confined to their home territory in terms of their overall business activities[1]. According to Ankie Hoogvelt the geographical reach of world capitalism has actually receded in the last decades of globalization. The percentage share of Latin America and Africa in world trade has, for instance, continuously been declining and with the same spirit, the global foreign investment in these countries has also receded since the colonial period. He says that expansive phase of world capitalism is now over; the extension of fundamentals of economic activities namely trades and productive investment into more and more areas of the globe at a standstill. The condition is now deepening, capital integration is not widening. Specifically in 1980s, the financial revolution was accompanied not merely by the powerful advances in telecommunications and information technology, but also disconnected from social relationships in which money and wealth were previously embedded. He underlines correctly, "It is because of this 'disembedding' that globalization entails a process of intensification of linkages within the core of the global system, while its counterpart 'peripheralisation' becomes a process of marginalization and expulsion that cuts across territories and national boundaries, rendering areas within the traditional core subject to the same processes of expulsion as large swathes of territories in Africa, Latin America and Asia. Hence the structure of core-periphery becomes a social division, rather than a geographic one."[2]

The economics of globalization provide a set of principles inducing a new order in the economic activities throughout the world. A global market principle comes into practice for smooth operation of the world economy. The earlier distance and location no longer becomes relevant in the present production and trade system because of annihilation of space through time compression. This results in easy and rapid movement of produced items from one place to another. The international mobility of money brings a further boost to this process. The shrinking of the world to a 'global village' produces definite social consequences. Giddens sums it up in the following way:

> "Globalization can thus be defined as the intensification of world wide social relations which link distant localities in such a way that local happenings are shaped by events occurring many miles away and vice versa."[3]

This cross-border social network is closely associated with the cross-border organization of economic production. The expansion in social space gives birth to the 'imagined' communities, cultures, and systems of authority and method of social control that crosses the border. It is the example of unification of the world humanity along the maintenance of distinct socio-cultural characteristics. Robertson analysed the cultural undertone of globalization identifying two of its predominant aspects, namely 'compression of the world' and 'global consciousness'. The compression of the world refers to the organic integration of human life with the world economy in such a way that any occurrence among the people of one area has immediate repercussions on the people of other side. This world compression intensifies 'global consciousness' which finds manifestation in the people's collective concern for world peace, 'human rights', 'issues of pollution' and other important facets of global life[4].

The history of the socio-political dimension of globalization may be traced back to the post-World War development. The emergence of nation-state was the significant phenomenon in this period, which not only brought out freedom in political participation but also expanded economic progress by making policies for large-scale industrialization. At the consequence level, the agenda of nation-state expressed concern for existing inequality in the society and involved in construction of a mainstream for fostering a general equality among the people of the state. The goal of this mainstream remained unfulfilled and it kept many of the social groups within the state apart; some of them were numerically a minority and some others were numerically a majority but politically marginalized. The people from both the categories emerged as a conscious social group resisting their ill representation in the constructed national mainstream. The emergence of ethnicity is the issue of this alienated group of people.

Understanding Ethnicity

For some scholars ethnic unit is a comparatively small community with a predominantly archaic character[5], which most probably refers to the tribal societies. A group of anthropologists of former USSR contradicted this view and argued that the term included not only small communities but also the members of larger social groups, embracing the primitive, backward people as well as the people from highly industrialized or 'developed' countries[6]. Besides the issue of the size, of the ethnic group is characterized with the number of cultural attributes. It is broadly 'defined as a historically formed aggregate of people having a real or imaginary association with a specified territory, a shared cluster of beliefs and values connoting its distinctiveness in relation to similar groups and recognized as such by others[7].

The term ethnicity has different connotations. To me it is a device of acquiring the political and economic share from the leading social groups, who have been dominating in the state process. Ethnicity then becomes the medium of group mobilization where the ethnic symbols are used as the base of socio-cultural and politico-economic purposes. In the cross-border situation, the formation of ethnicity precedes the migratory experience, the behaviour of the host country then stimulates the emergence of ethnicity. Particularly in the multi-ethnic nation-state, the ethnic attributes refer to differences between categories of people. The higher the concentration of multi-ethnic communities, larger the impulse of making differences between the ethnic groups.

The term ethnicity is most favoured and popular in USA, as the country is made up of a variety of people 'uprooted' or 'dislodged' from different nations. Here ethnicity is related more to the survival strategy than the simple political assertion.

Yancey et al correctly observe:

Ethnicity may have relatively little to do with Europe, Asia or Africa, but more to do with the requirements of survival and the structure of opportunity in this country[8].

The situation of Asian countries is different to USA in the context of emergence of nationhood. Oomen has observed that the issue of nationality is stronger in the US as compared to the Asian countries. The process of state formation has not yet been completed in Asian countries. As a result, assertion of national identity based on conventional categories like religion, language, region, tribe and so on are considered as 'communal', 'parochial' and even 'anti-national'[9]. In this context, the state identity remains above the ethnic identity although the force of 'sub-nationalism' or 'ethno-nationalism' is active in many parts of the Asian countries at present. Yet, it will not be correct to say that the ethnicity in the Asian state is always manifested in the form of collective movement for establishment of an exclusive ethnic-state. Ethnicity is also manifested in a variety of forms of activities ranging from the sphere of culture to business.

Migration and Ethnicity in Asia

The ethnic situation in Asian countries is based on the historic migration, both within these countries, as well as from the non-Asian countries. There was migration in prehistoric as well as in modern times. The centres of prehistoric migration were Southwest Asia and a region comprising the Mongolian plateaus and North China. Asiatic migration movements have always treaded primarily towards Southeast Asia. From Southwest Asia migration took place towards Central Asia, India and the European peninsula. Over a period of time, there occurred mixing of early European and Asiatic people in Central and West Asia. European migration to East Asia is evidenced by the present survival of the indigenous inhabitants of Japan known as the Ainu, who are considered to be the descendants of the European migrants. It is believed that the modern Japanese have taken birth from the intermixing of the early Asiatic migrants of Southeast Asia into Southern Korea and Japan with later Asiatic and Ainu people. Thus Asian regions have witnessed a complex pattern of ethnic identity and distribution of varying intermixing of regionally derived groupings. However, till the advent of the western powers, the migrants had already enriched the cultural diversities of Asia as well as integrated in its millennia the old civilization.

The modern movement of the migration cites that Russians penetrated into Central Asia and Western Europeans penetrated into the oceanic fringes of South and East Asia during the period of European imperialism. Seventeenth century onwards, inbreeding between host and migrant population produced ethnic mixture including Anglo-Indians of India and Burghers of Sri Lanka. The settlement of Chinese immigrants with the local women produced many hybrid peoples in Indonesia, Malaysia, Thailand and Philippines. The ethnic mosaic in China, Korea, Japan, Vietnam and the Philippines became further complicated because of entry of American white and black soldiers to East and Southeast Asia during and after World War II[10].

The ethnic diversity at present is at a primary stage in many parts of South Asian countries. Among them, the least populated state of the Maldives has the maximum degree of ethnic homogeneity followed by Bangladesh, Pakistan, Nepal, Bhutan and Sri Lanka. India is the country where, there prevails maximum ethnic heterogeneity.

Schermerhom lists Scheduled Castes, Scheduled Tribes, Jains, Jews, Sikhs, Muslims, Christians, Anglo-Indians, Parsees and Chinese as ten of the minorities as ethnic groups in India[11]. He excludes linguistic minorities. According to him, these linguistic groups are very fractionalized in nature that makes it impossible to treat them on societal basis. The Indian ethnic groups are mainly characterized by the attributes, of race, religion, tribe and language. Often many of the tribal groups integrate into a common ethnic group, e.g. Naga, Mizo or

Meiti community. Similarly many dialects merged into standardized language group like Tamil, Telugu, Malayalam, Kannada, Nepali, Bengali, Oriya and Assamese. A number of religious groups developed into ethnically self-conscious communities, e.g. Muslim, Sikhs and Parsees.

The ethnic diversity of Pakistan consists of four major ethnic communities, e.g., Punjabis, Pathans, Baluchis and Sindhis. The Punjabis are numerically predominant in Pakistan accounting for about two-third of the total population. They faced strong resistance from Sindhis, Pushtoons, Balochs and Seraikis who thronged into a conference at Islamabad in 1998 and decided to launch "Pakistan Opressed Nations Movement (PONM). They stressed on releasing themselves from the utter domination of the Punjabis. The conference issued a joint statement termed as "Islamabad Declaration" insisting on the split of Pakistan into five nations of Punjabis, Sindhis, Baluchs, Pushtoons and Seraikis with autonomous and sovereign power[12].

The ethnic structure in Bangladesh is more homogenous to that of Pakistan. There are around 86 per cent Bengali Muslims in this country. The main tribal ethnic communities that constitute one per cent, less than a million, are the Chakmas, the Marmas (Maghs), the Tipperas (Tipras) and the Mros (Moorangs). In its border country of Bhutan, the Bhotias of Tibetan origin who migrated following the political upheaval in Tibet, the earlier immigrant Ngalops and Sharchops the major inhabitants of Indo-Mongoloid origin contribute to the ethnic diversity.

The population in Nepal is threefold 'Mongoloid' or Tibeto-Burman', Indo-Aryan' and 'Austro-Asiatic'. The existing ethnic groups are the Newars, Magars, Tamangs, and Gurungs who foster both Hindu and Buddhist religions. The non-Tarai region of Nepal is inhabited by a larger number of Hindus comprising about half the population and the Tarai Hindus are only one-fourth of the population. The Tamangs with the Kiratis are five per cent; Newars as well as Tharus are about four per cent each of the total population. The Tarai Hindus are speakers of many Hindi dialects including Maithili, Bhojpuri, Awadhi etc. The Tharu tribe is mainly concentrated in the forest belt of the Tarai. The Newaris are believed to be an autonomous group of Nepal. The Muslim community of Nepal has migrated from the south at various times.

The Island State of Sri Lanka has experienced the ethnic diversity in the process of colonization. The Veddahas are the indigenous population of the country, who are no more than a few thousand individuals. The larger share of population is of the Sinhalese about 74 per cent claiming Aryan descent and Tamils are 18 per cent claiming Dravidian descent. Indian migration to Sri Lanka has been the ongoing phenomenon for centuries. This migration has changed the mosaic of the ethnic structure of Sri Lanka. It is believed that more than 90 per cent of Sri Lankans have Indian antecedents. The migration of Arab traders forms a larger part of the Muslim community in the country. The population of Burghers in the country originates from the intermarriage between natives and Portuguese as well as Dutch colonists.

The intensity of ethnic diversity in Central Asia became transparent with the dissolution of Soviet Russia on December 21, 1991. The six states, i.e. Kazakhstan, Uzbekistan, Turkmenistan, Tajikstan and Kyrgyzstan emerged as sovereign independent nation -state known as Central Asian States. Many of the descendants of the ethnic groups of these states are the German migrants who migrated in 16th, 17th and 18th centuries and scattered across the CIS countries, mainly Kazakhstan (960,000), Russia (859,000), Kyrgystan (102,000), Uzbekistan (40,000) and Ukraine (38,000). Since the implementation of glasnost and perestroika in 1989 a large number of ethnic Germans in Soviet Russia started to return to their home country. Germany has taken almost 690,000 of them. One long-term objective is to re-establish the autonomous Volga republic, which was wiped out by Joseph Stalin after Germany attacked the former Soviet Union in 1941, with 40,000 Volga Germans removed to Central Asia. The migration that leads to growing up of ethnic consciousness also becomes the cause of creating a challenge for the nation-state.

Recently, China apprehended the rise of separatism in its sensitive border province of Xinjiang where 70 lakh Ughyurs live. They are the largest single ethnic group in the province. Their places of concentration are Kashgar, Hotan, Southeast of Kashgar along with Turpan and Hami, which are not far from Central Asian border with Kazakhstan. The province has huge reserves of oil at around 20.8 billion and natural gas at 10.3 billion cubic meters, which is likely to emerge as an economic powerhouse in the future. The Ughyurs along with the Han Chinese have now expressed their need for a new state and sovereign after separation from China.

Thus, ethnic diversity and ethnic consciousness of separate state is a widely prevalent phenomenon in the Asian countries. The societal and cultural basis provide the predominant support to the ethnic configuration. This is one part of the story of the emergence and survival of ethnicity in Asian region. Another part of the story is the inter and intra aspects of ethnic integration in development of entrepreneurship.

Ethnic Entrepreneurship

The classical connotation of entrepreneurship refers to the combining of resources in a systematic way so as to create something of value. Its modern connotation encompasses nearly all stages in the life cycle of business although the entrepreneurial dimensions of innovation and risk remain salient in ethnic business. Finally, entrepreneurship means innovation, leadership, taking bold and courageous initiatives. It presumes hope, self-confidence and trust. Pessimism, fatalism, siege mentality, a pervading sense of being persecuted, are its arcenemies. Greenfield et al define entrepreneurs operationally as owners and operators of business enterprise, which further includes self-employed persons who employ family labour as well as those who employ outsiders[13]. It is observed that some ethnic groups particularly among first and second-generation immigrants have higher rates of business formation and ownership than others.[14]

The development of ethnic business is built on three interactive components; opportunity structures, group characteristics and strategies'. Opportunity structure encompasses many of the entrepreneurial opportunities, which supports the ethnic business. They include the favourable market condition and access to ownership. The favourable market condition implies to the condition where the big businesses are leaving the way for the growth of small business. The immigrant ethnic groups and their children usually turn to small business. In Asian situations these immigrants are both tribal and non-tribal categories. The tribal ethnic groups are involved in selling their ethnic consumer products. The Lepchas, Bhotias and many from the Ladakh region of India migrate into plain areas and continue the woollen business. Similarly, a section of the Rajasthani Muslims migrate to the remotest parts of the country for the business of iron utensils.

The ethnic residential concentration has come into practice in many of the cities and industrial complex after decades long migration. In the industrial cities of Rourkela and Jamshedpur of India, the tribal groups from the adjacent areas have come to settle in the slums for decades. Some of them turn their traditional habit of drinking Handia — country liquor prepared from rice — as business. They do not merely provide it to their ethnic members but to the non-ethnic clientele too. In this context, the ethnic business is associated with low margin of economic transaction and substantially less benefit.

The lack of market opportunities affects the ethnic people and their traditional trade. The same is evidenced in the foothills of the Menpat Hill of Madhya Pradesh in India where the Oraons and the Tibetans live together. The Tibetans migrated to this place about three decades ago. They had passed on the fine art of carpet weaving to the local tribe, Oraon. Carpet weaving has been flourishing in this region since this time. The lack of attractive incentives for carpet weavers coupled with the absence of a lucrative market in Madhya Pradesh forced the local tribes to migrate to areas such as Bhadoi and Mirzapur in neighbouring Uttar Pradesh, to seek employment in the numerous carpet factories situated there. They were paid less and worked like "bonded labour there.[16]

The immigrant traders often distort the local ethnic consciousness. This is exemplified in the Khasi Hill of Northeast India. Here a considerable number of non-tribal businessmen married to Khasi women during their stay in the area. As the Khasi society follows the norms of matriarchy, the inheritance descends in the female line; mainly the youngest daughter becomes the owner of the family property that has also been accepted by the male members over the generations. But these non-tribal businessmen tried to distort this custom and claimed the continuity of inheritance in male line. The Khasi Student Union (KSU) issued quit notice to Khasi women married to non-tribals on January 13, 1994 and transactions were stopped with immediate effect[17].

The ethnic business provokes ethnic assault in many parts of Asian countries. This happens when the host ethnic group feels marginalized and subordinated. The insurgent ethnic groups in the Northeast of India have amassed tremendous wealth by extortion, abduction of the Marwaris and other businessmen, providing safe passage to narcotics and gun running[18]. The conflict between the 'old Sindhi' and 'new Sindhi' in Pakistan is because of the competition in holding key positions in business.

Besides the opportunity structure, group characteristics play a significant role in ethnic entrepreneurship. The selective nature of migration is one of the important reasons for evolving an ethnic group as a success entrepreneur. For example, the initial Cuban migration to the United States was highly selective, as middle and upper-middle class Cubans — many with substantial education, business experience, and capital[19]. The Sikhs of India who migrated to Canada, Britain, Hong Kong and Singapore were not selective. In fact, the Asian migration and their subsequent involvement in ethnic business are non-selective and haphazard. Ethnic social structure consists of the networks of kinship and friendship around which ethnic communities are arranged. This network helps to mobilize the resource and business transaction. It is ascertained that vertical and horizontal linkages reduce transaction costs and lower intra-ethnic competition[20].

Ethnic businessmen should follow certain strategies to overcome the problems they face in handling the business. This includes acquiring training skills needed to run a small business; recruiting and managing efficient, honest, and cheap workers; managing relations with customers and suppliers; surviving strenuous business competition; and protecting themselves from political attacks.

Conclusion

A number of research articles have thrown light on multiple impact of globalization on Asian countries, their societies, culture and largely on economy. In this article it is attempted to underline how ethnic groups acquire self-consciousness day by day which is manifested in the term ethnicity. The effect of globalization may increase its intensity because of widening gap at the level of economy. But the same process may decrease the scope of enhancement of ethnic production and ethnic trade but it can not kill it completely. That is because the core of globalization hardly touches the perspective of the ethnic production. The ethnic trades, which have been run by the strong ethnic groups who are, sound in capital and possess worldwide network, will rather receive a better opportunity to increase the business prospect.

References

1. Paul Hirst and Grahame Thompson, *Globalization in Question*, London, Polity Press, 1999, p. note 1, pp. 95-7.

2. Ankie Hoogvet, *Globalization and the Post-colonial World Houndmills*, Macmillan, 1997, p. 129.

3. A.Giddens, *The Consequences of Modernity*, Cambridge Polity 1990, p. 64.

4. R. Roberston, *Globalization*, London: Sage, 1992.

5. Raoul Naroll, "On Ethnic Unit Classification", Current Anthropology, (October 1964): 1, in Wesvolod W. Isajiw's "Definitions of Ethnicity" in *Ethnicity*, 1 July 1974) No. 4, p. 111.

6. Yulion Broimley, "The Obiect and Subreet Matter of Ethnography in Ethnography and Related Science Problems of the Contemporary World", 49 (Muscow: Social Sciences today, Academy of Sciences, 1977): 10.

7. Urmila Phadris, *Ethnicity and Nation-Building in South Asia*, New Delhi, Sage, 1989, p. 14.

8. Yasgcey .L William. Ericksen, Eugene and Richard. Jullani" 1976: Emerging Ethnicity: a Review and Reformation, *American Sociological Review*, 41(3), p. 401.

9. T.K. Oomen, *Citizenship, Nationality and Ethnicity*, Cambridge Polity Press, 1997, p. 39.

10. *Encyclopaedia Britannia*, Vol. 2, "Sex Asia".

11. RA Schermerhom, *Ethnic Plurality in India*, Tucson, Arizona: University of Arizona Press, 1978, P. 14.

12. *The Times of India*, October 5, 1998.

13. Creenfleld, S.M, Strickon, A., Aubey, R.T., "Entrepreneurs in Cultural Context", Albuquerque: univ. No. Mex. Press, 1979.

14. Howerd E. Aldriach and Roger Waldinger, Ethnicity and Entrepreneurship, in *Annual Review of Sociology*, 1990, 16:113.

15. Waldinger, R., Asdrich, H.W.,Ward R., *Immigrant Entrepreneurs, Immigrant and Ethnic business In Western Industrial of Society* Severly Hill, CA, Sage, 1990.

16. *The Statesman*, March 11, 1993.

17. *The Telegraph*, January 15,1994.

18. *The Pioneer*, August 20,1997

19. Portes , A., "The Social Origins of the Cuban enclave Economy of Malm", *Sociological Perspect*, 1987, 30: 340-72.

20. Wilson, K., Maritn W.A., "Ethnic Enclores : A Comparison of Cuban and Black Economies in Miami" Am J. Social, 1982, 88: 135-60.

‹23›

Ethnicity and Globalization

*K. Borichpolets**

Ethnicity in its various dimensions became one of the most popular issues of scientific discussions. Multiple conflicts, which had been suffered before and are being suffered now, convene about a necessity to continue efforts not only to study the phenomenon of ethnicity but also to make a reliable linkage of scientific projects with practical requirements of peace.

The report brought to your attention is devoted to the problem of analysis of some political dimensions of the ethnicity in the epoch of globalization.

Over the last 20 years there has been a rapid unexpected and unprecedented growth of what has generally been characterized as ethnic consciousness, ethnic conflict and ethnic violence. This period brought forward a large number of factors and strategies. At the same time the scientists presented many relative stable concepts of definite ethnic developments in different social conditions and under different circumstances.

1. Ethnicity is a social problem, a kind of consciousness about the status and needs of an ethnic group which has a common language, religion, kinship, etc. These cultural symbols provide a distinct identity to it and separate it from other such groups. There are two sets of theoretical formulations regarding ethnicity: premordialists who believe

* Professor, Moscow State Institute of International Relations (MGIMO University), Lobachewsky, Moscow, Russia.

that because of different race, religion, language and kinship each ethnic group has a different historical experience and its position in the society is determined by that. Another point of view, represented by so-called instrumentalists, is that ethnic identity is multi-dimensional and its engagement in collective action is contextual. At times we can see some integrated concepts, including primordialists and instrumentalist's approaches.

2. Ethnic identity itself involves considerable variation. Some forms of ethnic identity may in fact represent, not the hardening but a weakening of ethnic boundaries. Ethnicity is an unstable and contested category. Ethnic nationalism contains a plurality of meanings that cannot be reduced to a single core. Factors of particular significance are inter-ethnic relations and the role of the state, both interacting with the dynamics of modernization.

3. In divided societies around the world, regional and ethnic disparities in wealth and in the distribution of government resources have become major political issues. But ethnic conflict does not merely involve disputes over material goods. Disputes over seemingly symbolic issues, such as recognition of one or another language as the official language or one design or another in a national flag, are more severe.

4. Given the widespread character of ethnic conflict, efforts to reduce it are common. Although different political systems handle ethnic problems differently or not all— the existence of the problems is not confined to any region or any system.

5. International conditions and foreign examples create a setting that makes ethnic demands more realistic. But such influences cannot create a conflict where one does not exist. The existence of ethnic conflict depends instead on a tangled skein of objective and subjective conditions— the relative position of groups and how they feel about that position.

6. The international security implications of ethnic conflicts
    are of different origins. The most common threats to state
    borders are secessionist movements and irredentist
    movements. Although irredentism has not been a serious
    threat in most areas so far and probably will not become
    one, because most states that are potential annexationists
    are themselves multiethnic. Embarking upon such
    international adventures jeopardizes ethnic balances at
    home. But, in some regions, restraints on international
    involvement in ethnic disputes may be declining. The
    motives that induce foreign states to provide aid to
    secessionists are various. If global power balances can
    play a role, it stands to reason that regional and local
    balances can also play a big role.

7. The general dynamics underlying the contemporary wave
    of ethnic politics include: a) post nationalism, or a shift
    of allegiance from the nation to units or networks smaller
    or larger than the nation, b) retreat of the state, due to
    the general crisis of development and to globalization
    under the sign of neoliberalism and deregulation. This
    may be interpreted as a general de-centering of the
    state, c) democratization. Ethnic politics may represent
    a deepening of democracy as a mobilization of alienated
    constituencies in reaction to regional uneven
    development or internal colonialism. Ethnicization may
    also be a consequence of a shift to multiparty democracy;
    conversely, it may be used and manipulated as a means
    to sabotage multiparty democracy.

Ethnicity poses great challenges to political creativity.
Different modes of ethnicization take place in the context of
colonialism, postcolonial development, industrial society, and
globalization. Development does not eliminate ethnicity but
makes for its refiguration. Different modes of modernization
and development produce different forms of ethnic association
and mobilization. But in any case ethnicity is the mobilization
and manipulation of group identity against certain structural

inequality. These inequalities may be inherent in the social structure or are created due to the fallout of modernization and development or due to discriminatory representation in the power structure. In result the domestic and international policy-makers have to do with different manifestations of so called nationalism phenomena.'

The problem of nationalism is of greatest interest in contemporary discussions on ethnicity. The main idea consists of one side presumption that the era of the nation is past its peak, and nationalism is not a very perspective model of political behavioural. At the same time nationalism is interpreted as the main obstacle for globalization processes.

Now researchers mostly appreciate nationalism as one phenomena which has an objective and long-term character, and not as a product of conspiracy and a kind of terrorism.

Nationalism doesn't manifest the opposition to globalization. It is global as the global economic network is. We must change stereotype characteristics of nationalism as phenomena opposite to globalization. Nationalism is connected with globalization. It doesn't produce a challenge for globalization but for autocratic structures. It is integrated in the process and is an integrative part of social changes connected with global contacts and cooperation. At the same time nationalism represents strong challenges for globalization not as independent substantial factor, but because conflicts originated by them.

Studding the nationalist phenomena we can operate two types of its manifestations. The nationalism of local community and the nationalism of the state. But both bring conflicts. Post cold war realignments produced some general models of ethnic demands and movements: ethnonationalism, indigenous peoples movements, regional autonomy movements, migrant workers movements, white ethnic identity movement in the USA. All of them can produce domestic and international rubbles. The dynamics of ethnic politics in these clusters are diverse but there is one factor common to all these varieties of ethnicization: they all protest some form of monoculture control (real or eventual).

On the base of these models we can see that the state has lost the monopoly on representation and control of cultural and emotional loyalty of their citizens. But the actor pretending to chair this monopoly politically and theoretically is not clearly defined. I would like to call them ethnopolitical elites and at the same time I would like to propose some concerns about applied studies of this powerful actor.

The consideration brought to your attention in this connection is devoted to a very concrete aspect - clanic differentiation of ethnopolitical elites and its influence on the modern political process. An influence of the clanic factor on actual life is widely recognized. Nevertheless systematized wives about a mechanism of functioning of political clans in a system of power distribution have not appeared yet.

The word "political clan" means stable informal associations; built on the personal connections of their members, quite often have an important part to play in the process of decision-making. Based as they are on a real (or imaginary) kinship, clans number up to several hundred people rallied round a single leader (head, elder, or chief). Although market relations undermine the significance of family groups as primary social units, clan organization still survives on a fairly wide scale. This essentially patriarchal institution of public control is fitted in one way or another into the system of contemporary ethnic, social and political links of the majority of contemporary states. Local group solidarity quite often takes on the same form as traditional clan organization.

The division of the social elite into clans makes itself particularly manifest in countries which have strong stereotypes of traditional political culture. Their governing stratum is very heterogeneous. Both at national and local level, it consists of groupings combining the features of the patriarchal family units and political organizations contending for power. Each elite clan rests on a ramified network of members and supporters in middle and even lower sections of the social pyramid, enhancing its immunity from outside influences, notably, from ·the processes of centralization of state power. Therefore, clan differentiation in the ruling establishment always poses a potential threat to the country's internal political stability.

It normally represents two basic types of clan groups at national and local levels. On the one hand, these are the groups whose representatives have been in the upper and middle echelons of power for a long time. Besides, there are new entities which have emerged as a result of major social change and collisions in society. In most cases, the major struggle stages between the old and new groupings, the system of relations established between traditional clans serving as a backdrop. The results of the competitive struggle of clans depends not only on the subjective characteristics of their potential but also on the ability of each clan to conduct an adequate political struggle. In this context, the principal means of achieving strategic objectives characteristic of the old and new clans variously influence the country's internal political stability.

For instance, old clans normally want all contradictions to be resolved exclusively at the level of elitist social strata. Drawn as they are into a conflict with other clans, they quite seldom resort to a simultaneous mobilization of all the members of their own grouping and its clients. Therefore the political struggle waged by the clans assumes the character of trench warfare in most cases.

At the same time, new clans, even at the initial stages of confrontation, are inclined to bring in not only all of their own members but also the great mass of subordinated social segments. The appeal primarily to the democratic sections of the population enables the clans to make up, if in part, for the weakness of their positions in the upper echelons of power. But at the same time such a turn of front is fraught with the danger of the inter-clan struggle quickly escalating into more or less extensive social and political conflicts.

Intensified activity of the new clans, regardless of their original motives, always substantially compounds the community's internal political instability.

The sharpening struggle in the midst of the ruling stratum always entails a disruption of the country's internal political stability. It takes on a particularly protracted and dangerous character with the confrontation involving the clans, which have achieved the position of a political leader on the scale of an individual region or ethos.

A clan, which has established itself as a collective ethnic or regional leader gains practically unlimited control over the major (and continuously renewable) manpower resources. This circumstance does not in any way contribute to the prompt resolution of inter-clan contradictions, either when these develop in the country's outlying regions or when they assume the character of a centre-periphery confrontation. Both the old and the new clans are inclined rather to whip up the confrontation than to work towards easing tension, especially if it develops against the backdrop of a social – political or economic crisis.

That creates a vicious circle. The unstable basis makes it impossible to install a durable, if conservative, superstructure, and the absence of a solid superstructure causes the consolidation of the basis to be postponed indefinitely. Therefore, the struggle of clans within the realm of politics has been and will remain, for a long time to come, a factor of instability of social development of an appreciable proportion of states. But the most serious problems arising in connection of the clanic factor during conflict regulation are national reconciliation, peacekeeping process, and preventive conflict management in ethnic divided societies.

The study of different informal social structures and relations differing widely from the modern institutional system has come to the fore in political science. The recent studies in ethnic problems of the world after cold war approves the opinion that a large variety of political life dimensions seems to be condemned with the clientelism and clanic ties. In my briefly report I tried to demonstrate not only general considerations about ethnicity and globalization but also refer to different aspects of informal relations which are of great importance in ethnic, fragmentized systems.

Ethnicity, nationalism and their different political manifestations are unacceptable only when used for reasons unacceptable to dominant social interests. Ethnicity is protean in all its aspects. There are as many ethnicities and nationalism models as there are boundaries that societies generate, and positions to take along them. Living with shifting boundaries means living with ethnicity and nationalism. The main political problem is to minimize the eventual losses and rationalize political actions.

The overcoming of destructive nationalism, manifestations cannot be the matter of one single state. Nationalism must be controlled and governed. The concept of this governing on a global scale is largely formulated as the policy of cultural autonomy for ethnic minorities, legitimating of native languages in the public sphere, the large-scale isolation of authoritarian leaders. Another line is connected with the international life, with the efforts aimed to integrate ethnic minorities in global communication, namely the enforcement of their participation in UNO structures, and on the regional level the development of trans blunderer's contacts.

Analysing ethnicity in connection with globalization in a broad way we can interpret contemporary political situation as a continuation of the dialectics of empire and emancipation.

‹24›

The Prospects of Interaction in the Triangle Russia-India-China

*Sergei Lounvev**

After the collapse of the Soviet Union the political domineering of the North seemed overwhelming. The socialist block has disappeared. With structural readjustment in the economy of the North and growing involvement of many countries of the South into international division of labor in 1980-90s, the opposition of the South to the North has weakened and, most importantly, has lost organized mode. Very little attention was paid to the historical and civilizational parameters as they were neglected in political theories, both in the West and former Soviet block.

It seems that the assumptions of many economists and political scientists are coming true: we mean alleged formation of monotype and monosystem world economy (so called «all-mankind» civilization), members of which in the foreseeable fixture will differ only in the level of development and the degree of involvement in the international division of labor. The present and future of the universe have been often interpreted by Western scholars and policy-makers as a progressing unification of economic and political changes in the direction of a specified "ideal model" of Europo-centrism. This wish has been

* Research Fellow, Institute of Oriental Studies, Institute of World Economy and International Relations, Russian Academy of Sciences, Moscow, Russia.

characteristic of the Western society ever since the times of colonization. This emerging civilization is conceived as constantly losing individual (traditional) peculiarities, even in the countries close enough to the Western world, such as Russia.

But the reality shows quite a different picture. The end of the millennium witnesses the erection of industrial (in the South) and post-industrial (in the North) modes of production which, according to many existing notions, constitutes the foundation of civilization common to all mankind. Meanwhile, multi-variation of socio-economic development is getting stronger, opposite vectors appeared in developed and developing countries. Even more, in the latter case we see the formation of different types of national capitalisms. These trends make doubtful - from the angle of socio-economic dimensions - the perspective of new civilization common to all mankind.

The end of the second millennium has signaled more clearly that neither bipolar, nor unipolar world, does meet culture-civilizational realities and differences of the countries. Moreover, civilizational divergence has grown recently in many regions and the South demonstrates accentuated tendency towards alienation from numerous values of European civilization. At the present moment, the advance of the European technology, science, education and mass (Americanized) culture, on the contrary, results in a certain reaction of rejection in the South. The revival of civilizational values, started after the achievement of political independence, within the last two decades has transformed to alienation from the foundations of European civilization. The trend was strengthened by the beginning of Islamic revolution in Iran. The priority of Islamic values and erection of Islamic Republics (Pakistan, Iran, Mauritania etc.) added to gradual revival of the idea of superiority of the yellow race (shown by surveys in Japan from the 80s), rise of militant Hinduism in India, emergence of militant Buddhism in Sri Lanka, restoration of traditional cults in some African countries.

The process of revival of traditional values accompanied by alienation from many European values is caused by a number of factors. They include: the existence of large low strata within the system of traditional relations, living below poverty line especially in large countries; the attempts of some elites to obtain political goals by creating the image of the foreign external enemy; initial euphoria from the first evident successes; the erosion of absolute superiority of European civilization and so on. Once emerged these factors are reproduced. So, it looks likely that the growth of alienation will take a relatively long period. In turn, these diverging civilizational vectors have their impact on the formation of development, its methods and modes. As a result, national-production structures of different types are formed, civilizational differences become firmer.

Attention is often given to superficial factors. Really, fashion and taste habits of young people are practically the same everywhere in the world. European business style is characteristic of businessmen of any nationality. There are practically no countries, where elections to legislative bodies do not correspond to Western democratic principles in outward appearance. But if we take the essential level, one can see the drifting away from common basic norms of Western "European" democracy in quite a lot of regions.

Thus, cultural factors, as well as economy and politics, determine regionalization as a leading trend in world development. Transition of the global system to multi-polar and multi-civilizational world looks as the highest probability, with more integration within regions, and the emergence of contradictions between them - civilizational, economic, political and others.

The North needs the complete openness of economy of transit and developing countries for the absolutely free movement of finance and goods (with the lack of free market of labor). With increasing differences and contradictions between the main centers of the North, all these countries are extremely interested in the preserving of the domineering in the system of international economic and political relations, in the augmenting of the processes of globalization that are weakening the positions of a nation state. Moreover, there are justified concerns that violence will be made the, constant instrument of governance over the world system. The picture by itself is not new - compulsion and violence were basic features of the world system, which started formation about five centuries ago - to be destroyed by the World War II. What is really new at present is political and military consolidation of the developed nucleus and emergence of the growing number of states, which are being pushed out of the system in economic terms and have no visible ways to be reintegrated. For these (grey zones), major world centers do not wish (or are not able) to take any responsibility. It is a sharp contrast to the period of the confrontation of two (socio-political systems) when both superpowers considered the whole globe as a place of their interests and were eager to push the opponent out of every most distant and backward country.

The largest Eurasian countries oppose the monopolistic position of the North and its present policy. The strategic objective of Indian foreign policy - the emerging as a global power - was determined half-a-century ago. Only during the first years after independence there were discussions on this macro goal. The lack of heated arguments on the problems of foreign policy during a very long period witnessed that national interests and the objectives of foreign policy were rightly understood by a government and were adequately reflected in Indian politics. Foreign policy was a subject of (above-party) concord and all-Indian consensus. The collapse of socialist system and bipolar configuration of the world, the break-up of the Soviet Union and practical disintegration of the Non-aligned Movement led to certain reorientation of Indian foreign strategy. But it applies rather to the mechanisms and instruments of the achievement of the macro objectives than to the essence of these strategic aims. The continuation of independent foreign policy is still considered to be extremely important for the promotion of the status of the Republic.

China was able to reject all the attempts of the USSR to impose its will on the country when Peoples Republic of China was an extremely weak state. Strong China will not allow any attempts of hegemonism all the more.

The over-all strengthening of the economic links with the North has become one of the main directions of India and China from the beginning of the nineties. But the vast internal market, the existence of considerable part of population whose consumption is equal to European standards gives the states an opportunity to obtain big successes without complete integration into the world economy. Taking into consideration the number of population and internal resources that are not yet mastered wholly - i.e. considerable opportunities of expanding of internal market - one has to acknowledge that only some extreme circumstances can cause long deceleration of the rates of Chinese and Indian growth.

There are many myths about the impact of globalization on Asian countries, about their movement towards open economy. I'll give only two figures for China: In the early 90's only 8% of Chinese Gross Domestic Product relate to external economic activity and in the late 90's 7%, more than 80% of all foreign investments come from Greater China, from Chinese Diaspora. The figures for India are much smaller. Moreover, China and India have no desire at all to be a part of the North. The Asian giants, slightly integrated in the world economy and half closed, are ready to take part only in some dimensions of the process of globalization. Both countries, with the lack of inferiority complex, are turning into separate subsystems of international relations.

Two Asian giants were the first ones to criticize the desire of the creation of unipolar world. China and India, these strategic competitors, have begun the process of normalization of bilateral relations. Russia joined them in the criticism of the concept of unipolar world with certain time-lag but was the first to suggest the construction of the strategic alliance between Russia, China and India.

I may remind that first appeals to Asian nations as global partners came out of half-destroyed Russia in 1920 from V. Lenin in somewhat similar situation - the country found itself out of Europe in political sense, and the economy was ruined after the civil war. The collapse of Russian illusions about the integrity into Europe was one of the major factors that have caused the shifts in Russian policy.

Since the late 80-ies ordinary consciousness in Russia has considered the country as part of the West. The views of the great majority of the population (and foreign political leaders) were based on the understanding of Russia's belonging to the all-European civilization. They actively supported the idea of Russias accelerated turning into a "legal state", the creation of a "civil society" (without being aware of the fact that this process takes several decades), an accelerated forced modernization in the direction of market economy. In the sphere of foreign policy the reaction of public consciousness to the loss by Russia of its important geopolitical role was rather quiet. On the whole the population supported the course aimed at developing ties with Europe and the USA and moving away from Asia, and believed that there was no point in consolidating partnership even with the republics of Central Asia, since they were considered to be a kind of "civilization ballast". The Western civilization was regarded as an "ideal type" and as the final aim of Russia's development. Hence the officially approved idea of the "entry to the European house".

A sharp aggravation of the socio-economic sphere, the absence of concrete wide assistance of the West, considerable weakening of the country's positions on the world arena has led to steadily growing anti-Westernism of the population. These sentiments cannot fail to tell on the positions of Russian political leaders, who strive most of all to expand their social base in conditions of preservation of democratic elections procedure. As far as Russia proper is concerned, internal political democratization will inevitably lead to certain friction with the north. What is characterized by the latter as "democratic policy" of Russia in first part of the 1990s, in Russia itself is called the "policy of unilateral concessions". Russia began very slow and inconsequent turn towards Asia. Its apotheosis was the suggestion of ex-prime minister E. Primakov to construct strategic alliance of three major Eurasian countries.

There is an objective base for the rapprochement of three countries. The prospects of the creation of unipolar world make the countries feel special apprehensions. Further, broadening of the use of violence in the policy of the North will inevitably lead to the strengthening of relations inside the triangle. In 1998 the reaction of Indian and especially Chinese leaders towards the suggestion of Primakov was very cool. But after the beginning of bombardments of Yugoslavia by NATO Indian prime-minister A. B. Vajpayee called immediately upon the necessity to return to the idea of the strategic alliance. The same was the reaction of the Chinese press.

The growth of Islamic fundamentalism will also push rapprochement of these states (the governments of China and India began to discuss frankly the possibilities of the establishment Islamic fundamentalist regimes in Central Asia on the eve of the 1990s). The Moslem are stretches from North-West of Africa to South-East of Asia. India (with more 100-million Moslem population), Russia (with Moslem population in Volga-Urals region) and China (with Moslem population in Sinkiang) face the similar problems and tasks, if there is the rise of Muslim extremism.

One should point out the relative closeness of three countries in the sphere of cultural life. I mean that spiritualism, this immanent element of their civilizations, opposes the materialism and consumerism of the developed countries. There are good relations between Russians and Indians, between Russians and Chinese at the grass root level. The Public opinion surveys in India and China show that Russia is still among the most popular countries. Chinese haven't forgotten about the colossal economic aid of the USSR in the 1940s-1950s, and Indians - in the 1960s-1980s. It is a good base for Russia for further rapprochement with Asian giants.

There are great obstacles on the way of strategic alliance as a political- military axis. During the last decade China goes to the gradual levelling of the relations with India and Pakistan. But India still considers China as an ally of Pakistan and as a main strategic opponent in Asia from the point of view of long-term perspective. Indian military doctrine prescribes the possibility of waging (one and a half) wars - with China and Pakistan. In 1998 Minister of Defense J. Fernandes called China the danger number one» for India. There are many limitations of over-all development of bilateral relations. There is no significant progress in Indo-Chinese negotiations on border problems. India is highly anxious about the continuation of Chinese-Pakistani military cooperation (especially in a nuclear sphere), the perfection of nuclear weapon in China. In its turn, China reacted extremely negative to the testing of nuclear devices by India in May 1998: the agency (Sinhua) named the Republic (a South Asian hegemonist).

The evaluation of China by India as its strategic opponent, the reluctance of the Chinese authorities to challenge openly the USA and consider India and especially Russia as equal partners make the establishment of (the strategic political-military partnership) of three giants of Eurasia practically impossible in the foreseeable future. But the perspectives of the comprehensive cooperation (without military aspect) have improved.

There is no necessity and no opportunity of creating a new military block that will be very counterproductive for all countries as no one wants to challenge the North to an open fight. Still, the danger of the creation of a military-political alliance can be very useful and make the North to go to a lot of significant concessions to three Eurasian giants.

Moreover, the possibilities of mutual cooperation in the military field are great for Russia. India is an ideal partner in this sphere. The volume of Russian military export to China (more than 1 billion $per a year) has no tendency for decline. Of course, one should add that there are a lot of apprehensions about China. Russian nationalistic forces and some regional elites of Siberia mistrust China and oppose the cooperation in military-political subsystem of bilateral relations.

On the whole the propects of the comprehensive co-operation inside the triangle have improved, economic, political and cultural spheres are more favorable for the development of the Russian-Indian-Chinese ties. Collective expression of views by three countries may be more persuasive than individual bargaining. For global strategic balance bilateral treaties on friendship and cooperation are very important: an agreement to start preparation of a new Sino-Russian document was reached during V. Putin's visit to Beijing in 2000, and in Oct. 2000, a new Indo-Russian document was signed.

The last summits on the problems of globalization and the events around them have shown the unification of different opponents to the process, mainly social movements, such as trade unions, etc. May be, it is time for Russia, India and China to combine their efforts in the struggle against the aspects of globalization that are of serious danger to national interests of the countries.

The economic cooperation in continental Asia is extremely important. All three countries are compelled to think of development of infrastructure in backward regions - without quick financial returns and direct participation of foreign investors. Historically this task was performed by national states. At present it is a subject of broader approaches, including also international cooperation in continental Asia. However, these approaches are sharply different from those applied in Pacific Asia - due to the essence of continental conditions, another type of resource endowment, difficult access to foreign markets, specific political and cultural situation. The coming modernization in Asia's heartland poses the necessity to broaden the existing potential for continental cooperation and, perhaps, to implement the system of preferential treatment of trade and investment between three countries in some geographical areas and industrial branches.

In conclusion it is necessary to note that in the sphere of foreign policy pragmatism and increase of "profitability", the creation of conditions to ensure normal internal functioning are much more important than the attempts to achieve recognition of the status of a "great power" or to become a member of the most prestigious international organizations. Russia will not be in such a bad situation if it is able to use the contradictions between different world centers and major countries. The return to Asia, especially to Asian countries, should not be (vocal): it is the main way for solving external and internal problems.

‹25›

Global Governance by Formation of
Global Policy Institutions
The Tasks of the Third World

Bhaskar Majumdar*

The world economy experienced major orientations twice in the twentieth century. The first one followed the end of the Second World War in 1945 and the second one followed the disintegration of the USSR and reunification of Germany in 1989. The first one helped the formal independence or decolonization of countries that were under the tutelage of mainly the British and French powers. The US and the USSR, which emerged as the biggest power twins immediately after the Second World War, initiated this decolonization. This decolonization is also believed to have imposed shocks on the Third World Countries (TWCs) by converting them into post-decolonized battlefields between the two warring groups, the US-led First World and the USSR-led Second World. The end of the cold war in 1989 imposed a shock on most of the TWCs by converting them into an apparently non-existent group who have 'nowhere to go' (Burbach, 1997, p. 77).

The International Economic Order (IEO) that emerged immediately after the Second World War relied on world financial institutions like the World Bank, the IMF, the world trade bodies like the GATT and later the WTO, for execution of the IEO.

*   Govind Ballabh Pant Social Institute, Jhusi, Allahabad, Uttar Pradesh, India.

Transnational Corporations (TNCs) became the new actors in the world market. There came the Multinational Banks (MNBs) that mobilise savings of national economies on a world scale and follow the TNCs for realization of the savings. All these were the offshoots of the efforts of the major or dominant countries in the post-Second World War world economy. These economies are formally in the Organization for Economic Cooperation and Development (OECD). The way in which and when the WTO came to be formed also shows the requirement of the Developed Market Economies (DMEs). In our view, the most significant factor that came to influence the post-second World War IEO was the leadership of US supported by her allies and the formation of global policy institutions. As a late participant in the Second World War the leader knew what she would have to do so as not to repeat the kind of errors the former imperial power, UK, committed. The leader rationally planned to form a system where she accommodated not only the 'Allies' but also the 'Axis Powers'. Thus, the group of Seven Major Industrial Countries namely. U.S., U.K., Germany, Japan, France, Italy and Canada (G-7) came into existence.

The post-Second World War leader needed policy coordination institutions for legitimization of her decision and intervention in global governance. This governance had to be outside the United Nations (UN).

This paper has three sections. In Section 1 we examine the question of power sharing by formation of global policy institutions. In Section II we examine the relevance of global policy institutions formed only by the Third World Countries. Finally, in Section III we examine the tasks of the countries in the Third World.

I Global Policy Institutions and Power Sharing

The economic institutions that operate globally and impose major effects on world economic phenomena are the institutions constituted by the developed market economies.

These are the group of seven most industrialized countries (G-7) and on an extended horizon G-10. The institutions or policy coordination groups that also exist are G-22, G-26 and the most recently formed G-20. G-22 is an extension of G-7 by accommodation of some emerging market economies from both the Organization for Economic Cooperation and Development (OECD) and the non-OECD countries. G-26 is an extension of G-22 by inclusion of G-10 members who are not in G-7. Thus, functionally G-26 includes members of G-7, G-10, G-22. In this sense, G-26 is also an extension of G-7. G-20 came into being in September 1999. It is a peculiar group of individual countries, union of countries, and world financial institutions. The Finance Ministers of countries in G-7 initiated the Group that is really an extension of G-7 along with the inclusion of EU, emerging large market economies in the Third World, and the Bretton Woods twins. G-15, G-24 and G-77 are the groups formed by countries in the Third World. The newly formed G-20 is a group of 20 members constituted by 19 nation-states, a union of countries, and world financial institutions. The union of countries in G-20 is the European Union (EU) and the world financial institutions are the World Bank and the IMF. As such the calculation of relative power, both economic and political, of G-20 does not carry much meaning. There will be double counting for some countries, and zero counting for the Bretton Woods twins if quantitative indicators are taken like the size of population, volume and value of output, trade value' etc. If the problem of double entries of some countries by their being inside both G-7 and EU is eliminated, then the functioning of EU as an independent unit loses its significance in G-20. In general, G-20 came into existence within the framework of the post-Second World War IEO. These instruments to implement the IEO are the World Bank, the IMF, and the WTO (GOI, 1999-2000, p.108). The instability or disturbance in the world capitalist financial system may be a major reason for inclusion of the major market economies in the newly formed G-20. Since 1980s, the countries in G-7 had been anxious for non-representation of the emerging large market economies, particularly from the Third World. This non-

Box 1: Global Major Policy Institutions/ Groups of Countries (Membership of countries and status of groups)

Global Institutions/ Groups	Member Countries	Status of the Group/ Institutions	Year of Establish-ment
G-7	US, UK, France, Germany, Japan, Italy, Canada	Highest economic power	1975
G-10	G-7 plus Belgium, Netherlands, Sweden, Switzerland	Same as that of G-7	1962
G-22	G-7 plus emerging market economies from both OECD & non-OECD countries. This includes Argentina, Australia, Brazil, China, Hong Kong, India, Indonesia, Rep. of Korea, Malaysia, Mexico, Poland, Russian Fed., Singapore, South Africa, Thailand	Promising power of the emerging market econo-mies by economic-political alliance with G-7	1998
G-26	G-22 plus Belgium, Netherlands, Sweden, Switzerland	Same as that of G-22	NA
G-24	Algeria, Argentina, Brazil, Colombia, Dem-ocratic Republic of Congo, Cote d'Ivore, Egypt, Ethiopia, Gabon, Ghana, Guatemala,	Weak economic power	NA

Box 1 : Continued

Global Institutions/ Groups	Member Countries	Status of the Group/ Institutions	Year of Establish- ment
	India, Islamic Rep. of Iran, Lebanon, Mexico, Nigeria, Pakistan, Peru, Philippines, Sri lanka, Syrian, Arab Rep. Trinidad and Tobago, Venezuela, Yugoslavia.		
G-20	G-7 plus EU plus Argentina, Australia, Brazil, China, India, Indonesia, Mexico, Russia, Saudi Arabia, South Africa, South Korea, Turkey, the Bretton Woods Institutions.	A heterogeneous mixture of countries, economic groups like the EU and world financial institutions. Newly formed and yet to show power.	1999
G-77	Around 133 countries in the Third World	Yet to exert power	1964
G-15	Algeria, Argentina, Brazil, Chile, Egypt, India, Indonesia, Jamaica, Kenya, Nigeria, Malaysia, Mexico, Peru, Senegal, Sri Lanka, Venezuela and Zimbabwe.	Weak Economic Power	NA

Note : NA means "Not Available"

Source : GOI, Economic Survey, 1999-2000, p. 108 ; UNDP, 1999, Human Development Report, p. 109

representation constrains the ability of finance ministers in countries in G-7 to tackle issues related to developments in the international financial system. This became clearer from the financial crises of the first-tier and second-tier NICs faced during late 1990s. G-20 is a response to this urgency (Box 1).

It seems that there are two ways for the countries to assert for global power sharing. One way is global political-administrative governance, and the other way is through assertion of economic power. The formation of global policy institutions aims at global governance. We concentrate here on economic power and examine how the global policy institutions control world output, investment, exports, imports, and finance. This control will also show which countries are in command of the economic indicators selected for perusal.

Sharing of World Output

G-7 is by far the most powerful institution that commanded around two-third of world output during late 1990s although it had only one-tenth of the world population. G-10 as an institution does not show anything significantly different from that of G-7 in terms of size of population and output. Since G-22 and G-26 are both extensions of G-7 with the inclusion of large economies like China, India, Indonesia, Brazil, Russian Fed. etc and also small economies like Hong Kong, Singapore etc, each of them covers around two-thirds of world population. We classify the economies as large or small in terms of size of population. Each of G-22 and G-26 covers around four-fifths of world output during the late 1990s. During the same period, these groups had around two-third of world population. The output figures for G- 22 and G-26 for the mid-1990s show an improvement over what they were in 1980. If the shares of G-7 in world output are taken out, the remaining shares of each of G-22 and G-26 will be lower and will obviously be much less than that of G-7. For example, The output share of G-22 that excludes countries in G-7 was around one-sixth of world total in 1995, while for

G-7 it was more than one-sixth of world total. The same is true for G-26, and for all the years in the late 1990s. The groups, G-15 and G-24, represent respectively 17 and 24 countries from the Third World. The largest country in the third world, China, is not in G-24. G-24 commanded less than one-tenth of world output during 1995-1998, having

TABLE 1: Share of Policy Coordination Groups in World Population, 1980, 1995-98

GROUPS	PERCENTAGE SHARE				
	1980	1995	1996	1997	1998
G-7	13.59	11.87	11.76	11.8	11.61
G-10	14.47	12.59	12.49	12.5	12.32
G-22	55.92	52.66	64.33	64.8	63.29
G-26	56.80	53.38	65.06	65.5	64.00
G-20	NC	NC	NC	NC	NC
G-15	28.95	30.92	30.98	31.15	31.39
G-24	30.78	32.64	34.02	34.6	33.89*

Note: NC means 'Not Calculated'

* Excluded countries are Gabon, Syrian Arab Rep., Trinidad and Tobago, Yugoslavia

Source: World Bank, 1982, World Development Report, p. 110-111

World Bank, 1997, World Development Report, p. 214-215

World Bank, 1998, World Development Indicators, p. 12-14

World Bank, 1998/99, World Development Report, p. 190-191

World Bank, 1999/2000, World Development Report, p. 230-231

TABLE 2 : Share of Policy Coordination Groups in World Ouptut, 1980, 1995-98

GROUPS	PERCENTAGE SHARE				
	1980	1995	1996	1997	1998
G-7	43.43+	67.42	65.6	64.0	64.79
G-10	48.29	71.70	69.85	67.8	68.66
G-22	56.11*	82.61	82.11	81.7	77.40
G-26	60.97	86.89	86.30	85.8	81.27
G-20	NC	NC	NC	NC	NC
G-15	10.51	7.71	8.41	10.48	9.75
G-24	9.86	8.69	8.19	8.9	8.87**

Note: NC means 'Not Calculated'
+   means 'excluding Germany'
*   means 'excluding Russian Fed'
**   Excluded countries are Gabon, Syrian Arab Rep., Trinidad and Tobago, Yugoslavia

Source: World Bank, 1982, World Development Report, p. 110-111
World Bank, 1997, World Development Report, p. 236-232
World Bank, 1997, World Development Report, p. 236-237
World Bank, 1998, World Development Indicators, p. 180-182
World Bank, 1998/99, World Development Report, p. 212-214
World Bank, 1999/2000, World Development Report, p. 252-253

one-third of world population. The output data for G-24 for the late 1990s show a deceleration relative to what they were in 1980. China is not a member of G-15, as is the case with G-24. Naturally, the output share of G-15 came to be around one-tenth of world total during the late 1990s with around one-third of world population (Tables 1 and 2).

Sharing of World Trade

In 1980, G-7 had a little less than half of world exports. During late 1990s, G-7 maintained this share. For G-7 the export share is proportionately much less than its share in world output during late 1990s. Contrary to the high share in world exports of G-7 and G-10, the groups formed only by the TWCs like G-15 and G-24 had less than one-tenth of world exports. The export shares of G-15 and G-24 in world exports have a correspondence with their shares in world output. Each of G-22 and G-26 covers more than two-third of world exports. This high share was because of the share of G-7, which is a constituent of each of G-22 and G-26. The export share of G-22 excluding the share of G-7 in 1995 was around one-fifth of world total, while it was a little less than half of world total for G-7. Similar is the scenario for sharing in world imports. In 1980, G-7 had more than two-third of world imports. Contrary to this, in world imports G-15 and G-24 shared much less than one-tenth. Particularly, the trade data for G-24 for the late 1990s show a deceleration relative to what they were in

TABLE 3: Share of Policy Coordination Groups in World Exports, 1980, 1995-98

GROUPS	PERCENTAGE SHARE				
	1980	1995	1996	1997	1998
G-7	47.9	48.66	46.1	47.99	48.85
G-10	58.55	58.16	55.54	57.04	58.69
G-22	60.29	69.75	67.24	69.81	70.76
G-26	70.85	79.28	76.66	78.86	80.60
G-20	NC	NC	NC	NC	NC
G-15	7.54	7.19	9.88	7.67	10.21
G-24	7.91	7.19	6.00	6.44	6.53

Note: NC means 'Not Calculated'
  Data for 1997 refer to exports of goods and services. For all other years, it is merchandise exports.

Source: World Bank, 1982, World Development Report, p. 110-111
  World Bank, 1997, World Development Report, p. 242-243
  World Bank, 1998, World Development Indicators, p. 12-14, 180-182, 192-194
  World Bank, 1998/99, World Development Report, p. 228-230
  World Bank, 1999/2000, World Development Report, p. 268-269

TABLE 4: Share of Policy Coordination Groups in World
Imports, 1980, 1995-98

GROUPS	PERCENTAGE SHARE				
	1980	1995	1996	1997	1998
G-7	49.0	47.31	45.65	47.70	50.65
G-10	59.92	55.75	53.96	55.96	59.80
G-22	61.29	68.48	66.97	69.72	69.81
G-26	72.14	76.92	75.28	77.98	78.96
G-20	NC	NC	NC	NC	NC
G-15	6.74	7.23	9.73	8.32	9.96
G-24	8.86	7.56	6.63	7.40	7.83

Note: NC means 'Not Calculated'

Data for 1997 refer to exports of goods and services. For all other years, it is merchandise exports.

Source: World Bank, 1982, World Development Report, p. 110-111

World Bank, 1997, World Development Report, p. 242-243

World Bank, 1998, World Development Indicators, p. 12-14, 180-182, 192-194

World Bank, 1998/99, World Development Report, p. 228-230

World Bank, 1999/2000,World Development Report, p. 268-269

1980. The mixed groups like G-22 and G-26 by inclusion of large emerging market economies show more than two-third share in world imports. The reason is same. The share of G-7 explains the high shares of these mixed groups. For example, in 1995, the import share of G-22 in world imports was around one fifth of world total, which was a little less than one-fifth of world total for G-7. The same is true for G-26, and for all the years of the late 1990s (Tables 3 and 4).

Sharing of World Investment

Except for a few countries in the Third World, the developed market economies control most of the world foreign direct investment (FDI). In 1980, for example, G-7 had around 60.0 per cent of total FDI that came to be 45.0 per cent in 1996. G-10 had a little less than 70 per cent of FDI in 1980 which came down to half of total FDI in 1996. Low-income countries, excluding China and India, had less than one per cent of FDI in 1980 that increased to three per cent in 1996. The share of China in the low-income TWCs in FDI increased significantly, from around two per cent to around 12.0 per cent. This happened in a state of more than 50 per cent increase in FDI in world economy (World Bank, 1998/99, P.230-231). On average, in FDI outflows during 1986-91, G-7 contributed more than 70.0 per cent. During 1992-96 this share oscillated around two-third of total FDI. The share of the developing countries in world FDI outflows increased from around six per cent on average during 1986-91 to around 15.0 per cent during the first half of the 1990s. In FDI inflows, G-7 had a share of around 60 per cent on average during 1986-91 that later declined. The share of the developing countries in inflow of FDI increased steadily from less than one-fifth of the total during 1986-91 on the average to two-fifth during the first half of the 1990s (UNCTAD, 1998, p. 361-371). The message is clear. The DMEs represented by G-7 or G-10 contribute most of the FDI outflows while the emerging market economies in the Third World attract increasing FDI inflows. The fact remains that most of the FDI inflows also continues to remain confined to the DMEs as these DMEs contribute to the lion's share of FDI outflows. Most of the FDI that goes to the TWCs, whatever insignificant it is, goes to the relatively advanced market economies.

Sharing of World Finance

The world financial institutions that came into existence immediately after the Second World War following the initiatives of the US and the UK in the Conference of the Bretton Woods are the IMF and the World Bank. Each member country in the IMF has a quota determined by the country's GNP, foreign trade and foreign exchange reserves. This quota determines the voting rights of each country and its borrowing facilities (Anell and Nygren, 1980, p. 42; Hoogvelt, 1982, p. 83-84). For the DMEs the dollar vote declined from 78.5 per cent in 1950 to 66.5 in 1980 while for US alone it declined from 34.7 per cent to 21.5 per cent (Sauvant, 1981, p.293). The share of US in 1996 came to be 18.25, slightly above what is required to stall any major decision in the IMF (CMIE, 1996, July, p. 75). Membership in the World Bank is restricted to Governments that are also the members of the IMF. As in the case of IMF, the percentage subscription of members to the total capital stock in the World Bank, determines their voting shares. For example, in 1972 the voting share of the US in World Bank was 23.2 per cent and of G-7 (excluding Italy) was 49.3 per cent (Press and information Office of the Federal Government, n.d., p. 59-60). The power of the countries/groups of countries thus depends on, among other things, maintaining the voting share in world financial institutions. The countries in G-7 are surely ahead of others in this power structure. In fact, members in G-7 control the Bretton Woods institutions through voting rights. There is no developing country equivalent to the G-7 (UNDP, 1999, p. 11).

The idea may be that investment made by the TNCs that cover most of the global economic space needs safety in such investment. Once the world financial institutions are accommodated in the policy groups, the policy formation network becomes stronger. The other idea behind formation of groups like G-20 may be safety of output produced by the DMEs by its realisation at least on the space covered by these policy institutions. Both FDI and trade work as supporting tools for this realization.

Exclusion of Small Economies from Global Policy Institutions

The aspect that is common to all the groups initiated by G-7 is the exclusion of countries in Africa, excepting South Africa, which has been included in the newly formed G-20. This is valid for G-10, G-22, and G-26. The formation of these groups confirms also the credibility of countries for inclusion in terms of actual and potential market size. This may be the reason why in the latest group G-20, the group that was initiated by G-7, the city-states like Hong Kong, and Singapore have been excluded. These city-states were the members in G-22 and hence remained members of G-26. The groups formed by the countries in the Third World, namely, G-15, G-24, and on an extended scale G-77, show the natural inclusion of countries in Asia, Africa, and Latin America. The reason why the small economies have been excluded is probably the exhaustion of 'intensive globalization'. Let us see why.

The first-tier Newly Industrialized Countries (NICs) are the export-dependent small economies that developed a peculiar economic structure by the mid-1990s. They make up less than one per cent of the world population, and around two per cent of world output. Their import-GDP ratio (excluding Taiwan) in 1995 was as high as 76.0 per cent while export-GDP ratio was 81.0 per cent. At the given import-ratio, these NICs can absorb 17 per cent of G-7 exports, if these NICs (including Taiwan) import only from G-7. This was valid for the early 1990s (World Bank, 1995. p. 166-167, 186-187; 1996, p. 210-211, 216-217; 1997, p. 214-215, 236-237, 242-243). The key factor facilitating the Export-Oriented Industrialization (EOI) strategy adopted by the NICs was their access to their major markets of DMEs, particularly Japan and US. More generally, these NICs depended on access to the markets of the US and Japan on the one hand and operation of command capitalism on the other. The US and the International Financial Institutions (IFIs) had cited these NICs as examples of export-led growth. Even until recently, it was argued that the reasons for the export-cum-investment-led success of the countries in East Asia lay in their increasing integration in the regional division of labour (UNCTAD, 1998a, p. 204). The leader however understands that these are the small economies by size of population and natural resources. NICs as growth centres or trade centres thus can not offer the leader a durable base for her expansion. This is also because the astronomically high import-GDP and export-GDP ratios achieved by the NICs do not seem to be feasible for any country or group of countries in the end. This extremely high trade ratio of the NICs corresponded to very low share in world output. The DMEs as destinations of extremely high dose of exports by the NICs may deny after a point easy access to the latter. This is more so if the output share of these NICs increases because of increasingly population-cum-material neutral technology. The action planned by G-7 clarifies this. Excepting South Korea, no country in the first-tier NICs has been included in G-20. The non-exclusion of South Korea from G-20 may rest more on political reasons. Excepting G-15 and G-24, which are constituted solely by the TWCs all the other policy groups are the brainchildren of G-7. Thus, inclusion or exclusion of countries in the groups that influence global policy and governance depends on the ambitions of G-7. On the supposition that possibilities of intensive globalization have exhausted, what we infer is inclusion of large economies with large actual or potential markets in the forthcoming G-7 initiated groups. Not only the first-tier NICs, the second-tier NICs also have been excluded from the newly formed G-20. This second-tier NICs are the countries in ASEAN. The exception is South Korea. By size of population, Indonesia is a large country while the others are not small in comparison with Turkey or Australia or South Korea, which have been included in G-20. The economic reason for exclusion of these countries can not be cited in terms of the financial crises and hence financial mismanagement, which the ASEAN countries suffered from in 1997. It may be that G-20 has come as a test case by the G-7 to legitimise the global governance by the latter. Some other non-small countries may be included in future if G-20 in its present structure succeeds. What is the probable indicator of success? It is the protection of interests of capital of the TNCs and, in turn, of the DMEs. The argument behind the regional integration networks is free movement of capital, including FDI, that should aim at easy investment by the TNCs 'beyond those induced by trade liberalization or growth alone' (UNCTAD, 1998, p. 118). The inclusion of large market economies, actual and promising, in the policy groups initiated by G-7, ensure standardization of products, harmonization of consumers and the homogenization of markets, and hence make it easier for the TNCs to serve larger markets. The interests of dominant policy groups like G-7 thus are clear. These are to protect the markets for the countries in G-7 through not only exports but also investment on a regional and global scale. This ensures long term uninterrupted economic growth of countries in G-7. Annexing the large market economies in this network shows a path of 'extensive globalization'.

II Relevance of Global Policy Institutions formed only by the TWCs

The groups that include only the TWCs are G-15, G-24 and G-77. G-15 is a group of 17 countries from Asia, Africa and Latin America. The group was set up to enhance cooperation and provide input for other international policy groups. The country biggest by size and probably the most powerful in terms of economic-political indicators inside the TWC is China. China is not in G-15. The representatives of the countries in G-15 do not often see eye to eye on all trade, development and finance issues, but are supposed to have confidence in cooperation and speak with a single voice at international gatherings (www.theodora.com/maps). Similar is for G-24. The Group of 77 that was established in June 1964 by 77 developing countries signatories of the Joint Declaration of the Seventy-seven countries, did not include China. Subsequently, China came to be inside G-77, as this Group expanded to encompass 133 countries from the Third World so far. G-24 is a follow up action group based in Washington D.C. on behalf of G-77. G-24, as G-15, does not include China. However, this non-inclusion weakens the power of G-15 and G-24. The relative economic strength of these two policy groups is also clear from their shares in output, investment, trade vis-a-vis the groups formed by the DMEs and the groups where the large market economies are included.

If the purpose of the global policy institutions is global governance by establishing economic-financial stability, the G-7 initiated G-20, matters the most. We assume here the significant role played by the world financial institutions, mainly the World Bank and the IMF. The inclusion of the President of the World Bank, the Managing Director of the IMF, and the Chairpersons of the International Monetary and Financial Committee and the Development Committee implies that formation of G-20 in 1999 was well orchestrated. It acknowledges the power of the European Union, in addition to G-7, and hence both are there in G-20. In fact, it is a G-7 plan that accommodates EU and the emerging large market economies to thwart any economic-financial disaster. In this frame, groups like G-22 and G-26 seem also to be not of much relevance, though their shares in world output and trade are high. As we explained, this is because of shares of G-7. The groups like G-15 and G-24 that are constituted only by the TWCs are irrelevant in shaping and influencing the global governance so far.

III Tasks of the Third World

It is now clear that the G-7 directly influences international financial and trade institutions by virtue of its disproportionate economic power. For example, the agreements reached by the G-7 leaders deeply influence the direction of policy within such international bodies as the World Bank, the IMF, the OECD, the WTO, and the NATO. This is the case in spite of the fact that, unlike these bodies the G-7 has no formal set up, understood as having no permanent staff, no headquarters, no set of rules governing its operations, and no legal set up. The influence of G-7 derives from its disproportionate economic power and strategic position.

The post-Second World War, particularly the post-Cold War world economy has witnessed a distinct trend towards formation of policy institutions. The decolonized countries in the Third World realized the implications of formation of these groups and started forming groups much later than the developed countries. The reason for the delay in the initiative of the TWCs is that 'more than 70 countries moved from colonial status to political independence' from the late 1940s to the early 1970s

(UNDP, 1999, p. 99). This also shows that most of the TWCs had no say in shaping the IEO that came into existence immediately after the Second World War. The fact is that the groups that include only the TWCs are weak while inclusion of some of the TWCs in the groups initiated by DMEs does not add to the economic power of the TWCs in general. The power of the groups that accommodate both the countries from the DMEs and the TWCs does not seem to be more than the power enjoyed by groups that accommodate only the DMEs. While G-22 and G-26 represent the former case, G-7 and G-10 represent the latter. This is not only because of the heterogeneous interests of the former but also because that the formation of the former depends on the choice of groups like G-7. Some of the small countries in the Third World insignificant in terms of economic power are expendable in these regional formations. They are either excluded straightaway or made dependent for a while as 'transnational city states'. The first category includes most of the countries in Africa while the second category includes countries like Singapore and Hong Kong. The entry of small countries or countries in the Third World also takes time if the country at all gets the chance to enter where she likes to. For example, the Canada-US Free Trade Agreement took more than ten years to include one extra member, namely, Mexico, through NAFTA. At the same time, Chile's attempts to join it met with serious resistance (ADB, 1999, p. 226). In principle, the formation of multinational regional groups is 'an intermediate step between the nation state and a single integrated world economic system' (Brown, 1973, p. 204). In reality, it shows the consolidation of the power of the DMEs. The already existing powerful policy groups may impose trade and investment restrictions on the non-members, block entry on non-members or impose stringent conditions for entry of non-members. The already existing powerful groups thus may be obstructionists for the countries not yet included in any policy group. The power of the nation state is also not weakened relative to other regional bodies and the rest of the world if the country is one of the DMEs. The best example at this moment is the power of the countries in EU (The Economist, 1999, Nov. 13-19, p. 56). The decolonized lesser independent countries in the Third World have to accept extra-nation ideology and hence have to shed the essence of nationhood and statehood before they realize the responsibilities of such nation-cum-statehood.

On the one hand, both the IEO and the global policy coordination groups are weighted in favour of the DMEs. On the other any extension by inclusion or exclusion of countries in these existing groups and in the new groups that are formed by the DMEs is naturally determined by the latter. The countries in the Third World have little say in these formations of policy groups. Once these groups are formed that include some of the TWCs, some of who are large by size, the TWCs have no choice but to obey the rules and norms of the groups of which they are members. The most recent case is G-20 where they have to obey to work within the framework of the post-Second World War IEO. It is known that that IEO was shaped essentially by the US with support from the UK and possibly also from the War allies. What is more glaring is the exclusion of the small countries from these policy groups, the bypassing of the UN as a supra-national body and increasing weightage of the Bretton Woods twins. The inclusion of the twins in G-20 and the agenda of G-20 confirm this. Post-Second World War globalization is centered on formation of policy coordination groups. In the context of exclusion or marginalisation of most of the TWCs in this network, one may question the relevance and worth of participation of countries not only excluded but also of countries included at present in the groups. Because the inclusion of countries from the Third World is also subject to the choice and confirmation by G-7 or by the leader. What can be the tasks of the countries in the Third World in this context?

If the TWCs are to be open door, formation of trade-cum-investment groups is a vital step for them in the right direction. The infra-group trade and investment may be taken as a first step for the TWCs for collective self-reliance in their interaction with the DMEs and groups formed by the latter. However, the choice is not easy. For a small economy, initial dependence on a single dominant country may lead to crises of different types. For a small economy it is impossible to be closed even in the very short run. Some of the small countries may be really resource starved. This leads to concentrated use of resources in a few commodities. Once these commodities are produced more than what is required for home consumption the corollary is export-led production. For example, even in the mid-seventies, two-thirds of Chad's exports were cotton, two-thirds of Chile's exports were copper, two-thirds of Congo's exports were wood, two-thirds of Ghana's exports were cocoa, four-fifth's of Cuba's exports were sugar. Similar were the export baskets for the small economies like Sri Lanka, Zambia, Liberia, Mauritius etc (Hamson, 1980, p. 338). A small county like Surinam is dependent only on export of bauxite and that too through the TNCs. Nevertheless, in accordance with the resource bases the small countries in the Third World can plan for the continuation and expansion of existing production lines. The structural imbalances in one small country can be solved when countries combine for trade and industrialization. What can not be achieved by a few activities can be achieved by a composition of activities, activities that ensure linkage effects on a higher scale. Increased regional trade and investment indeed offer a means of overcoming the constraints on individual countries related to their small size and of breaking away from their traditional export structure' (UNCTAD, 1998a, p. 204). The idea is that increasing practice of regional division of labour is a step forward for global division of labour.

The income-poor TWCs can generate only a small percentage of world output that is hardly adequate to generate enough purchasing power that can absorb a significant, if not a rising, percentage of output produced within non-TWCs. For example,

40.0 percent of world population settled in G-22 excluding countries in G-7 commanded 15.0 per cent to of world output in 1995. The population-output disproportionate share between G-7 and non-G-7 countries remain unaltered even when the latter are accommodated in broader groups like G-22, G-26 etc (Tables 1 and 2). In addition to legitimizing the command and control of G-7, the accommodation of the large economies from the Third World in the newly formed broad policy groups rests on growth reasons.

Abbreviations Used

ASEAN	Association of South East Asian Nations
CMIE	Centre for Monitoring Indian Economy
DMEs	Developed Market Economies
EU	European Union
FDI	Foreign Direct Investment
G-7	Group of Seven most Industrialized Countries
GATT	General Agreement on Tariffs and Trade
GNP	Gross National Product
IEO	International Economic Order
IFIs	International Financial Institutions
IMF	International Monetary Fund
ITO	International Trade Organization
NATO	North Atlantic Treaty Organization
NICs	Newly Industrializing Countries
NIEO	New International Economic Order
OECD	Organization for Economic Cooperation and Development
TNCs	Transnational Corporations
TNCs	Third World Countries
WB	World Bank
WTO	World Trade Organization

References

1. Anell L. and Nygren, B., 1980, 'The Developing Countries and the World Economic Order', Nethuen, London.
2. Asian Development Bank, 1999, *Asian Development Outlook*, Oxford Univ. Press, New York.
3. Brown, Lester R., 1973, 'World without Borders', Affiliated East-West Press Pvt. Ltd., New Delhi.
4. Burbach, R,, Nunez, 0. and Kagarlitsky, B. 1997, 'Globalization and its Discontents', Pluto Press, London.
5. CMIE, 1996, India's Balance of Payments', July.
6. Government of India, Ministry of Finance, *Economic Survey,* 1999-2000.
7. Harrison, Paul, 1980, 'Inside the Third World, The Anatomy of Poverty', The Harvester Press, UK.
8. Hoogvelt, Ankei, M. N., 1982, The Third World in Global Development', Macmillan, London.
9. Press and Information Office of the Federal Government, n.d., The Federal Republic of Germany, Member of the United Nations' (A Documentation), Siegler& Co.. Bonn.
10. Sauvant Karl P., 1981, Sauvant Karl P. (Ed), 'Changing Priorities on the International Agenda, The New International Economic Order', Pergamon Press, Oxford.
11. *The Economist,* 1999, Nov. 13-19, London.
12. UNCTAD, 1998, World Investment Report, Trends and Determinants, Bookwell, Delhi.
13. UNCTAD, 1998a, Trade and Development Report, Bookwell, Delhi.
14. UNDP, 1999, Human Development Report, Oxford University Press, New York.
15. World Bank, 1995, World Development Report, Oxford University Press.
16. World Bank. 1996, World Development Report, Oxford University Press.
17. World Bank, 1997, World Development Report, Oxford University Press.
18. World Bank, 1998/99, Wo rld Development Report, Oxford University Press
19. www.theodora. corn/maps

‹26›

India-Vietnam Relationship
Past and Present

*Tran Thi Ly**

The relationship between India and Vietnam is traditional relationship. From prehistoric times India already had some relations with Vietnam as evidenced by archaeological and linguistic of our era. By that time, relations were rather unilateral, i.e. Indian merchants, and priests came to some areas in the coastal and riverside plains in Vietnam for trade, religious preaching and settlements, while the reverse, i.e. Vietnamese archaeologists since 1975 up to the present time have unearthed a great bulk of variegated artifacts originating from India or produced under the influence of Indian culture in Southern Vietnam. That influence may not be so marked in the Northen as in the South and the center, is not considerable. The Buddhist center in Luy Lau, Thuan Thanh Districts, Bac Ninh Province, established by Indian monks has been considered as the earliest Buddhist center in Southeast Asia. According to many researchers the cultural; factors of Buddhism which the Vietnamese adopted from India in the context of their Chinese cultural reception have made great contributions to the shaping of the cultural identity of the Vietnamese enabling them not to be assimilated by any alien culture.

* Head, Centre for Indian Studies, Institute for South East Asian Studies, Hanoi, Vietnam

In the contemporary times, both Vietnam and India'suffered the domination of colonialism. Vietnam became colonies of French colonialism and India, of British colonialism. The relations between the two nations were then expressed in the sympathy towards each other for the condition of country-logers and the concern of Vietnamese patriots in learning from the struggle movement for national liberation of Indian people as it is a typical movement resounding through Asia. Ho Chi Minh has dedicated many of his essays to the struggle of Indian people. Right from 1924, he asserted *"how useful it is for Vietnamese people if they could know how their Indian brothers have organized for the struggle against British domination"*. Interestingly, it is just under the harshness of colonialist domination that a most noble friendship among other ones between patriots in the world had blossomed between President Ho Chi Minh and Prime Minister J. Nehru.

In the second half of 20th century Vietnam and India had both recovered their national independence; Vietnam on 19 August 1945, India on 15 August 1947. The relationship between the two countries then stepped into a new chapter of history. That is, the official diplomatic relations between two countries. In the past half a century, relations between Vietnam and India had gradually developed, marked by the mutual support and assistance in various fields, political as well as socio-economic and science, technology. In the period from the 50s up to the time when Vietnam could secure victoriously her country's unification (1975), relations between the two countries were extended chiefly in the political field. In spite of different paths of development embraced, both countries have had many a convergence and consensus of opinion on various world and regional issues, as both of them were aiming at the same target of opposing any oppression of imperialism, backing the national liberation struggle movement for peace and stability in the region and the world over. India had heartily given support to the resistance war of the Vietnamese people against French and American invaders. Such events as the visit of Prime Minister Nehru to Hanoi, who was the first head of state all over the world to do so, a week after the liberation of the capital city and the official recognition of the Provisional Revolutionary Government of the Republic of South Vietnam by the Indian Government right on 30 April 1975 are a manifestation of India's sympathy for Vietnam. From her side, Vietnam has also heartily backed the struggle for independence and territory sovereignty of Indian people, and at the same time set great store by the contribution of India to the preservation of peace and security in the region and the world.

Relation between two countries have expanded since the full country reunification of Vietnam. Besides being in unison with each other on various world and regional strategic issues, the two countries have both undertaken closer cooperation in cultural, economic and scientific and technological fields. To begin with, a sequence of agreement on cultural and economic cooperation have been signed between the two countries from 1976 to 1980, such as the Agreement on Culture Cooperation in 1976, Trade Agreement and Science and Technology Cooperation Agreement in 1978, and especially the setting up of a Mixed Committee for Cultural, Economic and Science and Technology Cooperation in 1982. Many cultural and art festivals have been organized in both countries since 1980 up to the present time, to the spread out those agreements. Various meetings and seminars on President Ho Chi Minh and Prime Minister Nehru have been held solemnly by Governments of India and Vietnam respectively to celebrate the birthday of these two great men. Many groups of economic and technological experts of India have come for help to Vietnam.

After the collapse of the Soviet Union and the end of the cold war, both India, Vietnam have to readjust their socio-economic policy to look for the best position in the New World order. Vietnam carried out the Renovation in 1986 and India began to carry out the Economic reform in 1991. Both countries have gained considerable achievement on the economic as well as foreign policy field.

The relationship between the two counties has been

maintained and developed, because it is a cooperative, amicable and traditional relationship, that has been time tested. The relationship is based on a strong foundation which is the compatibility of strategic mutual interest of the two countries. Both Vietnam and India are developing countries in Asia and members of Non-Alignment. Vietnam and India have similar point of views on important regional, international issues, especially those concerning peace, stability and security in Southeast Asia and Asia-Pacific. Both countries join forces and support each other in regional, international and United Nations For a, strive for peace, international security and for an equal, progressive world over. Both countries have to cope with a lot of challenges including the negative impacts of the globalization process and the pressure of developed countries attempt to impose unequal trade and financial relations against developing countries.

The economic cooperation between the two countries is limited and not yet compatible with the good political relations because both Vietnam and India are in transition period from a central planning and subsidized economy to an open liberalized and market economy.

However with achievements of the renovation process in Vietnam and the economic reform in India, the strength of India as one of the 7 world economic powers in the early 21st century as predicted by the world Bank, with Indian great assistance to Vietnam, we believe that the traditional friendship between the two countries will be further promoted in the new millennium.

Index